iPhone Application Development For Dummies

D1119358

Customizing `UIKit` Framework Behavior

The `UIKit` framework provides a great deal of functionality — and you can use it to customize application behavior with three distinct mechanisms:

- ✔ Subclassing: This allows you to add instance variables and methods.
- ✔ Target-Action: This is the pattern you use to give the app its controls.
- ✔ Delegation: The way you implement application-specific behavior in generic objects.

One challenge facing a developer is to determine which of these mechanisms to use when. I wish I'd had the following what-to-do-when tips when I first got into developing applications — and now you do . . . .

Subclassing

Subclassing involves two stages: (1) creating a new class that inherits properties from another (super) class and then (2) adding properties as needed for your application. In general, you'll want to subclass

- ✔ `UIView`, to create your (more complex) content views, which you may fill with controls, graphics or the like.
- ✔ `UIViewController`, to manage the content views and connect it to the model.
- ✔ `NSObject`, to create Model views and delegates.

Target-Action

If you're going to use any of these controls . . .

- ✔ `UITabBarItem` (for items on the tab bar)
- ✔ `UIBarButtonItem` (for items on the navigation bar and tool bar)
- ✔ `UIButton`
- ✔ `UIDatePicker`
- ✔ `UIPageControl`
- ✔ `UISegmentedControl`
- ✔ `UITextField`
- ✔ `UISlider`
- ✔ `UISwitch`

. . . then you'll be using the Target-Action pattern. Typically you'll want to specify the target as the view controller (which you'll have already subclassed) because it controls the view in which these controls reside.

iPhone Application Development For Dummies®

Cheat Sheet

Delegation

If you use any of the views listed in the following table, you'll almost always use a delegate; exceptions to that rule are shown in the Special Use column.

Using Delegates with Views

Class	Delegate(s)	Special Use
UIAccelerometer	UIAccelerometerDelegate	
UIActionSheet	UIActionSheetDelegate	
UIAlertView	UIAlertViewDelegate	
UIApplication	UIApplicationDelegate	
UIImagePicker	UIImagePickerControllerDelegate	
UINavigationBar	UINavigationBarDelegate	To push or pop view controllers
UIPickerView	UIPickerViewDataSource	
	UIPickerViewDelegate	
UIScrollView	UIScrollViewDelegate	Under some circumstances
UISearchBar	UISearchBarDelegate	
UITabBar	UITabBarControllerDelegate	To customize a tab bar
UITableView	UITableViewDataSource	
	UITableViewDelegate	
UITextField	UITextFieldDelegate	To put away the keyboard
UITextView	UITextViewDelegate	To examine text being edited
UIWebView	UIWebViewDelegate	

For Dummies: Bestselling Book Series for Beginners

iPhone™ Application Development

FOR

DUMMIES®

iPhone™ Application Development FOR DUMMIES®

by Neal Goldstein

WILEY

Wiley Publishing, Inc.

iPhone™ Application Development For Dummies®

Published by
Wiley Publishing, Inc.
111 River Street
Hoboken, NJ 07030-5774

www.wiley.com

Copyright © 2009 by Wiley Publishing, Inc., Indianapolis, Indiana

Published by Wiley Publishing, Inc., Indianapolis, Indiana

Published simultaneously in Canada

For general information on our other products and services, please contact our Customer Care Department within the U.S. at 877-762-2974, outside the U.S. at 317-572-3993, or fax 317-572-4002.

For technical support, please visit www.wiley.com/techsupport.

Wiley also publishes its books in a variety of electronic formats. Some content that appears in print may not be available in electronic books.

Library of Congress Control Number: 2009925424

ISBN: 978-0-470-48737-2

Manufactured in the United States of America

10 9 8 7 6 5 4

WILEY

About the Author

Neal Goldstein is a recognized leader in making state-of-the-art and cutting-edge technologies practical for commercial and enterprise development. He was one of the first technologists to work with commercial developers at firms such as Apple Computer, Lucasfilm, and Microsoft to develop commercial applications using object-based programming technologies. He was a pioneer in moving that approach into the corporate world for developers at Liberty Mutual Insurance, USWest (now Verizon), National Car Rental, EDS, and Continental Airlines, showing them how object-oriented programming could solve enterprise-wide problems. His book (with Jeff Alger) on object-oriented development, *Developing Object-Oriented Software for the Macintosh* (Addison Wesley, 1992), introduced the idea of scenarios and patterns to developers. He was an early advocate of the Microsoft .NET framework, and successfully introduced it into many enterprises, including Charles Schwab. He was one of the earliest developers of Service Oriented Architecture (SOA), and as Senior Vice President of Advanced Technology and the Chief Architect at Charles Schwab, he built an integrated SOA solution that spanned the enterprise, from desktop PCs to servers to complex network mainframes. (He holds three patents as a result.) As one of IBM's largest customers, he introduced them to SOA at the enterprise level and encouraged them to head in that direction. He is currently leading an iPhone startup that is developing an application to help minimize the cost (and pain) of global travel for both leisure and corporate travelers.

Dedication

To my mother, Anne, who was really looking forward to reading this book.

To my brother, Jay, who has been a pillar of support and enabled me to stay focused.

To my children, Sarah and Evan, who have always inspired me and never let me get too carried away with my own magnificence.

But most of all, to my wife Linda, who understands my absences, even when I am in the same room, and has enthusiastically accompanied me on all my adventures.

Acknowledgments

Carole Jelen, agent extraordinaire, put this together in record time.

Acquisitions Editor Katie Feltman was a pleasure to work with and a great sounding board and originator of ideas. Senior Project Editor Paul Levesque helped me turn my sometimes random musings into an orderly romp through iPhone development. Senior Copy Editor Barry Childs-Helton did a great job in helping me make things clearer. Technical reviewer Glenda Adams added a great second pair of eyes.

Early beta testers Jeff Behrens and Michael Bentley were extremely helpful in pointing out places where my explanations weren't clear enough. Jeff Behrens also helped me refine the HTML code.

And finally, Evan Goldstein did a great job of reviewing the nontechnical parts of the book. It was a real treat to be on the receiving end of his editorial comments after being on the giving side for so many years.

Publisher's Acknowledgments

We're proud of this book; please send us your comments through our online registration form located at http://dummies.custhelp.com. For other comments, please contact our Customer Care Department within the U.S. at 877-762-2974, outside the U.S. at 317-572-3993, or fax 317-572-4002.

Some of the people who helped bring this book to market include the following:

Acquisitions, Editorial

Senior Project Editor: Paul Levesque

Senior Acquisitions Editor: Katie Feltman

Senior Copy Editor: Barry Childs-Helton

Technical Editor: Glenda Adams

Editorial Manager: Leah Cameron

Media Development Assistant Producers: Angela Denny, Josh Frank, and Shawn Patrick

Editorial Assistant: Amanda Foxworth

Sr. Editorial Assistant: Cherie Case

Cartoons: Rich Tennant (www.the5thwave.com)

Composition Services

Project Coordinator: Lynsey Stanford

Layout and Graphics: Carl Byers, Reuben W. Davis, Sarah Philippart

Proofreaders: Amanda Graham, John Greenough, Joni Heredia

Indexer: Slivoskey Indexing Services

Publishing and Editorial for Technology Dummies

Richard Swadley, Vice President and Executive Group Publisher

Andy Cummings, Vice President and Publisher

Mary Bednarek, Executive Acquisitions Director

Mary C. Corder, Editorial Director

Publishing for Consumer Dummies

Diane Graves Steele, Vice President and Publisher

Composition Services

Debbie Stailey, Director of Composition Services

Contents at a Glance

Table of Contents

Introduction

· ·

*W*hen Apple opened up the iPhone to developers, I got as excited about developing software as I did when I first discovered the power of the Mac. The iPhone was a new platform, one that opened up possibilities for applications that never existed before. It was more than a phone, and not just simply a small computer. Its hardware and software made it possible to wander the world, or your own neighborhood, and stay connected to whomever and whatever you wanted to. It enabled a new class of here-and-now applications that allowed you to do what you needed to, based on what was going on around you and where you were.

Of course, at first I thought developing for the iPhone would be like developing for the Mac. And, in the beginning, developing software on the Mac was like crawling over broken glass in midsummer at high noon in Death Valley. (I remember it fondly.) But when I downloaded the iPhone Software Development Kit (SDK), I was amazed. Here was a set of mature, easy-to-use, and (the best part) *free* tools. The frameworks were amazing! I had used frameworks before, but the ones that came with the iPhone were especially rich and mature. All I really had to do was add my application's user interface and functionality to the framework, and then *poof* . . . an instant application.

I had discovered an (almost) easy and fun way to develop software. Of course, I say that now in hindsight.

If that seemed too good to be true, well, okay, it *was*, sort of. All that convenience came at a cost. It was really difficult to get my head around the whole thing, conceptually speaking; sometimes I found it hard to figure out exactly where (and how) to add my application's functionality to that supplied by the framework.

And while there were lots of resources, the problem was exactly that: There were *lots* of resources! As in, *thousands* of pages of documentation I could read, and lots of sample code to look at. I could only get through a small fraction of the documentation before I just couldn't stand the suspense anymore and started coding. Naturally enough, there were a few false starts and blind alleys until I found my way, and it has been (pretty much) smooth sailing ever since.

That's why, when the *For Dummies* folks asked me to write a book on developing software for the iPhone, I jumped at the chance. Here was an opportunity for me to write the book I wish I'd had when I started developing iPhone software.

About This Book

iPhone Application Development For Dummies is a beginner's guide to developing iPhone applications. And not only do you *not* need any iPhone development experience to get started, you don't need any Macintosh development experience either. I expect you to come as a blank slate, ready to be filled with useful information and new ways to do things.

Because of the nature of the iPhone, you can create small, bite-sized applications that can be really powerful. And since you can start small and create real applications that do something important for a user, it's relatively easy to transform yourself from "I know nothing" into a developer who, though not (yet) a superstar, can still crank out quite a respectable application.

But the iPhone can be home to some pretty fancy software as well — so I'll take you on a journey through building an industrial-strength application and show you the ropes for developing one on your own.

This book distills the hundreds (or even thousands) of pages of Apple documentation, not to mention my own development experience, into only what's necessary to start you developing real applications. But this is no recipe book that leaves it up to you to put it all together; rather, it takes you through the frameworks and iPhone architecture in a way that gives you a solid foundation in how applications really work on the iPhone — and a acts as a roadmap to expand your knowledge as you need to.

It's a multicourse banquet, intended to make you feel satisfied (and really full) at the end.

Conventions Used in This Book

This book guides you through the process of building iPhone applications. Throughout, you use the provided iPhone framework classes (and create new ones of course) — and code them using the Objective-C programming language.

Code examples in this book appear in a monospaced font so they stand out a bit better. That means the code you'll see will look like this:

```
#import <UIKit/ UIKit.h>
```

Objective-C is based on C, which (I want to remind you) *is* case-sensitive, so please enter the code that appears in this book *exactly* as it appears in the text. I also use the standard Objective-C naming conventions — for example, class names always start with a capital letter, and the names of methods and instance variables always start with a lowercase letter.

Let me throw out that all URLs in this book appear in a monospaced font as well:

```
www.nealgoldstein.com
```

If you're ever uncertain about anything in the code, you can always look at the source code on my Web site at `www.nealgoldstein.com` — from time to time, I'll provide updates for the code there, and post other things you might find useful. (You can grab the same material from the *For Dummies* Web site at `www.dummies.com/go/iphonedevfd`.)

Foolish Assumptions

To begin programming your iPhone applications, you'll need a Macintosh computer with the latest version of the Mac OS on it. (No, you can't program iPhone applications on the iPhone.) You will also need to download the iPhone Software Development Kit (SDK) — which is free — but you do have to become a registered iPhone developer before you can do that. (Don't worry; I show you how to do both.) And, oh yeah, you'll need an iPhone. You won't start running your application on it right away — you'll use the Simulator that Apple provides with the iPhone SDK during the initial stages of development — but at some time you'll want to test your application on a real live iPhone.

I'm going to assume that you have some programming knowledge and that you have at least a passing acquaintance with object-oriented program-ming, using some variant of the C language (such as C++, C#, or maybe even Objective-C). If not, I'll point out some resources that can help you get up to speed. The examples in this book are focused on the frameworks that come with the SDK; the code is pretty simple (usually) and straightforward. (I won't use this book as platform to dazzle you with fancy coding techniques.)

I'm also going to assume that you're familiar with the iPhone itself, and that you've at least explored Apple's included applications to get a good working sense of the iPhone look and feel. It would also help if you browse the App Store to see the kinds of applications available there, and maybe even download a few free ones (as if I could stop you).

How This Book Is Organized

iPhone Application Development For Dummies has five main parts.

Part I: Getting Started

Part I introduces you to the iPhone world. You'll find out what makes a great iPhone application, and how an iPhone application is structured. You also find out how to become an "official" iPhone developer and what you need to do to in order to be able to distribute your applications through Apple's App Store.

Part II: Using the iPhone Development Tools

I start Part II by showing you how to download the Software Development Kit (SDK) — and then help you unpack all the goodies contained therein, including Xcode (Apple's development environment for the OS X operating system) and Interface Builder. (You'll soon discover that the latter is more than your run-of-the-mill program for building graphical user interfaces.) I'll also explain how everything works together at runtime, which should give you a real feel for how an iPhone application works. Parts I and II give you the fundamental background that you need to develop iPhone applications.

Part III: From "Gee, That's a Good Idea" to the App Store

With the basics behind you and a good understanding of the application architecture under your belt, it's finally time to have some fun doing something useful. In this part, I show you how to create a simple application that people can actually use — it displays a phone number to call if you lose your iPhone. (My friends thought it was sheer genius.) What's more, the Good Samaritan who finds your phone only has to tap that number where it's shown on-screen, and the phone dials the number automatically. Putting this handy little app together will give you some practice at creating a useful, single-screen program with controls. It's a great application to learn about iPhone development — big enough to be useful, but small not to make your head explode.

I've submitted the application to the App store, and I show you how to do that as well.

Part IV: An Industrial-Strength Application

Part IV takes you into the world of applications that contain major functionality. I show you how to design an application with lots of data, views, and access to the Web. I won't go slogging through every detail, but I will demonstrate almost all the technology you need to master if you're going to create a compelling application like this on your own. I also touch on a few advanced topics — such as creating self-configuring objects so you don't find your classes multiplying like rabbits.

Part V: The Part of Tens

Part V consists of some tips to help you avoid having to learn everything the hard way. It talks about approaching application development in an "adult" way right from the beginning (without taking the fun out of it I assure you). I also take you on a tour of the iPhone sample code, pointing out some samples I really like and have found to be the most useful.

Icons Used in This Book

When you see this icon, you can be sure that the code on my (or the *For Dummies* Web site) applies to the current example. The Web sites contain the code for all projects in this book — perfect for those who don't feel like typing the code. Just go to www.nealgoldstein.com or www.dummies.com/go/iphonedevfd and download what you need.

This icon indicates a useful pointer that you shouldn't skip.

This icon represents a friendly reminder. It describes a vital point that you should keep in mind while proceeding through a particular section of the chapter.

This icon signifies that the accompanying explanation might be informative (dare I say, interesting?), but it isn't essential to understanding iPhone application development. Feel free to skip past these tidbits if you'd like (though skipping while leaning may be tricky).

This icon alerts you to potential problems that you may encounter along the way. Read and obey these blurbs to avoid trouble.

Where to Go From Here

It's time to explore the iPhone! If you're nervous, take heart: One of the better-selling apps in the App Store was written by a nine-year-old. So just get in touch with your inner nine year old, and let's go have some fun.

Part I
Getting Started

The 5th Wave   By Rich Tennant

"It's like any other pacemaker, but it comes with an internal iPhone docking accessory."

In this part . . .

So you've decided you want to develop some software for the iPhone. You have good idea for a utility — one that lets you know your net worth in Zimbabwean dollars, or a data-driven application (say, one that knows where to find the best coffee in Seattle). Now what?

This part lays out what you need to know to get started on the development journey. First of all, what makes a great iPhone application? Knowing that, you can evaluate your idea, see how it ranks, and maybe figure out what you have to do to transform it into something that knocks your users' socks off. Next, before you can actually build that sucker, you look under the hood at how iPhone applications work — what goes on behind the screen that ends up with a user seeing something in a window and interacting with controls. You get a look at the user interface frameworks and how to use them (and how they want to use you). Finally, to get all that free development software from Apple, and get your application into the App Store, you'll have to become "legal" — it's time to become an official iPhone developer.

Chapter 1

Creating Killer iPhone Applications

*I*magine that you've just landed at Heathrow Airport. It's early in the morning, and you're dead tired as you clear customs. All you want to do now is find the fastest way to get into London, check into your hotel, and sleep for a few hours.

You take out your iPhone and touch the MobileTravel411 icon. On the left in Figure 1-1, you can see it asks whether you want to use Heathrow Airport as your current location. You touch Yes, and then touch Getting To From (as you can see in the center of Figure 1-1). Since it already knows that you're at Heathrow, it gives you your alternatives. Because of the congestion in and out of London, it suggests using the Heathrow Express, especially during rush hour.

You touch the Heathrow Express tab and it tells you where to get the train and also tells you that the fare is £14.50 if you buy it from the ticket machine and £17.50 if you buy it on board the train. (The iPhone on the right in Figure 1-1 is proof that I'm not making this up.) It turns out that you're so jetlagged that you can't do the math in your head so you touch the Currency button and it tells you that £14.50 is around $21.35 if you took it from the ATM, $21.14 on your no-exchange-rate-fee credit card, or $22.31 at the *bureau de change* at the airport.

Another touch gets you the current weather, which prompts you to dig out a sweater from your luggage before you get on the train.

When you get to Paddington Station, you really don't have a clue where the hotel that someone at the office booked for you might be. You touch Getting Around, and the application allows you to use the hotel address that is in your iPhone Contacts, and then gives you your options when it comes to finally finding that big, comfortable, English bed. These include walking, taking a taxi, and public transit. You touch Tube and it directs you to the nearest Tube stop, and then displays fares, schedules, and how to buy a ticket.

Figure 1-1:
The Mobile-Travel411 application can use your current location.

How much of a fantasy is this?

Not much. Except for automatically determining your location and giving you public-transit directions as well as real-time exchange rates (stuff I'll be adding in the near future) this application already exists. What's more, it took me only a little over two months to develop that application, starting from where you are now, with no iPhone programming experience.

What Makes a Great iPhone Application

You'll find a lot of different kinds of applications on the iPhone, ranging from utilities like the Weather Application, to games, to the New York Times reader, to the application I just described. Each one of these applications also falls on another continuum.

At one end of this continuum is what I think of as the *mobile desktop*. These are applications you might use if you were using your desktop or laptop — applications you could *port to* (rewrite for) the iPhone. For example, I have a weather application on my MacBook Pro on which I can read the New York Times as well — and it doesn't take any major imaginative leap to see how one can do the Weather/New York Times thing on an iPhone. Although I wouldn't think about writing this book on my iPhone, I can easily picture the iPhone as a handy home for note-taking applications, spreadsheet apps, and even stock-trading apps.

At the other end of this continuum are those applications that you would never want to do on the desktop (or even a laptop), either because you don't have the hardware or because, even if you did, doing it that way would be way too inconvenient. Imagine being at Heathrow, dead tired, taking out your laptop in the middle of a crowded terminal, powering it up, launching the application, and then navigating through it with the touch pad to get the information I got easily while holding the iPhone in one hand. I want that kind of information quickly and conveniently; I don't want to have to dig my way to it through menus or layers of screens (or even going through the hassle of finding a wireless Internet connection). Seconds count. By the time any road warrior tied to a laptop did this at Heathrow, I would already be on the Heathrow Express.

I like to think of these kinds of applications as *here-and-now* applications. You want to do a specific task, with up-to-date information, which the iPhone can access over the Internet through a cell network or Wi-Fi connection. You may even want the information or tasks tailored to where you are, which the iPhone can determine with its location hardware.

With all that in mind, I can think of two things that you need to consider — besides functionality, of course — when it comes to creating a great iPhone application:

✔ Create a compelling user experience.

✔ Exploit the platform.

The next few sections dig a little into my Two-Part Rule of Great iPhone Applications.

Creating a Compelling User Experience

The iPhone allows an immediacy and intimacy as it blends mobility and the power of the desktop to create a new kind of freedom. I like to use the term *user experience* because it implies more than a pretty user interface and nice graphics. A *compelling* user experience enables users to do what they need to do with a minimum of fuss and bother. But more than that, it forces you to think past a clean interface and even beyond basic convenience (such as not having to scroll through menus to do something simple). It includes meeting the expectations of the user based on the *context* — all the stuff going on around a user — in which they are using the application.

A guidebook application may have a great user interface, for example, but it may not give me the most up-to-date information, or let me know a tour of Parliament is leaving in 5 minutes from the main entrance. Without those added touches, I'm just not willing to consider an app compelling.

Exploiting the Platform

The iPhone's unique software and hardware allow you to create an application that enables the user to do something that may not be practical, or even possible with a laptop computer. Although the iPhone is a smaller, mobile personal computer, it is not a replacement for one. It is not intended to produce documents, proposals, or research. The iPhone has the capability to be an extension of the user, seamlessly integrated into his or her everyday life, and able to accomplish a singly focused task, or step in a series of tasks, in real time, based on where he or she is.

Device-guided design

While the enormous capabilities of the iPhone that make it possible to deliver the compelling user experience, you must take into account the limitations of the device as well. Keeping the two in balance is *device-guided design*. The next two sections describe both the features and limitations of the iPhone — and how to take them into account as you plan and develop an application. But understanding these constraints can also inspire you to create some really innovative applications. After a closer look at device-guided design, I come back to what makes a compelling user experience.

Exploiting the features

One of the keys to creating a great application is to take advantage of what the device offers. In the case of a new platform with new possibilities, such as the iPhone, this is especially important. Think about the possibilities that open up to you when your application can easily do the following:

- Access the Internet
- Know the location of the user
- Track orientation and motion
- Track the action of the user's fingers on the screen
- Play audio and video
- Access the user's contacts
- Access the user's pictures and camera

Accessing the Internet

The ability to access Web sites and servers on the Internet allows you to create applications that can provide real-time information to the user. It can tell me, for example, that the next tour at the Tate Modern is at 3:00 o'clock. This kind of access also allows you, as the developer, to go beyond the limited memory and processing power of the device and access large amounts of data stored on servers, or even offload the processing. I don't have to have all the information for every city in the world stored on my iPhone, and don't have to strain the poor CPU to compute the best way to get someplace on the Tube. I can send the request to a server and have it do all that work.

This is *client-server computing* — a well established software architecture where the client provides a way to make requests to a server on a network that's just waiting for the opportunity to do something. A Web browser is an example of a client accessing information from other Web sites that act as servers.

Knowing the location of the user

The iPhone Operating System (OS) and hardware allow a developer to determine the device's current location, or even be notified when that location changes. As people move, it may make sense for your application to tailor itself to where the user is moment by moment.

There are already iPhone applications that use location information to tell you where the nearest coffee house is, or even where your friends are. The MobileTravel411 application uses this information to tell you the nearest Tube stop and give you directions to your hotel.

Tracking orientation and motion

The iPhone contains three *accelerometers* — devices that detect changes in movement. Each device measures change along one of the primary axes in three-dimensional space. You can, for example, know when the user has turned the device from vertical to horizontal, and change the view from portrait to landscape if it makes for a better user experience. You can also determine other types of motion such as a sudden start or stop in movement (think of a car accident or fall), or the user shaking the device back and forth. It makes some way cool features easy to implement — for example, the Etch-A-Sketch® metaphor of shaking a device to reset it, and controlling a game by moving the iPhone like a controller.

Tracking the action of the user's fingers on the screen

People use their fingers, rather than a mouse, to select and manipulate objects on the iPhone screen. The moves that do the work, called *gestures*, give the user a heightened sense of control and intimacy with the device. There is a set of standard gestures — taps, pinch-close and pinch-open, flicks, and drags — that are used in the applications supplied with the iPhone.

I suggest strongly that you use *only* the standard gestures in your application. Even so, the iPhone's gesture-recognition hardware and software allows you to go beyond standard gestures when appropriate. Because you can monitor the movement of each finger to detect gestures, you can create your own, but use that capability sparingly — only when it's undoubtedly the right thing to do in your application.

Playing audio and video

The iPhone OS makes it easy to play and include audio and video in your application. You can play sound effects, or take advantage of the multichannel audio and mixing capabilities available to you. You can also play back many standard movie file formats, configure the aspect ratio, and can specify whether or not controls are displayed. This means your application can not only use the iPhone as a media player, but also use and control pre-rendered content. Let the games begin!

Accessing the user's contacts

Your application can access the user's contacts on the phone and display that information in a different way, or use it as information in your application. As a user of the MobileTravel411 application, for example, you could enter the name and address of your hotel, and the application would file it in your Contacts database. That way you have ready access to the hotel address — not only from MobileTravel411, but also from your phone and other applications. Then, when you arrive at Paddington Station, the application can retrieve the address from Contacts and display directions for you.

Accessing the user's pictures and camera

As with Contacts, your application can also access the pictures stored on the user's phone — and not only display them, but also to use or even modify them. The Photos application, for example, lets you add a photo to a contact, and there are several applications that enable you to edit your photos on the iPhone itself. You can also incorporate the standard system interface to actually use the camera as well.

Embracing the limitations

Along with all those features, however, the iPhone has some limitations. The key to successful applications — and to not making yourself too crazy — is to understand those limitations, live (and program) within them, and even learn to love them. (It can be done. Honest.) These constraints help you understand the kinds of applications that are right for this device.

Often it's likely that if you *can't* do something (easily, anyway) because of the iPhone's limitations, then maybe you shouldn't.

So learn to live with and embrace some facts of iPhone life:

✔ The small screen.

✔ Users with fat fingers (me included).

✔ Limited computer power, memory, and battery life.

The next sections can help get you closer to this state of enlightenment.

Living with the small screen

While the iPhone's screen size and resolution allows you to deliver some amazing applications, it is still pretty small. Yet while the small screen limits what you can display on a single page, I have managed to do some mental jujutsu on myself to really think of it as a feature.

When your user interface is simple and direct, the user can understand it more easily. With fewer items in a small display, users can find what they want more quickly. A small screen forces you to ruthlessly eliminate clutter and keep your text concise and to the point (the way you like your books, right?).

Designing for fingers

While the Multi-Touch interface is an iPhone feature, it brings with it limitations as well. First of all, fingers aren't as precise as a mouse pointer, which makes some operations difficult (text selection, for example). User interface elements need to be large enough (Apple recommends that anything a user has to select or manipulate with a finger be a minimum of 44x44 pixels in size), and spaced far enough apart so that user fingers can find their way around the interface comfortably.

You also can only do so much using fingers. There are definitely a lot fewer possibilities using fingers than the combination of multi-button mouse and keyboard.

Because it's so much easier to make a mistake using just fingers, you also need to ensure that you implement a robust — yet unobtrusive — undo mechanism. You don't want to have your users confirm every action (it makes using the application tedious), but on the other hand, you don't want your application to let anybody mistakenly delete a page without asking, "Are you *sure* this is what you *really* want to do?" Lost work is worse than tedious.

Another issue around fingers is that the keyboard is not that finger-friendly. I admit it, using the iPhone keyboard is not up there on the list of things I really like about my iPhone. So instead of requiring the user to type some information, Apple suggests that you have a user select an item from a list. But on the other hand, the items in the list must be large enough to be easily selectable, which gets back to the first problem.

But again, like the small screen, this limitation can inspire (ok may force) you to create a better application. To create a complete list of choices, for example, the application developer is forced to completely understand the context (and be creative about) what what the user is trying to accomplish. Having that depth of understanding then makes it possible to focus the application on the essential, eliminating what is unnecessary or distracting. It also serves to focus the user on the task at hand.

Limited computer power, memory, and battery life

As an application designer for the iPhone, you have several balancing acts to keep in mind:

✔ Although significant by the original Macintosh's standards, the computer power and amount of memory on the iPhone is limited.

✔ Although access to the Internet can mitigate the power and memory limitations by storing data and (sometimes) offloading processing to a server, those operations eat up the battery faster.

✔ Although the power-management system in the iPhone OS conserves power by shutting down any hardware features that are not currently being used, a developer must manage the trade-off between all those busy features and shorter battery life. Any application that takes advantage of Internet access using Wi-Fi or the 3G network, core location, and a couple of accelerometers, is going to eat up the batteries.

The iPhone OS is particularly unforgiving when it comes to memory usage. If you run out of memory, it will simply shut you down.

This just goes to show that not *all* limitations can be exploited as "features."

A Compelling User Experience

When you've got a handle on the possibilities and limitations of the iPhone, your imagination is free to soar to create a compelling user experience. Which reminds me: It's worth considering what "compelling user experience" really means.

For openers, a compelling user experience has to result from the interaction of several factors:

✔ Interesting, useful, plentiful content.

✔ Powerful, fast, versatile functionality.

✔ An intuitive, well-designed user interface.

Compelling content

As I said earlier, there are a lot of different kinds of applications on the iPhone. What most of the really good ones have in common is focus. They address a well defined task that can be done within a time span that is appropriate for that task. If I need to look something up, I want it right now! If I am playing a game while waiting in line, I want it to be of short duration, or broken up into a series of short and entertaining steps.

The application content itself then, especially for here-and-now applications, must be streamlined and focused on the fundamental pieces of the task. Although you *can* provide a near-infinity of details just to get a single task done, here's a word to the wise: Don't. You need to extract the essence of each task; focus on the details that really make a difference.

Here's an example: The other night, my wife and I were standing with some friends inside the lobby of a movie theater, trying to decide where to go to grab some dinner. It was cold (at least by California standards) but we wanted to walk to the restaurant from the theater. We had two iPhones going, switching from application to application, trying to get enough information to make a decision. None of the applications gave us what we really needed — restaurants ranked by distance and type, with reviews and directions.

One of the applications was a great example of how to frustrate the user. It allowed you to select a restaurant by distance and cuisine. After you selected the distance, it gave you a list of cuisines. So far, so good. But the cuisine list was not context-based; when I tapped *Ethiopian*, all I got was a blank screen. Very annoying! I took it off my iPhone then and there — I don't want an application that makes me work only to receive nothing in return. Your users won't either.

Every piece of a good application is not merely important to the task, but important to *where you are in the task*. For example, if I'm trying to decide how to get to central London from Heathrow, don't give me detailed information about the Tube until I need it.

That doesn't mean your applications shouldn't make connections that ought to be made. One aspect of a compelling user experience is that all the pieces of an application work together to tell a story. If the tasks in your application are completely unconnected, perhaps they should be separate applications.

An application such as MobileTravel411 is aimed at people who may not know anything about their destination. If the application informs them that one reason to take the Heathrow Express is that it offers convenient Tube access on arrival in London, the users then have a bite-size bit of valuable information about how to get around London once they're in the city. Save the train routes for when they're in the station.

By limiting the focus to a single task, it also enables you to leave behind some iPhone constraints, and the limitations of the iPhone can guide you to a better application design.

Consistency with the user's world

Great applications are based on the way people — users — think and work. When you make your application a natural extension of the user's world, it makes the application much easier and pleasant to use — and to learn.

Your users already have a mental model that describes the task your software is enabling. The users also have their own mental models of how the device works. At the levels of both content and user interface, your application must be consistent with these models if you want to create a superb user experience (which in turn creates loyalty — to your application).

The user interface in MobileTravel411 was based on how people divide up the experience of traveling. Here are typical categories:

- ✔ Foreign currency — how much it really costs and what's the best way to convert money and buy things abroad.
- ✔ Getting to and from the airport with maximum efficiency and minimum hassle.
- ✔ Getting around a city, especially an unfamiliar one.
- ✔ Finding any special events happening while you're in the city.
- ✔ Handling traveler's tasks — such as making phone calls, tipping, or finding a bank or ATM — with aplomb.
- ✔ Checking the current weather and the forecast.
- ✔ Staying safe in unfamiliar territory — places you shouldn't go, what to do if you get in trouble, and so on.

This is only a partial list, of course. I get into this aspect of application design in more detail when I take you through the design of MobileTravel411.

I suppose there are other ways to divide up the tasks, but anything much different would be ignoring the user's mental model — which would mean the application wasn't meeting some of the user's expectations. It would be less pleasant to use because it would impose an unfamiliar way of looking at things instead of building on the knowledge and experiences those users already have.

When possible, model your application's objects and actions on objects and actions in the real world. For example, the iPhone has a set of iPod-style playback controls, tapping controls to make things happen, sliding on-off switches, and flicking through the data shown on Picker wheels. All of these are based on physical counterparts in the real world.

Your application's text should be based on the target user. For example, if your user isn't steeped in technical jargon, avoid it in the user interface.

This does not mean that you have to "dumb down" the application. Here are some guidelines:

✔ If your application is targeted for a set of users who already use (and expect) a certain kind of specialized language, then sure, you can use the jargon in your application. Just do your homework first and make sure you use those terms *right*.

For example, if your application is targeted at high-powered foreign-exchange traders, your application might use *pip* ("price interest point" — the smallest amount that a price can move, as when a stock price advances by one cent). In fact, a foreign exchange trader expects to see price movement in pips, and not only *can* you, but you *should* use that term in your user interface.

✔ If your application requires that the user have a certain amount of specialized knowledge about a task in order to use your application, identify what that knowledge is up front.

✔ If the user is an ordinary person with generalized knowledge, use ordinary language.

Gear your application to your user's knowledge base. In effect, meet your users where they are; don't expect them to come to you.

The user interface – form following function

Basing your application on how the user interacts and thinks about the world makes designing a great user interface easier.

Don't underestimate the effect of the user interface on the people who are trying to use it. A bad user interface can make even a great application painful to use. If users can't quickly figure out how to use your application, or if the user interface is cluttered or obscure, they're likely to move on and probably complain loudly about the application to anyone who will listen.

Simplicity and ease of use are fundamental principles for all types of software, but in iPhone applications they are critical. Why? One word: multitasking. iPhone OS users are probably doing other things simultaneously while they use your application.

The iPhone hardware and software is an outstanding example of form following function; the user interfaces of great applications follow that principle as well. In fact, even the iPhone's limitations (except for battery life) are a result of form following from the functional requirements of a mobile device user. Just think how the iPhone fulfills the following mobile device user wish list:

- Small footprint
- Thin
- Light weight
- Self contained — no need for an external keyboard or mouse
- Task oriented

It's a pretty safe bet that part of the appeal of the iPhone to many people — especially to non-technical users (like most of my friends) — is aesthetic: The device is sleek compact, and fun to use. But the aesthetics of an iPhone application aren't just about how "beautiful" your application is on-screen. Eye candy is all well and good, but how well does your user interface match its function — that is, do its job?

Consistency

As with the Macintosh, users have a general sense of how applications work on the iPhone. (The Windows OS has always been a bit less user-friendly, if you ask a typical Mac user.) One of the early appeals of the Macintosh was how similarly all the applications worked. So Apple (no fools they) carried over this similarity into the iPhone as well. The resulting success story suggests the following word to the wise. . . .

A compelling iPhone user experience usually requires familiar iPhone interface components offering standard functionality, such as searching and navigating hierarchical sets of data. Use the iPhone standard behavior, gestures, and metaphors in standard ways. For example, users tap a button to make a selection and flick or drag to scroll a long list. iPhone users understand these gestures because the built-in applications utilize them *consistently*. Fortunately, staying consistent is easy to do on the iPhone; the frameworks at your disposal have that behavior built in. This is not to say that you should never extend the interface, especially if you're blazing new trails or creating a new game. For example, if you were creating a roulette wheel for the iPhone, why not use a circular gesture to spin the wheel, even if it isn't a "standard" gesture?

Making it obvious

Although simplicity is a definite design principle, great applications are *also* easily understandable to the target user. If I'm designing a travel application, it has to be simple enough for even an inexperienced traveler to use. But if I'm designing an application for foreign-exchange trading, I don't have to make it simple enough for someone with no trading experience to understand.

- The main function of a good application is immediately apparent and accessible to the users it's intended for.

✔ The standard interface components also give cues to the users. Users know, for example, to touch buttons and select items from table views (as in the contact application).

✔ You can't assume that users are so excited about your application that they are willing to invest lots of time in figuring it out.

Early Macintosh developers were aware of these principles. They knew that users expected that they could rip off the shrink-wrap, put a floppy disk in the machine (these were *really* early Macintosh developers), and do at least something productive immediately. The technology has changed since then; user attitudes, by and large, haven't.

Engaging the user

While we're on the subject of users, here's another aspect of a compelling application: direct manipulation and immediate feedback.

✔ **Direct manipulation makes people feel more in control.** On the desktop, that meant a keyboard and mouse; on the iPhone, the Multi-Touch interface serves the same purpose. In fact, using fingers gives a user a more immediate sense of control; there's no intermediary (such as a mouse) between the user and the object on-screen. To make this effect happen in your application, keep your on-screen objects visible while the user manipulates them, for example.

✔ **Immediate feedback keeps the users engaged.** Great applications respond to every user action with some visible feedback — such as highlighting list items briefly when users tap them.

Because of the limitations imposed by using fingers, applications need to be very forgiving. For example, although the iPhone doesn't pester the user to confirm every action, it also won't let the user perform potentially destructive, non-recoverable actions (such as deleting all contacts or restarting a game) without asking, "Are you sure?" Your application should also allow the user to easily stop a task that's taking too long to complete.

Also: Notice how the iPhone uses animation to provide feedback. (I especially like the flipping transitions in the weather application when I touch the Info button.) But keep it simple; excessive or pointless animation interferes with the application flow, reduces performance, and can really annoy the user.

Why Develop iPhone Applications?

Because you can. Because it's time. And because it's fun. Developing my iPhone applications has been the most fun I've had in many years (don't tell my wife!). Here's what makes it so much fun (for me, anyway):

✔ **iPhone apps are usually bite-size — small enough to get your head around.** A single developer — or one with a partner and maybe some graphics support — can do them. You don't need a 20-person project with endless procedures and processes and meetings to create something valuable.

✔ **The applications are crisp and clean, focusing on what the user wants to do at a particular time and/or place.** They're simple but not simplistic. This makes application design (and subsequent implementation) much easier — and faster.

✔ **The free iPhone Software Development Kit (SDK) makes development as easy as possible.** I reveal its splendors to you throughout this book.

If you can't stand waiting, you *could* go on to Chapter 3, register as an iPhone developer, and download the SDK . . . but (fair warning) jumping the gun leads to extra hassle. It's worth getting a handle on the ins and outs of iPhone application development beforehand.

The iPhone has three other advantages that are important to you as a developer:

✔ **The App Store.** Apple will list your application in the App Store, and take care of credit-card processing, hosting, downloading, notifying users of updates, and all those things that most developers hate doing. Developers name their own prices for their creations; Apple gets 30% of the sales price, with the developer getting the rest.

Apple has an iPhone developer program. To get your application into the store, you have to pay $99.00 join the program. But that's it. There are none of the infamous "hidden charges" that you often encounter, especially when dealing with credit-card companies. I explain how to join the developer program in Chapter 3, and how to work with the App Store in Chapter 13.

✔ **It's a business tool.** The iPhone has become an acceptable business tool, in part because it has tight security, as well as support for Microsoft Exchange and Office. This happy state of affairs expands the possible audience for your application.

Examining the Possibilities

Just as the iPhone can extend the reach of the user, the device possibilities and the development environment can extend your reach as a developer. Apple talks often about three different application styles:

✔ **Productivity applications** use and manipulate information. The MobileTravel411 application is an example.

✔ **Utility applications** perform simple, highly defined tasks. The weather application is an example.

> ✔ **Immersive applications** are focused on delivering — and having the user interact with — content in a visually rich environment. A game is a typical example of an immersive application.

Although these categories help you understand how Apple thinks about iPhone applications (at least publicly), don't let them get in the way of your creativity. You have probably heard ad nauseam about stepping outside the box. But hold on to your lunch; the iPhone "box" isn't even a box yet. So here's a more extreme metaphor: Try diving into the abyss and coming up with something really new.

The Sample Applications

When I started writing this book, I decided that there was no way I was going to do what legions of computer-book authors have done from time immemorial. You know — some kind of insipid "Hello World" application.

With a little more (although not much more) work, you can use the development environment to actually create something of value.

In Figure 1-2, you can see the first application that I show you how to develop — the one I thought about after I lost my iPhone for the first time. I realized that if anyone found it and wanted to return it, well, returning it wouldn't be easy. Sure, whoever found it could root around in my Contacts or Favorites and maybe call a few of them and ask if any of their friends had lost an iPhone. But to save them the work, I decided to create an application called *ReturnMeTo*, whose icon sat on the upper-left corner of the home screen and looked like something you would want to select if you had found this phone. It would show a phone number to call and create a very happy person at the receiving end of the call.

Originally I thought I would simply create this application and then get on with the rest of the book. It turned out, however, that as I showed my friends the application, I got a lot of feedback and made some changes to it. I'll include those changes as well — because they'll give you insight to the iPhone application-development process. All my friends also told me that they'd love to have the application (hey, they're my friends, after all).

To pay them back for using them as a test group, I'll be uploading it to the App store — I show you how to do the same with yours, in detail, in Chapter 13.

After I go through developing ReturnMeTo, I take you through the design of MobileTravel411 in Chapter 14. Then I show you how to implement a subset of this application, iPhoneTravel411, which shows you how to use much of the "technology" that implements the functionality of the MobileTravel411 application. You'll find out how to use table views (like the ones you see in the Contacts, iPod, Mail, and Settings applications that come with the iPhone), access data on the Web, go out to and return from Web sites while staying in your application, store data in files, include data with your application, allow users to set preferences, and even how to resume your application where the user last left off. I'll even talk about localization and self-configuring controllers and models. (Don't worry; by the time you get there, you'll know exactly what that means.)

Figure 1-2:
ReturnMeTo
— please!

What's Next

I'm sure that you are raring to go now and just can't wait to download the Software Development Kit (SDK) from the iPhone Developers Web site. That's exactly what I did back in the day — and later was sorry that I didn't spend more time up front understanding how applications work in the iPhone environment.

So I ask you to be patient. In the next chapter I explain what goes on behind the screen, and then, I promise, it's off to the races.

Chapter 2

Looking Behind the Screen

*O*ne of the things that makes iPhone software development so appealing is the richness of the tools and frameworks provided in the Apple's iPhone Software Development Kit for iPhone Applications (SDK). The *frameworks* are especially important; each one is a distinct body of code that actually implements your application's "generic" functionality — gives the application its basic way of working, in other words. This is especially true of one framework in particular — the UIKit framework, the heart of the user interface.

In this chapter, I'm going to lead you on a journey through most of the iPhone's user interface architecture — a mostly static view that explains what the various pieces are, what each does, and how they interact with each other. This will lay the groundwork for developing the ReturnMeTo application's user interface, which you get a chance to tackle in Chapter 5. After that's done — but before you start major coding — I'll take you on a similar tour of the iPhone application *runtime environment* — the dynamic view of all the pieces working together when, for example, the user launches your application or touches a button on the screen.

Using Frameworks

A framework is designed to easily integrate any of the code that gives your application its specific functionality — the code that runs your game or delivers the information that your user wants, for example. Frameworks are therefore similar to software libraries, but with an added twist. Frameworks also implement a program's flow of control, unlike in a software library, where it's dictated by the programmer. That means that, instead of the programmer deciding in what order things happen — what objects and methods get called and in what order when an application launches, or what objects and methods get called in what order when a user touches a button on the screen — all of that is already a part of the framework and does not need to be specified by the programmer.

When you use a framework, you give your application a ready-made set of basic functions; you've told it, "Here's how to act like an application." With the framework in place, all you need to do is add the application's specific functionality you want — the content and the controls and views that enable the user to access and use that content — to the frameworks.

The frameworks and the iPhone OS provide some pretty complex functionality, such as

- Launching the application and displaying a window on the screen
- Displaying controls on the screen and responding to a user action — changing a toggle switch for example, or scrolling a view, like the list of your contacts
- Accessing sites on the Internet, not just through a browser, but from within your own program
- Managing user preferences
- Playing sounds and movies
- The list goes on — you get the picture

Some developers talk in terms of "using a framework"; I think about the matter differently: You don't use frameworks so much as they "use" you. You provide the functions that the framework accesses; it needs your code in order to become an application that does something other than start up, display a blank window, and then end. This perspective makes figuring out how to work with a framework much easier. (For one thing, it lets the programmer know where he or she is essential.)

If this seems too good to be true, well, okay, it is — all that complexity (and convenience) comes at a cost. It can be really difficult to get your head around the whole thing, and know exactly where (and how) to add your application's functionality to that supplied by the framework. That's where *design patterns* come in. Understanding the design patterns behind the frameworks gives you a way of thinking about a framework, especially UIKit, that doesn't make your head explode.

Using Design Patterns

A major theme of this chapter is the fact that, when it comes to iPhone app development, the UIKit framework does a lot of the heavy lifting for you. That's all well and good, but it's a little more complicated than that: The framework is designed around certain programming paradigms, also known as *design patterns*. The design pattern is a model that your own code must be consistent with.

To understand how to take best advantage of the power of the framework — or (better put) how the framework objects want to use *you* best — you need to understand design patterns. If you don't understand them — or if you try to work around them because you're sure you have a "better" way of doing things — it will actually make your job much more difficult. (Developing software can be hard enough, so making your job more difficult is definitely something you want to avoid.) Getting a handle on the basic design patterns used (and expected by) the framework helps you develop applications that make the best use of the frameworks. This means the least amount of work in the shortest amount of time.

The iPhone design patterns can help you to understand not only how to structure your code, but also how the framework itself is structured. They describe relationships and interactions between classes or objects, as well as how responsibilities should be distributed amongst classes so the iPhone does what you want it to do.

The common definition of a design pattern is "a solution to a problem in a context." (Uh, guys, that's not too helpful.) At that level of abstraction, the concept gets fuzzy and ambiguous. So here's how I'll use the term throughout this book:

> In programming terms, a *design pattern* is a commonly used template that gives you a consistent way to get a particular task done.

There are three basic design patterns you need to be comfortable with:

- ✔ Model-View-Controller (MVC)
- ✔ Delegation
- ✔ Target-Action

Of these, the Model-View-Controller design pattern is the key to understanding how an iPhone application works. I'll defer the discussion of the last two until after you get the MVC under your belt.

The Model-View-Controller (MVC) pattern

The iPhone frameworks are *object-oriented*. The easiest way to understand what that really means is to think about a team. The work that needs to get done is divided up and assigned to individual team members (objects). Every member of a team has a job, and works with other team members to get things done. What's more, a "good" team doesn't butt in on what other members are doing — just like how objects in object oriented programming spend their time taking care of business and not caring what the object in the virtual cubicle next door is doing.

Object-oriented programming was originally developed to make code more maintainable, reusable, extensible, and understandable (what a concept!) by tucking all the functionality behind well-defined interfaces — the actual details of how something works (as well as its data) is hidden. This makes modifying and extending an application much easier.

Great — so far — but a pesky question still plagues programmers:

> *Exactly how do you decide on the objects and what each one does?*

Sometimes the answer to that question is pretty easy — just use the real world as a model (Eureka!). In the MobileTravel411 application that serves as an example later in this book, some of the classes I use are `Airport` and `Currency`. But when it comes to a generic program structure, how *do* you decide what the objects should be? That may not be so obvious.

The Model-View-Controller (MVC) is a well-established way to group application functions into objects. Variations of it have been around at least since the early days of Smalltalk, one of the very first object-oriented languages. The MVC is a high-level pattern — it addresses the architecture of an application and classifies objects according to the general roles they play in an application.

The MVC pattern creates, in effect, a miniature universe for the application, populated with three kinds of objects. It also specifies roles and responsibilities for all three objects and specifies the way they're supposed to interact with each other. To make things more concrete (i.e., to keep your head from exploding) imagine a big beautiful 60-inch flat screen TV. Here's the gist:

- **Model objects:** These objects together comprise the content "engine" of your application. They contain the application's data and logic — making your application more than just a pretty face. In the MobileTravel411 application, it stores the various ways to get from Heathrow Airport to London as well as some logic to decide the best alternative based on time of day, price, and some other considerations.

  You can think of the *model* (which may be one object or several that interact) as a particular television program. One that, quite frankly, does not give a hoot about what TV set it is being shown on.

In fact, the model shouldn't give a hoot. Even though it owns its data, it should have no connection at all to the user interface and should be blissfully ignorant about what is being done with its data.

✔ **View objects:** These objects display things on the screen and respond to user actions. Pretty much anything you can see is a kind of view object — the window and all the controls, for example. Your views know how to display information that it has gotten from the model object, and how to get any input from the user the model may need. But the view itself should know nothing about the model. It may handle a request to tell the user the fastest way to London, but it doesn't bother itself with what that request means. It may display the different ways to get to London, although it doesn't care about the content options it displays for you.

You can think of the *view* as a television screen that doesn't care about what program it is showing or what channel you just selected.

The UIKit framework provides many different kinds of views, as you'll find out later on in this chapter.

If the view knows nothing about the model, and the model knows nothing about the view, how do you get data and other notifications to pass from one to the other? To get that conversation started ("Model: I've just updated my data." View: "Hey, give me something to display," for example), you need the third element in the MVC triumvirate, the controller.

✔ **Controller objects:** These objects connect the application's view objects to its model objects. They supply the view objects with what they need to display (getting it from the model), and also provide the model with user input from the view.

You can think of the *controller* as the circuitry that pulls the show off of the cable, and sends it to the screen, or requests a particular pay-per-view show.

The MVC in action

Imagine that an iPhone user is at Heathrow Airport, and he or she starts the handy MobileTravel411 application mentioned so often in these pages. The view will display his or her location as "Heathrow Airport." The user may tap a button that requests the best way to get into London. The controller "interprets" that request and tells the model what it needs to do by sending a message to the appropriate method in the model object with the necessary parameters. The model computes a list of alternatives (taxi, bus, train) and the controller then delivers that information to the view, which promptly displays it. If the user selects "train," for example, that information is then sent to the model, which then sends back the details of the train.

All this is illustrated in Figure 2-1.

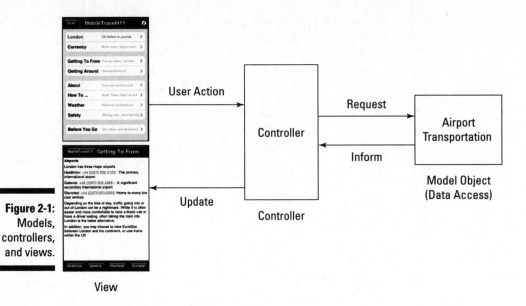

Figure 2-1:
Models,
controllers,
and views.

View

When you think about your application in terms of Model, View, and Controller objects, the UIKit framework starts to make sense. It also begins to lift the fog from where at least part of your application-specific behavior needs to go. Before I get more into that, however, you need to know a little more about the classes provided to you by the UIKit that implement the MVC design pattern — windows, views, and view controllers.

Working with Windows and Views

After an application is launched, it's going to be the only application running on the system — aside from the operating system software, of course. iPhone applications have only a single window, so you won't find separate document windows for displaying content. Instead, everything is displayed in that single window and your application interface takes over the entire screen. When your application is running, it is all the user is doing with the iPhone.

Looking out the window

The single window you see displayed on the iPhone is an instance of the UIWindow class. This window is created at launch time, either programmatically by you or automatically by UIKit loading it from a *nib* file — a special file that contains instant objects that are reconstituted at run time (You'll find out more about nib files starting in Chapter 5). You then add views and controls to the window. In general, after you create the window object (that is, if you create it instead of having it done for you), you never really have to think about again.

An iPhone window cannot be closed or manipulated directly by the user. It is your application that programmatically manages the window.

Although your application never creates more than one window at a time, the iPhone OS does use additional windows on top of your window. The system status bar is one example. You can also display alerts on top of your window by using the supplied Alert views

Figure 2-2 shows the window layout on the iPhone for the MobileTravel411 application.

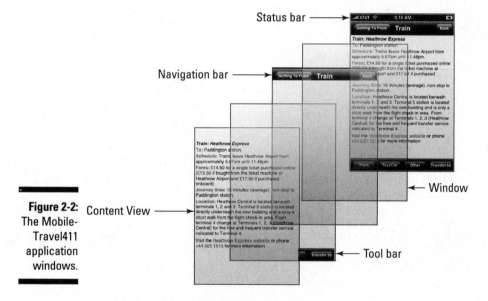

Status bar

Navigation bar

← Window

Figure 2-2: The Mobile-Travel411 application windows.

Content View

← Tool bar

Admiring the view

In an iPhone app world, View objects are responsible for the view functionality in the Model-View-Controller architecture.

A view is a rectangular area on the screen (on top of a window). I'll often refer to the *content view,* that portion of data and controls that appear between the upper and lower bars shown in Figure 2-2.

In the UIKit framework, windows are really a special kind of view, but for purposes of this discussion, I'm going to be talking about views that sit on top of the window.

As you will see, there are two ways you need to think about views. From the user perspective, the views sit on top of each other. From a programming perspective, however, the views that are on top of the windows visually are really subviews inside the window view. I'll explain that more as we continue on.

What views do

Views are the main way for your application to interact with a user. This interaction happens in two ways:

- ✔ **Views display content:** For example, making drawing and animation happen on-screen.

  In essence, the View object displays the data from the Model object.

- ✔ **Views handle touch events:** They respond when the user touches a button, for example.

  Handling touch events is part of a *responder chain* (a special logical sequence detailed in Chapter 6).

The view hierarchy

Views and subviews create a view hierarchy. There are two ways of looking at it (no pun intended this time) — visually (how the user perceives it) and programmatically (how you create it). You must be clear about the differences or you will find yourself in a state of confusion that resembles Times Square on New Year's Eve.

Looking at it visually, the window is at the base of this hierarchy with a *content view* on top of it (a transparent view that fills the window's Content rectangle). The content view displays information and also allows the user to interact with the application, using (preferably standard) user-interface items such as text fields, buttons, toolbars, and tables.

In your program that relationship is different. The content view is added to the Window view as a *subview*.

- ✔ Views added to the content view become *subviews* of it.
- ✔ Views added to the content view become the *superviews* of any views added to them.
- ✔ A view can have one (and only one) superview and zero or more subviews.

It seems counterintuitive, but a subview is displayed *on top of* its parent view (that is, on top of its superview). Think about this relationship as containment: a superview *contains* its subviews. Figure 2-3 shows an example of a view hierarchy.

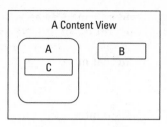

The visual hierarchy
... translates to a structural one:

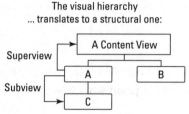

Figure 2-3:
The view
hierarchy
is both
visual and
structural.

Controls — such as buttons, text fields, and the like — are really view sub-classes that become subviews. So are any other display areas you may spec-ify. The view must manage its subviews, as well as resize itself with respect to its superviews. Fortunately, much of what the view must do is already coded for you: The UIKit framework supplies the code that defines view behavior.

The view hierarchy plays a key role in both drawing and event handling. When a window is sent a message to display itself, the window asks its sub-view to render itself first. If that view has a subview, it asks *its* subview to render itself first, going down the structural hierarchy (or up the visual struc-ture) until the last subview is reached. It then renders itself and returns to its caller, which renders itself, and so on.

You create or modify a view hierarchy whenever you add a view to another view, either programmatically or with the help of the Interface Builder. The UIKit framework automatically handles all the relationships associated with the view hierarchy.

I pretty much glossed over this visual vs. programmatic view hierarchy stuff when I started developing my applications — making it really difficult to get a handle on what was going on.

The kinds of views you use

The UIView class defines the basic properties of a view, and you may be able to use it as is — like I will in the ReturnMeTo application — by simply adding some controls.

The framework also provides you with a number of other views that are sub-classed from `UIView`. These views implement the kinds of things that you as a developer need to do on a regular basis.

It's important to use the View objects that are part of the `UIKit` framework. When you use an object such as a `UISlider` or `UIButton`, your slider or button behaves just like a slider or button in any other iPhone application. This enables the consistency in appearance and behavior across applications that users expect. (For more on how this kind of consistency is one of the characteristics of a great application, see Chapter 1.)

Container views

Container views are a technical (Apple) term for content views that do more than just lie there on the screen and display your controls and other content.

The `UIScrollView` class, for example, adds scrolling without you having to do any work.

`UITableView` inherits this scrolling capability from `UIScrollView` and adds the ability to display lists and respond to the selections of an item in that list. Think of the Contacts application (and a host of others). `UITableView` is one of the primary navigation views on the iPhone; you'll work a lot with table views starting with Chapter 14.

Another container view, the `UIToolbar` class, contains button-like controls — and you find those everywhere on the iPhone. In Mail, for example, you touch an icon in the bottom toolbar to respond to an e-mail.

Controls

Controls are the fingertip-friendly graphics you see extensively used in a typical application's user interface. Controls are actually subclasses of the `UIControl` superclass, a subclass of the `UIView` class. They include touch-able items like buttons, text fields, sliders, and switches, as well as text fields in which you enter data.

Controls make heavy use of the Target-Action design pattern, which I'll get to soon. (I talk more about controls and how they fit in to the Target-Action pattern in Chapter 10.)

Display views

Think of display views as controls that look good, but don't really do any-thing except, well, look good. These include `UIImageView`, `UILabel` (which I use in Chapter 5 to display the ReturnMeTo application's phone number), `UIProgressView`, and `UIActivityIndicatorView`.

Text and Web views

Text and *Web views* provide a way to display formatted text in your application. The `UITextView` class supports the display and editing of multiple lines of text in a scrollable area. The `UIWebView` class provides a way to display HTML content. These views can be used as the content view, or can also be used in the same way as a display view above, as a subview of a content view. I use a `UIWebView` in Chapter 11 to allow someone who has found an iPhone to call the owner's number by simply tapping it. `UIWebViews` also are the primary way to include graphics and formatted text in text display views. (I use them when I show you how to develop iPhoneTravel411.)

Alert views and action sheets

Alert views and a*ction sheets* present a message to the user, along with buttons that allow the user to respond to the message. Alert views and action sheets are similar in function but look and behave differently. For example, the `UIAlertView` class displays a blue alert box that pops up on the screen and the `UIActionSheet` class displays a box that slides in from the bottom of the screen.

Navigation views

Tab bars and *navigation bars* work in conjunction with View controllers to provide tools for navigating in your application. Normally you don't need to create a `UITabBar` or `UINavigationBar` directly — it's easier to use Interface Builder or configure these views through a tab bar or navigation bar controller.

The window

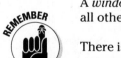

A *window* provides a surface for drawing content and is the root container for all other views.

There is typically only one window per application.

Controlling View Controllers

View controllers implement the Controller component of the Model-View-Controller design pattern. These Controller objects contain the code that connects the application's View objects to its Model objects. They provide the data to the view. Whenever the view needs to display something, the View controller goes out and gets what the view needs from the model. Similarly, view controllers respond to controls in your content view and may do things like tell the model to update its data (when the user adds or changes text in a text field, for example), or compute something (the current value of, sat, your US dollars in British pounds), or change the view being displayed (like when the user hits the detail disclosure button on the iPod application to learn more about a song).

As I'll describe in the Target-Action section later in this chapter, a view controller is often the (target) object that responds to the on-screen controls. The Target-Action mechanism is what enables the view controller to be aware of any changes in the view, which can then be transmitted to the model. For example, the user may decide — after looking at the Heathrow Express option — that he or she has too much luggage (or is too upscale) to take the train, and opts for a taxi or rental car instead.

Figure 2-4 shows what happens when the user taps the Taxi/Car tab in the MobileTravel411 application to request information about taking a cab or renting a car to get to London.

1. The method of that view's view controller is called to handle the request.

2. The view controller's method interacts with a Model object.

3. The Model object processes the request from the user for information on a taxi/car from Heathrow to London.

4. The Model object sends the data back to the view controller.

5. The view controller creates a new view to present the information.

View controllers have other vital iPhone responsibilities as well, such as:

✔ Managing a set of views — including creating them, or flushing them from memory during low-memory situations.

✔ Responding to a change in the device's orientation — say, landscape to portrait, — by resizing the managed views to match the new orientation.

✔ Creating *modal* views that require the user to do something (touch the Yes button, for example) before returning to the application.

You would use a modal view to ensure the user has paid attention to the implications of an action (for example, "Are you *sure* you want to delete all your contacts?").

View controllers are also typically the objects that serve as delegates and data sources for table views (more about those in Chapter 15).

In addition to the base `UIViewController` class, `UIKit` includes subclasses such as `UITabBarController`, `UINavigationController`, `UITableViewController`, and `UIImagePickerController` to manage the tab bar, navigation bar, table views, and access the camera and photo library.

Using naming conventions

When creating your own classes, it's a good idea to follow a couple of standard framework-naming conventions.

✔ Class names (such as `View`) should start with a capital letter.

✔ The names of methods (such as `viewDid Load`) should start with a lowercase letter.

✔ The names of instance variables (such as `frame`) should start with a lowercase letter.

When you do it this way, it makes it easier to understand from the name what something actually is.

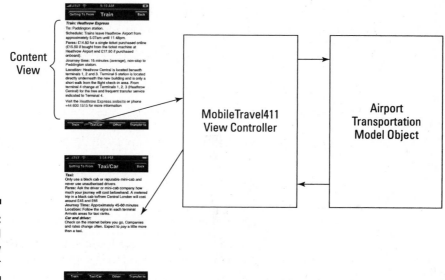

Content View

MobileTravel411 View Controller

Airport Transportation Model Object

Figure 2-4: The world of the view controller

  Even if your application is a graphics application, you'll want to use a view controller just to manage a single view and auto-rotate it when the device's orientation changes.

What About the Model?

As you have seen (and will continue to discover) a lot of the functionality you need is already in the Framework objects.

But when it comes to the Model objects, for the most part you're pretty much on your own. You're going to need to design and create Model objects to hold the data and carry out the logic. In my MobileTravel411 application, for example, you create an `Airport` object that knows the different ways to get into the city that it supports.

You may find classes in the framework that help you get the nuts and bolts of the model working. But the actual content and specific functionality is up to you. As for actually implementing Model objects, I show you how to do that in Chapter 17.)

Adding Your Own Application's Behavior

Earlier in this chapter (by now it probably seems like a million years ago), I mentioned two other design patterns used in addition to the Model-View-Controller (MVC) pattern. If you have a photographic memory, you won't need me telling you that those two patterns are the Delegation pattern and the Target-Action pattern. These patterns, along with the MVC pattern and subclassing, provide the mechanisms for you to add your application-specific behavior to the `UIKit` (and any other) framework.

I have already talked about the first way to add behavior, and that is through Model objects in the MVC pattern. Model objects contain the data and logic that make your application, well, your application.

The second way — the way people traditionally think about adding behavior to an object oriented program, if you want to know the truth — is through *subclassing,* — where you first create a new (sub) class that inherits behavior and instance variables from another (super) class and then add additional behavior, instance variables and *properties* (I'll explain properties in Chapter 6*)* to the mix until you come up with just what you want. The idea here is to start with something basic and then add to it — kind of like taking a deuce coupe (1932 Ford) and turning it into a hot rod. You'd subclass a view controller class, for example, to respond to controls.

The third way to add behavior involves using the Delegation pattern, which allows you to customize an object's behavior without subclassing by basically forcing another object to do the first object's work for it. For example, you could use the Delegation design pattern at application startup to automatically call a method `applicationDidFinishLaunching:` that gives you a place to do your own application-specific initialization. All you do is add your code to the method.

The final way to add behavior involves the *Target-Action* design pattern, which allows your application to respond to an event. When a user touches a button, for example, you specify what method should be called to respond to the button touch. What is interesting about this pattern is that it also requires subclassing — usually a view controller (see above) — in order to add the code to handle the event.

In the next few sections, I'll go into a little more detail about Delegation patterns and Target-Action patterns.

The Delegation pattern

Delegation is a pattern used extensively in the iPhone framework, so much so that it's very important to clearly understand. In fact, I have no problems telling you that, once you understand it, your life will be much easier. Until the light bulb went on for me, I sometimes felt like I was trying to make my way through one of those legendary London pea soup fogs.

As I said in the previous section, delegation is a way of customizing the behavior of an object without subclassing it. Instead, one object (a framework object) delegates the task of implementing one of its responsibilities to another object. You are using a behavior-rich object supplied by the framework as is, and putting the code for program-specific behavior in a separate (delegate) object. When a request is made of the framework object, the method of the delegate which implements the program-specific behavior is automatically called.

For example, the UIApplication object handles most of the actual work needed to run the application. But, as you will see, it calls your application delegate's applicationDidFinishLaunching: method to give you an opportunity to restore the application's window and view to where it was when the user previously left off. You can also use this method to create objects that are unique to your application.

When a framework object has been designed to use delegates to implement certain behaviors, the behaviors it requires (or gives you the option to implement) are defined in a *protocol*.

Protocols define an interface that the delegate object implements. On the iPhone, protocols can be formal or informal, although I'm going to concentrate solely on the former since it includes support for things like type checking and runtime checking to see if an object conforms to the protocol.

In a formal protocol you usually don't have to implement all of the methods; many are declared optional, meaning you only have to implement the ones relevant to your application. Before it attempts to send a message to its delegate, the host object determines whether the delegate implements the method (via a `respondsToSelector:` message) to avoid the embarrassment of branching into nowhere if the method is not implemented.

You'll find out much more about delegation and the Delegation pattern when you develop the ReturnMeTo and especially the iPhoneTravel411 applications in later chapters.

The Target-Action pattern

The *Target-Action* pattern is used to let your application know that a user has done something. He or she may have tapped a button or entered some text, for example. The control — a button, say — sends a message (the Action message) that you specify to the target you have selected to handle that particular action. The receiving object, or the Target, is usually a View Controller object.

If you wanted to start your car from your iPhone (not a bad idea if you have ever lived in some place like Minneapolis), you could display two buttons, Start and Heater. When you tapped Start, you could have used Interface Builder to specify that the target is the `CarController` object and that the method to call is `ignition`. Figure 2-5 shows the Target-Action mechanism in action. (If you're curious about `IBAction` and `(id) sender`, I'll explain what they are about when I show you how to use the target-action pattern in your application.)

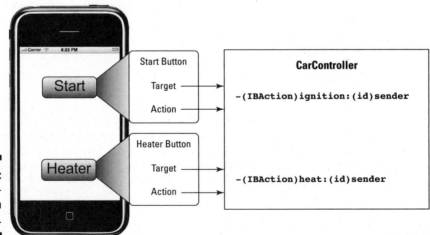

Figure 2-5: The Target-Action mechanism.

The Target-Action mechanism enables you to create a control object and tell it not only what object you want handling the event, but also the message to send. For example, if the user touches a "Ring Bell" button on-screen, I want to send a "Ring Bell" message to the view controller. But if the "Wave Flag" button on the same screen is touched, I want to be able to send the same view controller the "Wave Flag" message. If I couldn't specify the message, all buttons would have to send the same message. It would then make the coding harder and more complex, since I would have to identify which button had sent the message and what to do in response, and make changing the user interface more work and more error prone.

As you'll soon discover when creating your application, you can set a control's action and target through the Interface Builder application. This allows you to specify what method in which object should respond to a control without having to write any code.

You can also change the target and action dynamically by sending the control or its cell `setTarget:` and `setAction:` messages.

For more on the Interface Builder application, check out Chapter 5.

Doing What When?

The `UIKit` framework provides a great deal of ready-made functionality, but the beauty of `UIKit` lies in the fact that — as this chapter has made clear — and you can customize its behavior using three distinct mechanisms.

- ✔ Subclassing
- ✔ Target-Action
- ✔ Delegation

One of the challenges facing a new developer is to determine which of these mechanisms to use when. (That was certainly the case for me.) To ensure that you have an overall conceptual picture of the iPhone application architecture, check out the Cheat Sheet in the front of this book, where I give you a summary of which mechanisms are used when. (I wish I'd had this when I started developing my application — but at least you do now.)

Whew!

Congratulations! You have just gone through the Classic Comics version of hundreds of pages of Apple documentation, reference manuals, and how-to guides.

Well, you still have a bit more to explore — for example, how all these pieces work together at runtime (details, details . . .). But before that piece of the puzzle can make sense, you need to touch, feel, and get inside an application. As part of that process, I'm going to do a little demonstrating:

- ✔ I show you how to become a registered developer and download the SDK.
- ✔ I show you how to use the tools in the SDK to create an application framework and build the User Interface.
- ✔ I finish the conversation on iPhone architecture in Chapter 6.

When you've had a stroll through those adventures, you'll know everything you need to know about how to create a user interface and add the functionality to make your application do what you promised the user it would do. (How's that for a plan?)

Chapter 3

Enlisting in the Developer Corps

*P*ersonally, I'm not much of a joiner. I like to keep a low profile and just get on with having fun doing what I do.

But if you want to develop software for the iPhone, you do have to get involved with (yet another) major corporation and its policies and procedures. Although Apple's iPhone Software Development Kit (SDK) is free, you do have to register as an iPhone developer first. That will give you access to all the documentation and other resources found on the iPhone Developer Web site. This whole ritual transforms you into a *Registered iPhone Developer*.

Becoming a Registered Developer is free, but there's a catch: If you actually want to run your application on your iPhone, as opposed to only on the Simulator that comes with the SDK, you have to join the developer program. Fortunately, membership only costs $99, but then again, you have no choice if you want your application to see the light of day on the iPhone. This is called joining the *iPhone Developer Program*.

In this chapter, I lead you through the process of becoming a Registered Developer, signing on to — and then exploring — the iPhone Dev Center Web site, downloading the SDK so you can start using it, and then (finally) joining the developer program.

What you see when you go through this process yourself may be slightly different from what you see here. Don't panic. It's because Apple changes the site from time to time.

Becoming a Registered iPhone Developer

Although just having to become a registered developer is annoying to some people, it doesn't help that the process itself can be a bit confusing as well. You'll have to sign on several times, and occasionally it will seem as if you've somehow gotten off track. Fear not! Follow the steps and I will get you safely to the end of the road. (If you've already registered, skip to the next section where I show what the iPhone Dev Center has available as well as how to download the SDK.)

1. **Point your browser to** `http://developer.apple.com/iphone/`.

   Doing so brings you to a page similar to the one shown in Figure 3-1. Apple does change this site occasionally, so when you get here it may be a little different. You may be tempted by some of the links, but they aren't live, and won't be until you log in as a Registered Developer.

2. **Click the Not a Registered iPhone Developer? Start Now link in the top-right corner of the screen.**

   A login page appears.

3. **Using the login page, do what comes naturally — log in.**

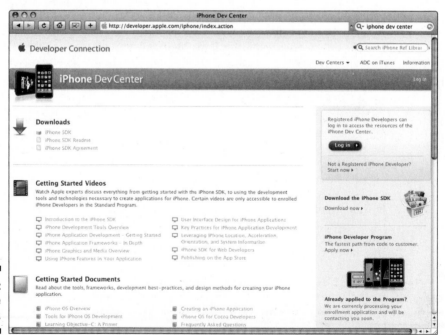

Figure 3-1:
The iPhone
Dev Center.

You can use your current Apple ID (the same one you'd use for iTunes or any other Apple Web site) or create an Apple ID and then log in:

- If you don't have an Apple ID, click the Create Apple ID button. Skip to Step 4 and you'll find yourself at the page shown in Figure 3-2.

- If you already have an Apple ID, click Log In to be taken to a screen where you can log in with your Apple ID and password. That will take you to Step 4 with some of your information already filled out. I know it looks like it is asking you to log in to the iPhone Dev center, even though you haven't registered yet, but that's the way it is.

4. **Fill out the personal profile form and then click Continue.**

If you have an Apple ID, most of the form will already be filled out.

You must fill in the country code in the phone number field. If you're living in the U.S., the country code is 1.

5. **Complete the next part of the form to register as a developer.**

You'll be asked some basic business questions. After you've filled everything in and clicked the Submit button, you're taken to an acknowledgment page, which mentions that a confirmation e-mail will be sent to the address you stipulated.

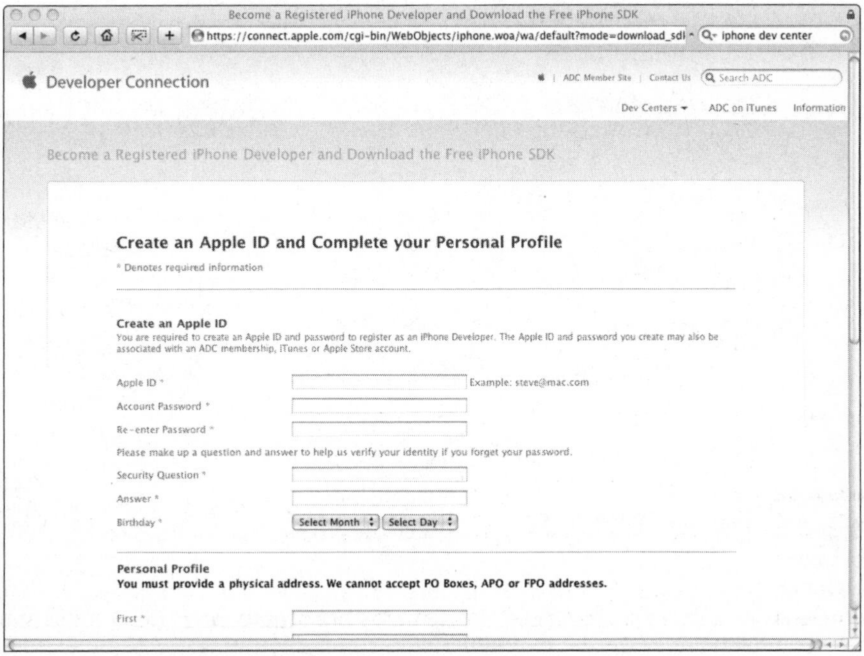

Figure 3-2:
Creating an
Apple ID.

> Don't forget to scroll to the bottom and check the confirmation that you have read and accept the terms and conditions.

6. **Using your e-mail application, open the e-mail from Apple and click the Download Free SDK button.**

   Clicking the Download Free SDK button automatically logs you in to the iPhone Dev center, as you see in Figure 3-3

If you want to do all this logging-in stuff later, navigate back to `http://developer.apple.com/iphone/` (as I did way back in Step 1), select Log In on the iPhone Dev Center home page, and then enter your Apple ID and password.

So, you are now an officially registered iPhone developer. The next section starts showing you what you can do with your new status.

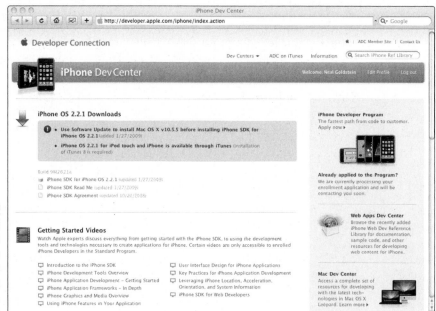

Figure 3-3:
Logged in to the iPhone Dev Center from the e-mail.

Exploring the iPhone Dev Center

I spend some time later in this section talking a little bit about some of the resources available to you in the iPhone Dev Center, but for the moment let's focus on what you are *really* after. I'm talking about your Phone SDK for iPhone OS 2.2.1 download, over there in that pink section bearing the title IPhone OS 2.2.1 Downloads. The SDK includes a host of tools for you to develop your application. Here's a handy list to help you keep them all straight:

✔ **Xcode:** This refers to Apple's complete development environment, which integrates all these features: a source editor, build system, graphical debugger, and project management. (I introduce you to the code editor's features in more detail in Chapter 7.)

✔ **Frameworks:** The iPhone's multiple frameworks help make it easy to develop for. Creating an application can be thought of as simply adding your application-specific behavior to a framework. The frameworks do all the rest. For example, the UIKit framework provides fundamental code for building your application — the required application behavior, classes for windows, views (including those that display text and Web content), controls, and view controllers. (All of the things I covered in Chapter 2, in other words.) The UIKit framework also provides standard interfaces to core location data, the user's contacts and photo library, accelerometer data, and the iPhone's built-in camera.

✔ **Interface Builder:** I use Interface Builder in Chapter 5 to build the user interface for the ReturnMeTo application. But Interface Builder is more than your run-of-the-mill program that builds graphical user interfaces. In Chapter 6, I show you how Xcode and Interface Builder work together to give you ways to build (and automatically create at runtime) objects for the user interface — as well as the objects that provide the infrastructure for your application.

✔ **iPhone Simulator:** The simulator allows you to debug your application and do some other testing on your Mac by simulating the iPhone. The Simulator will run most iPhone programs, but it doesn't support hardware-dependent features such as iPhone's accelerometer or camera — although it does allow you to *fake* having a camera.

✔ **Instruments:** The Instruments application lets you measure your application while it is running on a device. It gives you a number of performance metrics, including those for testing memory and network use. It will also work (in a limited way) on the iPhone Simulator, and you can test some aspects of your design there.

The iPhone Simulator does not emulate such real-life iPhone characteristics as CPU speed or memory throughput. If you want to understand how your application performs on the device from a user's perspective, you have to use the actual device, and the Instruments application.

Looking forward to using the SDK

The tools in the SDK support a development process that most people find comfortable. They allow you to rapidly get a user interface up and running to see what it actually looks like. You can add code a little at a time, and then run it after each new addition to see how it works. I take you through this incremental process as I develop the ReturnMeTo application; for now, here's a bird's-eye view of iPhone application development, one step at a time:

1. **Start with Xcode.**

   Xcode provides several project templates that you can use to get you off to a fast start. (In Chapter 5, I do just that to get my user interface up and running quickly.)

2. **Design and create the user interface.**

   Interface Builder has graphic-design tools you can use to create your application's user interface. This saves a great deal of time and effort. It also reduces the amount of code you have to write by creating resource files that your application can then upload automatically.

   If you don't want to use Interface Builder, you can always build your user interface by scratch, creating each individual piece and linking them all together within your program itself. Sometimes, Interface Builder is the best way to create on-screen elements; sometimes the hands-on approach works better. (In Chapter 17, you get a chance to create user interface elements with good old "by-hand" programming.)

3. **Write the code.**

   The Xcode editor provides several features that help you write code. I run through these features in Chapter 7.

4. **Build and run your application**.

   You build your application on your computer and run it in the iPhone Simulator application or (provided you've joined the Development Program) on your device.

5. **Test your application.**

   You'll want to test the functionality of your application as well as response time.

6. **Measure and tune your application's performance.**

   After you have a running application, you want to make sure that it makes optimal use of resources such as memory and CPU cycles.

7. **Do it all again until you're done.**

Resources on the iPhone Dev Center

You're not left on your own when it comes to the Seven-Step Plan for Creating Great iPhone Apps in the previous section. After all, you have me to help you on the way — as well as a heap of information squirreled away in various corners of the iPhone Dev Center. I've found the following resources to be especially helpful:

  ✔ **Links to the iPhone Reference Library:** This is all of the documentation you could ever want (except, of course, the answer to that one question you really need answered at 3:00 in the morning, but that's the way it goes). To be honest, most of this stuff only turns out to be really useful *after* you have a good handle on what you're doing. As you go through this book, however, an easier way to access some of this documentation will be through Xcode's Research Assistant and the Documentation window, which I show you in Chapter 7.

If you've never programmed in the Objective-C language before, here's the drill for getting up to speed:

1. *Choose iPhone Reference Library⇨Go to Reference Library.*

2. *On the Reference Library page, choose the Getting Started tab.*

3. *Choose Learning Objective-C: A Primer.*

   Here you'll also find links to an overview of Object-Oriented Programming with Objective-C, as well as an introduction to the Objective-C 2.0 Programming Language. (You can get to the same links in the iPhone Reference Library section by selecting Guides under Resource Types.)

✔ **iPhone programming videos:** These are relatively light on content.

✔ **Coding How-To's:** These tend to be a lot more valuable when you already have something of a knowledge base.

✔ **Sample code:** On the one hand, sample code of any kind is always valuable. Most good developers look to these kinds of samples to get themselves started. They'll take something that closely approximates what they want to do, and modify it until it does. When I started iPhone development, there were no books like this one; so much of what I learned came from looking at the samples and then making some changes to see how things worked. On the other hand, it can give you hours of (misguided) pleasure and can be quite the time waster and task avoider.

You can download the sample code in .dmg or .zip format. .zip is a lot easier to work with.

✔ **Getting started documents and videos:** Think of them as an introduction to the materials in the iPhone Reference Library.

✔ **A link to the developer forums:** I'd be the first to say that developer forums can be very helpful, but I'd also be the first to admit that they are a great way to avoid doing other things, like working. As you scroll through the questions people have, be careful about some of the answers you see. No one is validating the information people are giving out. But take heart: Pretty soon you'll be able to answer some of those questions better yourself.

Downloading the SDK

Enough prep work. Time to do some downloading. Make your way to that pink section of the iPhone Dev Center — the section that has IPhone OS 2.2.1 Downloads prominently displayed at the top. (Refer to Figure 3-3.).

By the time you read this book, it may no longer be version 2.2.1. You should download the latest (non-beta, non-prelease) SDK. That way you will get the most stable version to start with.

The actual download link for the iPhone SDK — the Software Development Kit for iPhone OS 2.2.1 — is underneath the pink section, but don't just ignore all the stuff in pink. It's pink for a reason: Pink highlights indicate pre-download info you really need to pay attention to. There is also a link under that — iPhone SDK Readme — that will explain what's new in the release and any compatibility issues.

> ✔ **Use Software Update to install Mac OS X v10.5.5 before installing iPhone SDK for iPhone OS 2.2.1 (added 1/27/2009):** It just makes sense for your computer's operating system to be as up-to-date as possible.
>
> ✔ **iPhone OS 2.2.1 for iPod touch and iPhone is available through iTunes (installation of iTunes 8 is required):** Nice to know if you haven't been keeping your iPhone software up to date.

After perusing the pink section — and updating your system's and iPhone's OS's, if necessary — click the iPhone SDK for iPhone OS 2.2.1 link right under the pink box. (Remember: It's right under the pink section as I write this, but it might not be in exactly the same place when you try it; a link proclaiming, "Download the SDK" will be prominently displayed, no matter what.)

After clicking the link, you're going to see the standard Downloads dialog, which lets you know how the download's going.

When it's done downloading, the iPhone SDK window appears onscreen, complete with an About iPhone SDK manual (in PDF form), and installer and various packages tied tot he install process. All you then have to do is double-click the iPhone SDK installer and follow the (really simple) installation instructions. After you do all that, you'll have your very own iPhone Software Development Kit on your hard drive.

You'll become intimately acquainted with the iPhone SDK during the course of your project, but for now there's still one more bit of housekeeping to take care of: Joining the official iPhone Developer Program. Read on to see how that works.

Joining the iPhone Developer Program

Okay, the simulator that comes standard with the iPhone SDK is a great tool for learning to program, but it does have some limitations. It doesn't support hardware-dependent features, such as iPhone's accelerometer or camera, and when it comes to testing, it can't really emulate such everyday iPhone realities as CPU speed or memory throughput.

Minor annoyances, you might say, and you might be right. The real issue, however, is that just *registering* as a developer doesn't get you one very important thing — the ability to actually run your application on your iPhone, much less to distribute your application through Apple's iPhone App Store. (Remember that the App Store is the only way for commercial developers to distribute their applications to more than a few people.) To run your app on a real iPhone or get a chance to profile your app in the iPhone App store, you have to enroll in either the Standard or Enterprise version of the iPhone Developer Program. There is much speculation behind the reason for this, but the bottom line is that that's simply the way it is. At least (I might note) it isn't all that expensive.

It used to be that that the approval process could take a while, and although the process does seem quicker these days, it's still true that you can't run your applications on your iPhone until you are approved. You should enroll as early as possible.

If you go back to the iPhoneDev Center page, you'll see a section of the right column that says iPhone Developer Program. (Refer to Figure 3-3.) Here's how you deal with that section:

1. **Click the Apply Now link.**

    The iPhone Developer program screen appears, as shown in Figure 3-4.

Figure 3-4:
The iPhone Developer Program overview.

2. **On the lower-right side of the screen, click the Learn More button.**

   A new page appears, outlining the details of each developer program, as shown in Figure 3-5.

   The Standard program costs $99. The Enterprise program costs $299 and is designed for companies developing proprietary, in-house applications for iPhone and iPod Touch. To be sure you're selecting the option that meets your needs; give the program details a once-over.

3. **Click the Apply Now button.**

   You don't actually get to choose Standard or Enterprise yet. But you do get a chance to log in again with your Apple ID and password.

4. **Do the logging-in stuff.**

   After logging in, you get a chance to go with either an Individual Enrollment or a Company Enrollment. Figures 3-6 and 3-7 show you the differences between the two options.

5. **Make your choice — Individual Enrollment or Company Enrollment — and then click Continue.**

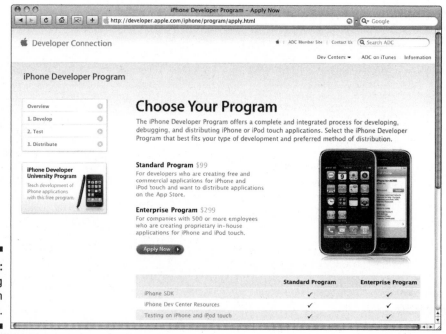

Figure 3-5:
Checking out program details.

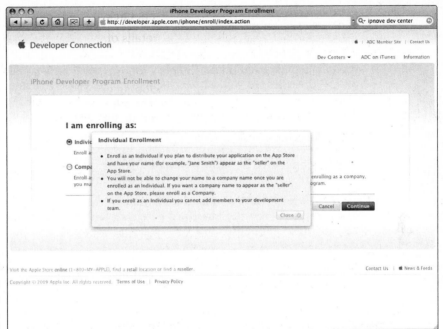

Figure 3-6:
Join as an individual.

Figure 3-7:
Join as a company.

Trust me, joining as an Individual is easier than joining as a Company. If you do go the Company route, you then have to choose whether you want the Standard program or Enterprise Program. (If you plan on distributing in-house applications, you'll need to enroll your company in the Enterprise program.) Although there are clearly some advantages to enrolling as a company — for example, you can add team members (which I discuss in connection with the developer portal in Chapter 13) — I'm a lone developer and want to sell applications on the App Store, so I joined up as an Individual.

When you join as an individual, your real name will show up when the user buys (or downloads for free) your application in the App Store. If you are concerned about privacy, or if you want to seem "bigger," the extra work invoked in signing up as a Company may be worth it for you.

6. **Confirm your enrollment in the Standard Program (if an Individual) or choose between the Standard Program and the Enterprise Program (if you are a Company) and then click Continue.**

   Doing so gets you to the iPhone Developer Program License Agreement page shown in Figure 3-8.

7. **Click the I Agree button to accept the terms and conditions.**

   You're taken through yet two more screens to confirm your information and select your currency. You finally end up on the Apple Store page (shown in Figure 3-9), where you get to fork over some of your hard-earned dough.

8. **Click the Check Out Now button to pay for your registration.**

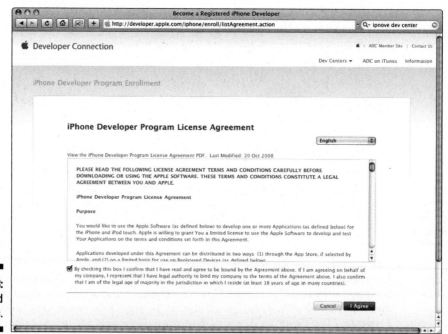

Figure 3-8:
Terms and
conditions.

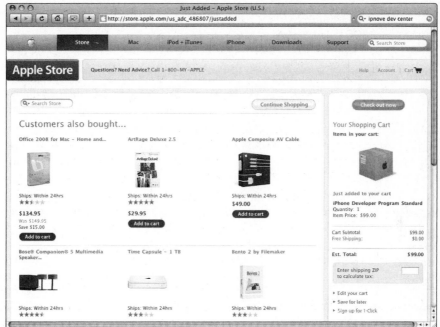

Figure 3-9:
Pay up.

Surprise, surprise, you are greeted by yet another log-in page, where you sign in using your Apple ID and password. You then get a new page where you get to enter your payment information.

A few hours later (four in my case), you get an e-mail from Apple thanking you for applying, and telling you that you need to click the e-mail's Activation Code link to finalize your registration.

9. Click your e-mail's Activation Code link.

The page you see in Figure 3-10 appears on-screen. Ignore all the stuff about receiving an e-mail — receiving the e-mail was the way you got there in the first place — and just click Submit.

You are taken to the iPhone Developer Program Portal page shown in Figure 3-11.

I wouldn't linger too long at the iPhone Developer Program Portal page, simply because it can be really confusing for a newbie. I explain this portal — which lets you provision your device, run your application on it, and prepare your creation for distribution to the App Store — in Chapter 13.

The next time you log in to the iPhone Dev Center you'll notice that the page has changed somewhat. As a freshly-minted Official iPhone Developer, you'll see the page shown in Figure 3-12. The download instructions have expanded a bit, and there's a new Program Portal link on the right side, under iPhone Developer Program. (The Program Portal is where you were sent when you first activated your iPhone Developer Program membership — refer to Figure 3-11.)

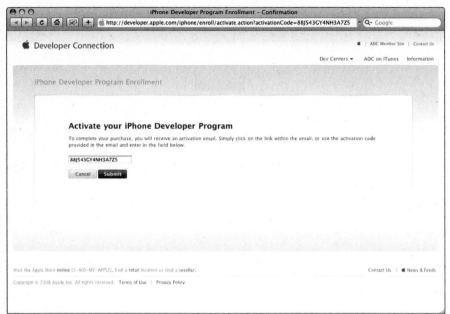

Figure 3-10:
Activating
your iPhone
Developer
Program.

Figure 3-11:
The iPhone
Developer
Program
Portal.

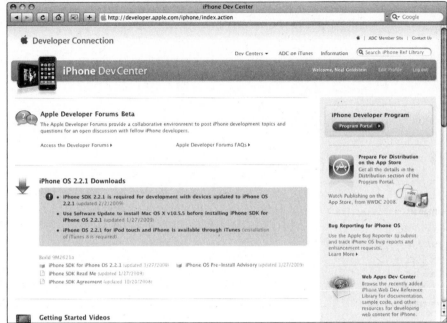

Figure 3-12:
The
Developer
Program
Portal
becomes
available.

Getting Yourself Ready for the SDK

Don't despair. I know the process is tedious, but it's over now. Going through this was definitely the *second* most annoying part of my journey toward developing software for the iPhone. The most annoying part was figuring out what Apple calls "provisioning" your iPhone — the hoops you have to jump through to actually run your application on a real, tangible, existing iPhone. I take you through the provisioning process in Chapter 13, and frankly, getting *that* process explained is worth the price of the book.

In the next chapter, I get you started using the SDK you just downloaded. I'm going to assume that you have some programming knowledge and that you also have some acquaintance with object-oriented programming, with some variant of C such as C++, C#, and maybe even with Objective-C. If those assumptions miss the mark, help me out, okay? Take another look at the "Resources on the iPhone Dev Center" section, earlier in this chapter, for an overview of some of the resources that could help you get up to speed on some programming basics.

I'm also going to assume that you're familiar with the iPhone itself, and that you've explored Apple's included applications to get a feel for the iPhone look and feel.

Part II
Using the iPhone Development Tools

The 5th Wave   By Rich Tennant

"You ever notice how much more streaming media
there is than there used to be?"

In this part . . .

When you've established yourself as one of the developer in-crowd, you can download the SDK. Of course once you do that, you will have to figure out how to use it, and you will. This part shows you how to download and use the iPhone Software Development Kit (SDK) and how to use Interface Builder — much more than your run-of-the-mill program for building graphical user interfaces — to start building a real interface. You can work along with me, and then take all that knowledge and start working on your own app. Of course, before you get into the guts of coding your app, you'll need to know about what goes on during runtime inside those itty-bitty chips — and I'll take you through that as well.

Chapter 4

Getting to Know the SDK

In This Chapter

▶ Getting a handle on the Xcode project

▶ Compiling an application

▶ Peeking inside the Simulator

▶ Checking out the Interface Builder

▶ Demystifying nib files

I've said it before and I'll say it again: One of the things that really got me excited about the iPhone was how easy it was to develop applications. The Software Development Kit (SDK) comes with so many tools, you'd think developing must be really easy. Well, to be truthful, it's *relatively* easy.

In this chapter, I introduce you to the SDK. It's going to be a low-key, get-acquainted kind of affair. I'll show you the real nuts-and-bolts stuff in later chapters, when I actually develop the two sample applications.

Developing Using the SDK

The Software Development Kit (SDK) supports the kind of development process that's after my own heart: You can develop your applications without tying your brain up in knots. The development environment allows you to rapidly get a user interface up and running to see what it looks like. The idea here is to add your code incrementally — step by step — so you can always step back and see how what you just did affected the Big Picture. Your general steps in development would look something like this:

1. Start with Xcode, Apple's development environment for the OS X operating system.

2. Design the user interface.

3. Write the code.

4. Build and run your application.

5. Test your application.

6. Measure and tune your application's performance.

7. Do it all again until you are done.

In this chapter, I start at the very beginning, with the very first step, with Xcode. (Starting with Step 1? What a concept!) And the first step of the first step is to create a project.

Creating Your Project

To develop an iPhone application, you work in what's called an *Xcode project*. So, time to fire one up. Here's how it's done:

1. **Launch Xcode**.

   After you've downloaded the SDK, it's a snap to launch Xcode. By default, it's downloaded to /Developer/Applications, where you can track it down to launch it.

   Here are a couple of hints to make Xcode handier and more efficient:

   • If I were you, I'd drag the icon for the Xcode application all the way down to the Dock, so you can launch it from there. You'll be using it a lot, so it wouldn't hurt to be able to launch it from the Dock.

   • When you first launch Xcode, you'll see the welcome screen shown in Figure 4-1. It's chock-full of links to the iPhone Development Center and iPhone documentation, news, and the like. You may want to leave this screen up to make it easier to get to those links, but I usually close it. If you don't want to be bothered with the welcome screen in the future, uncheck the Show at Launch checkbox.

   If you select iPhone Dev Center link at the top of the screen, you get a nice-looking guide to the Dev Center resources, as shown in Figure 4-2.

   Close the welcome screen for now; you won't be using it.

2. **Choose File⇨New Project from the main menu to create a new project.**

   You can also just press Shift+⌘+N.

   No matter what you do to start a new project, you are greeted with the New Project Assistant screen, as shown in Figure 4-3.

   The New Project Assistant window is where you get to choose the template you want for your new project. Note that the leftmost pane has two sections: One for the iPhone OS and the other for Mac OS X.

Figure 4-1:
The Xcode welcome screen.

3. In the New Project Assistant window, click Application under the iPhone OS heading.

Figure 4-2:
The iPhone Dev Center portal.

The main pane of the New Project Assistant window refreshes, revealing several choices, as shown in Figure 4-3. Each of these choices is actually a template that, when chosen, generates some code to get you started.

Figure 4-3:
The New
Project
Assistant.

4. **Select View-Based Application from the choices displayed and then click Choose.**

   Doing so brings up the New Project dialog.

   Note that when you select a template, a brief description of the template is displayed underneath the main pane. (Again, refer to Figure 4-3 to see a description of the View-Based Application. In fact, click some of the other template choices just to see how they are described as well. Just be sure to click the View-Based Application template again to get back to it when you're done exploring.)

5. **Using the New Project dialog, enter a name for your new project in the Save As field, choose a Save location (the Desktop works just fine) and then click Save.**

   I'm going to name my project ReturnMeTo. I suggest you do the same if you're following along with me.

   After you click Save, Xcode creates the project and opens the project window — which should look like what you see in Figure 4-4.

Exploring Your Project

To develop an iPhone application, you have to work within the context of an Xcode project. It turns out that you do most of your work on projects using the project window very much like the one in Figure 4-4. If you have a nice, large monitor, expand the project window so you can see everything in it as big as life. This is, in effect, Command Central for developing your application; it displays and organizes your source files and the other resources needed to build your application.

Toolbar   Detail view

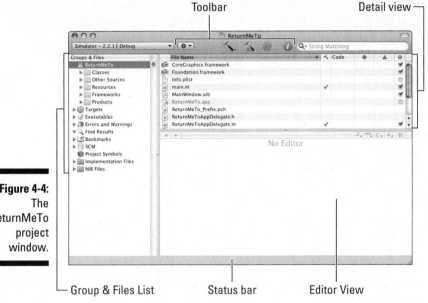

Figure 4-4:
The
ReturnMeTo
project
window.

Group & Files List   Status bar   Editor View

If you take another peek at Figure 4-4, you'll see the following:

- ✔ **The Groups & Files list:** An outline view of everything in your project, containing all of your project's files — source code, frameworks, and graphics, as well as some settings files. You can move files and folders around and add new folders. If you select an item in the Groups & Files list, the contents of the item are displayed in the topmost-pane to the right — otherwise known as the Detail view.

   You'll notice that some of the items in the Groups & Files list are folders, whereas others are just icons. Most have a little triangle next to them. Clicking the little triangle to the left of a folder expands the folder to show what's in it. Click the triangle again to hide what it contains.

- ✔ **The Detail view:** Here you get detailed information about the item you selected in the Groups & Files list.

- ✔ **The Toolbar:** Your one-stop place for quick access to the most common Xcode commands. You can customize the toolbar to your heart's content by right-clicking it and selecting Customize Toolbar from the contextual menu that appears. (I continue to use it just as delivered from the factory, but as you get more comfortable with it, feel free to change it.)

- ✔ **The Status bar:** Look here for messages about your project. For example, when you're building your project, Xcode updates the status bar to show where you are in the process — and whether the process completed successfully.

✔ **The Favorites bar:** Works much like other "favorites" bars you're certainly familiar with; so you can "bookmark" places in your project. This bar isn't displayed by default; to put it on-screen, choose View⇨ Layout⇨Show Favorites Bar from the main menu.

✔ **The Editor view:** Displays a file you've selected, in either the Groups & Files or Detail view. You can also edit your files here — after all, that's you'd expect from the "Editor view" — although some folks prefer to double-click a file in Groups & Files or Detail view to open the file in a separate window.

To see how Editor view works, check out Figure 4-5, where I've selected the Classes folder in the Groups & Files view, and the `ReturnMeToAppDelegate.h` class in the Detail view. You can see the code for the class in the Editor view.

If you look on the Editor toolbar (at the top of the Editor View window), you'll see a Lock icon on the far right of the bar. Immediately to the left of that is an icon that looks like two pages overlapping. Clicking that icon will switch you from the header (or interface) file, to the implementation file and vice versa. The header files define the class's interface by specifying the class declaration (and what it inherits from), *instance variables* (a variable defined in a class — at runtime every object has its own copy) and methods. The implementation file, on the other hand, contains the code for each method.

Right under the Lock icon is another icon that lets you split the editor view. That enables you to look at the interface and implementation files at the same time, or even the code for two different methods in the same or different classes.

If you have any questions about what something does, just position the mouse pointer above the icon and a tool tip will explain it.

Figure 4-5: The `Return MeToApp Delegate .h` file in the Editor view.

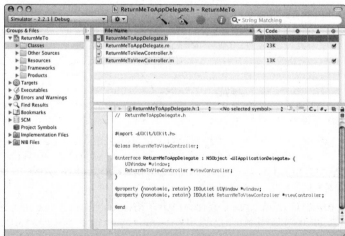

The first item in the Groups & Files view, as you can see in Figure 4-5, is labeled `ReturnMeTo`. This is the container that contains all the "source" elements for my project, including source code, resource files, graphics, and a number of other pieces that will remain unmentioned for now (but I get into those in due course). You can see your project container has five distinct groups (folders, if you will) — Classes, Other Sources, Resources, Frameworks, Products. Here's what gets tossed into each group:

- **Classes** is where you should place all of your code, although you are not obliged to. As you can see from Figure 4-5, this project has four distinct source-code files:

        ReturnMeToAppDelegate.h

        ReturnMeToAppDelegate.m

        ReturnMeToViewController.h

        ReturnMeToViewController.m

- **Other Sources** is where you typically would find the precompiled headers of the frameworks you will be using — stuff like `ReturnMeTo_ Prefix.pch` as well as `main.m`, your application's main function.

- **Resources** contains, well, resources, such as `.xib` files, property lists (which I will explain in Chapters 14 and 16), images and other media files, and even some data files.

    Whenever you'd choose the View-Based Application template (see Figure 4-3), Xcode creates the following three files for you:

        MainWindow.xib

        ReturnMeToViewController.xib

        Info.plist

    I explain `.xib` files in excruciating detail in this and following chapters. Soon you will learn to love the `.xib` files as I much as I do.

- **Frameworks** are code libraries that act a lot like prefab building blocks for your code edifice. (I talked lots about frameworks in Chapter 2 and will talk even more about them in Chapter 6.) By choosing the View-Based Application template, you let Xcode know that it should add the `UIKit framework`, `Foundation.framework`, and `CoreGraphics.framework` to your project, since it expects that you'll need them in a View-Based Application.

    I'm going to limit myself to just these three frameworks in developing my application, but if you need to add one, all you have to do is choose Project⇨Add to Project from the main menu and navigate to the framework you need.

- **Products** is a bit different from the previous three items in this list: It's not a source for your application, but rather *the compiled application itself*. In it, you'll find `ReturnMeTo.app`. At the moment, this file is listed in red because the file cannot be found (which makes sense, since you haven't built the application yet).

A file's name in red lets you know that Xcode can't find the underlying physical file.

If you happen to open the ReturnMeTo folder on your Mac, you won't see the "folders" that appear in the Xcode window. That's because those folders are simply "logical" groupings that help organize and find what you're looking for; this list of files can grow to be pretty large, even in a moderate-size project.

Once you have a lot files, you'll have better luck finding things if you create subgroups within the Classes group and/or Resources group, or even whole new groups. You create subgroups (or even new groups) in the Groups & Files listing by choosing New Project⇨New Group from the main menu. You then can select a file and drag it to a new group or subgroup.

Building and Running Your Application

It's really a blast to see what you get when you build and run a project that you yourself created using a template from the project creation window. Doing that is relatively simple:

1. **Choose Simulator - iPhone OS 2.2.1 from the Overview pop-up menu in the top-left corner of the project window to set the active SDK.**

   Figure 4-6 shows you what setting your active SDK looks like. While you're busy with that process, here are some important aspects of the iPhone SDK to keep in mind:

   • When you downloaded the SDK, you actually downloaded *eight* SDKs — a Simulator SDK and a device SDK for each of the current *four* iPhone OS releases.

   • Fortunately, for most of this book, I'll be using the Simulator SDK and iPhone OS 2.2.1. Even more fortunately, in Chapter 13, I show you how to switch to the device SDK and download your application to a real-world iPhone. But before you do that, there's just one catch . . .

   • You have to be in the iPhone Developer Program to run your application on a device, even on your very own iPhone.

2. **Using the same Overview pop-up menu, set the Active Build Configuration.**

   A *build configuration* tells Xcode the purpose of the built product. You can choose between Debug, which has features to help with debugging (duh) and Release, which results in smaller and faster binaries. I'll be using Debug for most of this book, so I recommend you go with Debug for now.

3. Choose Build ⇨Build and Go (Run) from the main menu to build and run the application.

You can also press ⌘+Return or select the Build and Go icon in the Project Window toolbar. The status bar in the project window tells you all about build progress, build errors such as compiler errors, or warnings — and (oh, yeah) whether the build was successful. Figure 4-7 shows that this was a successful build.

Because you selected Debug for the active build configuration, the Debugger Console launches for you, as shown in Figure 4-8. (I talk more about debugging in Chapter 10.). If you don't see the console, select Run⇨Console to unhide it.

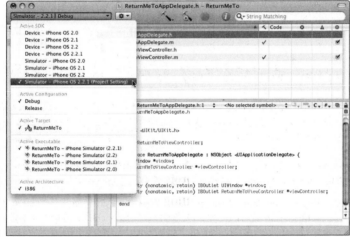

Figure 4-6: Setting the active SDK and build configuration.

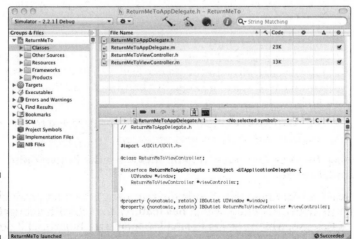

Figure 4-7: A successful build.

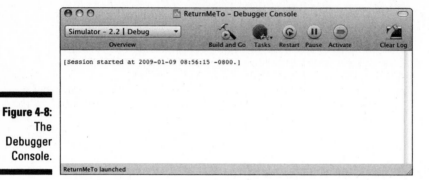

Figure 4-8:
The
Debugger
Console.

After it's launched in the Simulator, your first application looks a lot like what you see in Figure 4-9. You should see the Status Bar and a grey window, but that's it. (I know . . . this may look even more insipid than "Hello World," but I fix that big-time in Chapter 5). You can also see the Hardware menu; I'll explain that next.

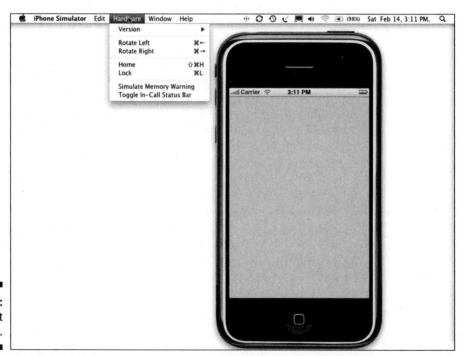

Figure 4-9:
Your first
application.

The iPhone Simulator

When you run your application, Xcode installs it on the iPhone Simulator (or a real iPhone device if you specified the device as the active SDK) and launches it. Using the Hardware menu and your keyboard and mouse, the Simulator mimics most of what a user can do on a real iPhone, albeit with some limitations that I point out shortly.

Hardware interaction

You use the iPhone Simulator Hardware menu (you can see it in Figure 4-9) when you want your device to

- ✔ **Rotate Left:** Choosing Hardware⇨Rotate Left rotates the Simulator to the left. This enables you to see the Simulator in Landscape mode.

- ✔ **Rotate Right:** Choosing Hardware⇨Rotate Right rotates the Simulator to the right.

- ✔ **Go to the Home screen**: Choosing Hardware⇨Home does the expected — you go to the home screen.

- ✔ **Lock the Simulator (device):** Choosing Hardware⇨Lock locks the simulator.

- ✔ **Send the running application low-memory warnings:** Choosing Hardware⇨Simulate Memory Warning fakes out your simulator by sending it a (fake) low-memory warning. I won't be covering this, but it is a great feature for seeing how your app may function out there in the real world.

- ✔ **Toggle the status bar between its Normal state and its In Call state**. Choose Hardware⇨Toggle In-Call Status Bar to check out how your application functions when the iPhone is not answering a call (Normal state) and when it supposedly *is* answering a call (In Call state).

The status bar becomes taller when you're on a call than when you're not. Choosing In Call state here shows you how things look when your application is launched while the user is on the phone.

Gestures

On the real device, a gesture is something you do with your fingers to make something happen in the device — such as a tap, or drag. Table 4-1 shows you how to simulate gestures using your mouse and keyboard:

Table 4-1	Gestures in the Simulator
Gesture	*iPhone action*
Tap	Click the mouse.
Touch and hold	Hold down the mouse button
Double tap	Double-click the mouse.
Swipe	1. Click where you want to start and hold the mouse button down. 2. Move the mouse in the direction of the swipe and then release the mouse button.
Flick	1. Click where you want to start and hold the mouse button down. 2. Move the mouse quickly in the direction of the flick and then release the mouse button.
Drag	1. Click where you want to start and hold the mouse button down. 2. Move the mouse in the drag direction.
Pinch	1. Move the mouse pointer over the place where you want to start. 2. Hold down the Option key, which will make two circles appear that stand in for your fingers. 3. Hold down the mouse button and move the circles in or out.

Uninstalling applications and resetting your device

You uninstall applications on the Simulator the same way you'd do it on the iPhone, except you use your mouse instead of your finger.

1. **On the Home screen, place the pointer over the icon of the application you want to uninstall and hold down the mouse button until the icon starts to wiggle.**

2. **Click the icon's Close button — the little x that appears in the upper left hand corner of the application's icon.**

3. **Click the Home button — the one with a little square in it, centered below the screen — to stop the icon from wiggling.**

You can also use move an application icon around by clicking-and-dragging with the mouse.

To reset the Simulator to the "original factory settings" — which also removes all the applications you've installed — choose iPhone Simulator⇨ Reset Content and Settings.

Limitations

Keep in mind that running applications in the iPhone Simulator is not the same thing as running them in the iPhone. Here's why:

- The Simulator uses Mac OS X versions of the low-level system frameworks, instead of the actual frameworks that run on the device.

- The Simulator uses the Mac hardware and memory. To really determine how your application is going to perform on an honest-to-goodness iPhone device, you're going to have to run it on a real iPhone device. (Luckily for you, I show you show you how to do that in Chapter 13.)

- Xcode installs applications in the iPhone Simulator automatically when you build your application using the iPhone Simulator SDK (you did that in Figure 4-7, for example). All fine and dandy, but there is no way to get Xcode to install applications from the App Store in the iPhone Simulator.

- You can't fake the iPhone Simulator into thinking it's lying on the beach at Waikiki. The location reported by the `CoreLocation` framework in the Simulator is fixed at

    Latitude: 37.3317 North

    Longitude: 122.0307 West

    Which just so happens to be 1 Infinite Loop, Cupertino, CA 95014, and guess who "lives" there?

- The Simulator does not support audio session behavior.

- There is no accelerometer data.

Using Interface Builder

Interface Builder is a great tool for graphically laying out your user interface. You can use it to design your application's user interface and then save what you've done as a resource file which is then loaded into your application at runtime. Then, this resource file is used to automatically create the single window, as well as all your views and controls, and some of your application's other objects — view controllers, for example. (For more on view controllers and other application objects, check out Chapter 2.)

If you don't want to use Interface Builder, you can also create your objects programmatically — creating views and view controllers and even things like buttons and labels in your own application code. I show you how to do that as well. Often Interface Builder makes things easier, but sometimes just coding it is the best way.

To see how Interface Builder works, go ahead an open up the program. You should use the ReturnMeTo app you started earlier in the chapter as your starting point:

1. **In your project window's Groups & Files list, expand the Resources group.**

   Don't make the mistake of opening the `mainWindow.xib`. You need the `ReturnMeToViewController.xib` file.

2. **Double-click the `ReturnMeToViewController.xib` file, as shown in Figure 4-10.**

Note that `ReturnMeToAppDelegate` is still in the Editor window; that's okay, because we're set to edit the `ReturnMeToViewController.xib` file in the Interface Builder, not in the Editor window. That's because double-clicking always opens a file in a new window — this time, the Interface Builder is the window that opens.

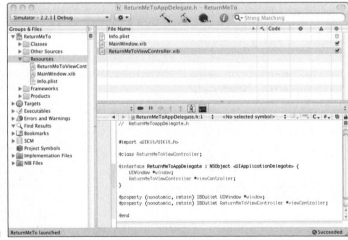

Figure 4-10: Selecting ReturnMe ToView Controller. xib.

What you see after double-clicking are the windows as they were the last time you left them. If this is the first time you've opened Interface Builder, you'll see three windows that look something like those in Figure 4-11. Not surprisingly, the View window looks exactly as it did in the iPhone Simulator window — as blank as a whiteboard wiped clean.

Interface Builder supports two file types: an older format that uses the extension .nib and a newer format that utilizes the extension .xib. The iPhone project templates all use .xib files. While the file extension is .xib, everyone still calls them *nib files*. The term "nib" and the corresponding file extension .xib are an acronym for "NeXT Interface Builder." The Interface Builder application was originally developed at NeXT Computer, whose OPENSTEP operating system was used as the basis for creating Mac OS X.

The window labeled ReturnMeToViewController.xib (the upper-left window in Figure 4-11) is the nib's main window. It acts as a table of contents for the nib file. With the exception of the first two icons (File's Owner and First Responder), every icon in this window (in this case, there's only one, but you'll find more as you get into nib files) represents a single instance of an Objective-C class that will be created automatically for you when this nib file is loaded.

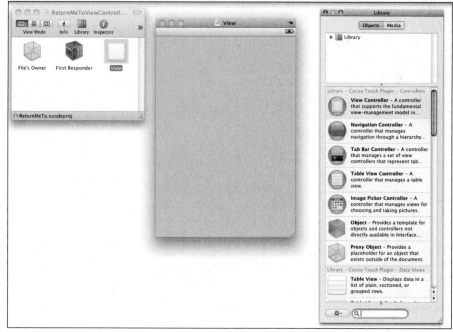

Figure 4-11:
The
ReturnMe
ToView
Controller
in Interface
Builder.

Interface Builder does not generate any code that you have to modify or even look at. Instead, it creates "instant" Objective-C objects that the nib loading code reconstitutes and turns into real objects at runtime.

If you were to take a closer look at the three objects in the `ReturnMeToViewController.xib` file window — and if you had a pal who knew the iPhone backwards and forwards — you'd find out the following about each object:

- ✔ **The File's Owner proxy object:** This is the controller object that is responsible for the contents of the nib file. In this case, the File's Owner object is actually the `ReturnMeToViewController` that was created by Xcode and will be the primary object you'll use to implement the application's functionality. The File's Owner is not created from the nib file. It's created in one of two ways — either from another (previous) nib file or by a programmer who codes it manually.

In Interface Builder, you can create connections between the File's Owner and the other interface objects in your nib file. For example, in Chapter 7, I create a connection between the `ReturnMeToViewController` and a text field (for entering a phone number) and a label (in which to display the phone number).

- ✔ **First Responder proxy object:** This object is the first entry in an application's dynamically constructed responder chain (a term I explain in Chapter 6) and is the object with which the user is currently interacting. For a view, it's usually going to start out as the View Controller object. If, for example, the user taps a text field to enter some data, the first responder would then become the Text Field object.

Although I use the first responder mechanism quite a bit as I build the ReturnMeTo application, there's actually nothing I have to do to manage it. It's automatically set and maintained by the `UIKit` framework.

- ✔ **View object:** The View icon represents an instance of the `UIView` class. A `UIView` object is an area that a user can see and interact with. In this application, you'll only have to deal with the one view.

If you take another look at Figure 4-11, you'll notice two other windows open besides the main window. Look at the window that has the word View in the title bar. That window is the graphical representation of the View icon. If you close the View window and then double-click the View icon, this window will open up again. This is your canvas for creating your user interface: It's where you drag user-interface elements such as buttons and text fields. These objects come from the Library window (the third window you see in Figure 4-11).

The Library window contains your palette — the stock Cocoa Touch objects that Interface Builder supports. Dragging an item from the Library to the

View window adds an object of that type to the View (and remember, as subview).

If you happen to close the Library window, whether by accident or by design, you can get it to reappear by choosing Tools⇨Library.

It's Time to Get to Work

Finally, at what may seem at long last (although it's really been only a few pages), you're ready to do some real work. In the next chapter, I lead you through creating the user interface for the ReturnMeTo application.

So take a break if you need to, but come back ready to work.

Chapter 5

Building the User Interface

As I've mentioned before in this worthy tome, and will say many times again (unless the editors stop me), the user interface, while critical for most applications, is less forgiving on the iPhone than on the desktop. That's because on-screen real estate is limited on the device. (Come on, as cool as the screen is, it's still smaller than a desktop monitor.) Given the space limitations, I always like to get a pretty good idea of what the user interface will be like, because it could have a definite impact on my software architecture. Before I start coding, I want to be sure the interface is going to work in its intended space.

When I started my little ReturnMeTo application, I thought the user interface would be a piece of cake — and to some extent, it was. But even the easiest of applications — apps like ReturnMeTo, that have focused functionality and a single window — can benefit from a little road-testing. As I go through the process of developing this application over the next few chapters (and take it for a spin now and then) I document what happens along the way — the good, the bad and the ugly. There's method to this madness: As I try out different implementations of the application, you get a close look at how easy it is to make those changes.

Starting Interface Builder

First things first: Start up Interface Builder so you can start laying out the user interface. Just so you know what you're aiming for, Figure 5-1 shows what the final application is going to look like in the Simulator.

Figure 5-1:
The Return
MeTo user
interface,
as it looks
in the
Simulator.

Isn't it a beauty? All modesty aside, you, too, can build cool-looking apps in no time. Here's what you need to do:

1. **Launch Xcode.**

   You'll find it located in /Developer/Applications. (If you listened to my advice in Chapter 3 and added the Xcode icon to the Dock, you can of course launch it from there.)

2. **With Xcode open, choose File⇨Open from the main menu, then use the Open dialog to navigate to (and open) the ReturnMeTo project created in Chapter 4.**

   The ReturnMeTo project window appears on-screen.

   If you haven't created the project yet, check out Chapter 4 — or, after you've launched Xcode, follow these steps:

   a. Choose File⇨New Project.

      You're asked to choose a template for your project.

   b. Choose a View-Based application.

   c. Name the application ReturnMeTo and then save it.

3. **In the Groups & Files list (on the left side of the project window), click the triangle next to the Resources folder to expand it, as shown in Figure 5-2.**

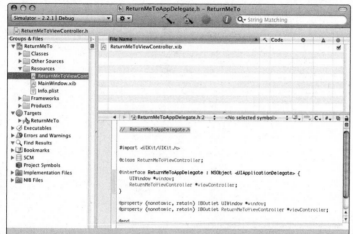

Figure 5-2:
The project
window.

4. **In the expanded Resources folder, double-click the** `ReturnMeToViewController.xib` **file.**

   Doing so launches Interface Builder — and if you've never run this pro-gram before, you end up with something that looks like Figure 5-3. (If you've already spent some time exploring Interface Builder, you'll see the windows as you last left them.)

5. **Check to see whether the Library window (at right in Figure 5-3) is open. If it isn't, open it by choosing Tools⇨Library.**

   The Library lists all the components you can use to build a user interface. Some of these you can see on-screen, such as buttons and text fields; other elements — view controllers, for example — stay out of sight.

6. **In the Library window, click the triangle next to the Library folder in the top pane.**

   The folder expands to show two more folders, labeled `Cocoa Touch Plugin` and `Custom Objects`.

7. **Click the triangle next to the** `Cocoa Touch Plugin` **folder, as shown in Figure 5-4.**

   The folder expands to show you a list of various object categories.

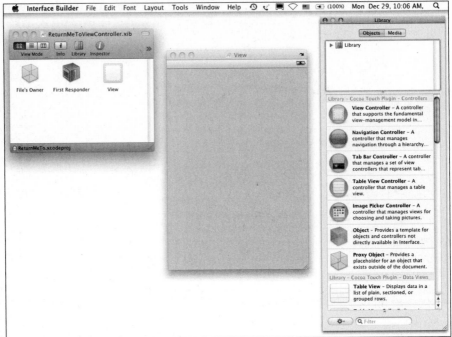

Figure 5-3:
Interface
Builder
windows.

8. **Click the** `Inputs & Values` **folder, as shown in Figure 5-4.**

   You get a list of user interface elements that you can drag onto the view to create your user interface. (I've rearranged my windows a bit to show you some things as I move along; you can arrange yours as you'd like.)

   `ReturnMeToViewController.xib` was created by Xcode when I created the project from the template. As you can see, the file already contains a view — all I have to do here is add the static text, images, and text fields. If you drag one of these objects to the View window, it will create that object when your application is launched.

9. **Drag the Label element from Library window over to the View window, as shown in Figure 5-4**.

   Labels display static text in the view (*static text* can't be edited by the user).

   You may notice a rectangle around the label when you are done dragging it over the View window. This rectangle won't show on-screen when the app is running. (You can turn this particular feature on or off by choosing Layout⇨Show/Hide Bounds Rectangle.)

   Your View should look something like Figure 5-4 when you're done.

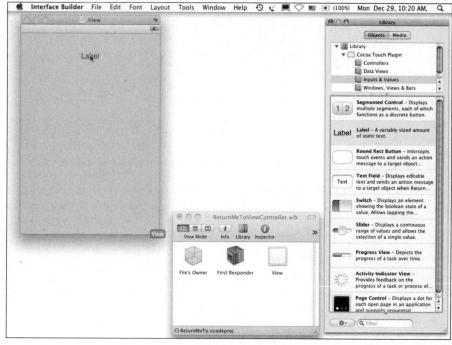

Figure 5-4:
Adding a
label to the
user
interface.

Labels are actually sub-views of your main view. Knowing that will make it a lot easier to understand some things I end up doing in the next few chapters. I'll remind you of this whole view/sub-view thing when it comes up again there.

10. Click to select the Label text, and then choose Tools⇨Attributes Inspector.

The Attributes Inspector appears on-screen, as shown in Figure 5-5.

Pressing ⌘+1 is another way to call up the Attributes Inspector.

Note the four icons across the top of the Attributes Inspector window. They correspond to the Attributes, Connections, Size and Identity Inspectors, respectively, in the Tools menu. The Attributes icon looks pushed down in Figure 5-5, which makes sense since the Attributes Inspector is the active one.

11. Enter If you find me in the Attributes Inspector's Text field, enter 34 in the Font Size field, and then press Return or Enter.

The minimum font size business can be confusing. Notice in the Attribute Inspector that the Adjust to Fit checkbox is checked. That means entering a font size here is really saying "I want the text to fit in the label, but don't make it any smaller than the size I've entered here in

Font Size." The resulting font size is a side effect of setting the minimum larger than the label. The problem is, if you uncheck the Adjust to Fit box and you want to specify the actual font size, using the Font Size field can increase it but not decrease it. (All you are doing in the Font Size field is setting the minimum, and it's already larger than that.) To actually specify a smaller font size, you have to choose Font ⇨ Show Fonts and set it from there.

Okay, at this point I could double-click the label in the View window and enter the new text, but I need the Attributes Inspector to change the font size. So I might as well change the text in the Attributes Inspector (I can also change other attributes there, such as color, if necessary).

What you see in response is something like Figure 5-5. Not very appealing is it? Where the heck is the text, for example? It turns out that you have to increase the size of the label to see the larger text.

12. With the label still selected, choose Layout⇨Size to Fit to increase the size of the label.

I could select the label and resize it by dragging the selection points you see in Figure 5-5, but I'm lazy enough just to choose Layout ⇨Size To Fit, which does exactly that: It adjusts the label size to fit the text.

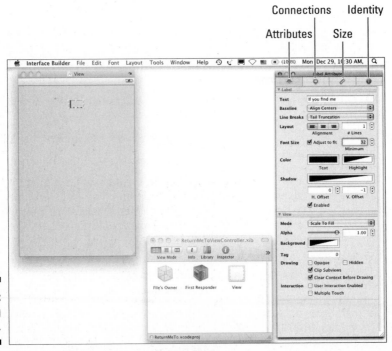

Figure 5-5:
Formatting
the label.

13. **Choose Layout ⇨Alignment ⇨Align Horizontal Center in Container to center the label in the View screen.**

    You have a couple of ways to center things in the View. If you had some other objects in place that were already centered, for example, you could use the guides provide by Interface Builder. (You can see them in Figure 5-10, if you peek ahead a few pages.) But in this case, there are no other objects to use as a reference; you're better off just using the Layout menu.

    Time now to specify a more appealing color for your View screen's background.

14. **With the view itself (rather than just the label) selected, click the Background field in the Attributes Inspector.**

    The Colors window appears in the form of a box of crayons, as shown in Figure 5-6.

    Note that selecting the view rather than the label changes the composition of the Attributes Inspector.

15. **Choose the white crayon in the Colors window to change the View background from grey to white.**

    (I know they call it "Snow," but white by any other name is still as white.) If the crayons remind you too much of kindergarten, you can get other color-palette views by clicking the icons at the top of the Colors window.

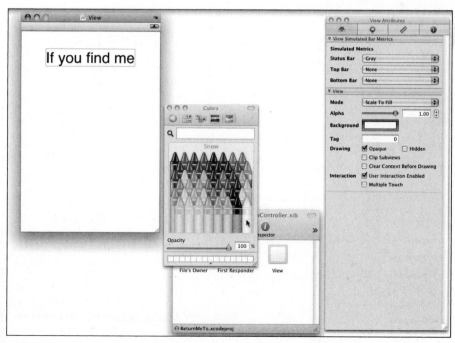

Figure 5-6:
Changing the background color.

16. **Choose File⇨Save to save what you have done.**

    You can also save your work by pressing ⌘+S.

    Ready to admire your work? For that, you'll need to build and run your application in Xcode.

17. **Make your Xcode window the active window again.**

    If you can't find it, or you minimized it, just click the Xcode icon in the Dock. The ReturnMeTo project should still be the active one. (You can always tell the active project by looking at the project name at the top of the Groups & Files pane.)

18. **In Xcode, click the Build and Go icon in the Project Window toolbar. (Refer to Figure 5-2.).**

    You can also choose Build⇨Build and Go (Run) from the main menu or press ⌘+Return.

    The Simulator launches automatically. It shows you something like Figure 5-7, depending on how creative you've been. (Maybe you went with the Cranberry Red crayon instead of Snow?)

Figure 5-7:
Admiring your work.

This is the general pattern I use as I build my interface — add stuff, Build and Go, and then check the results. Although I don't run the program in the Simulator after every change (unless, of course, I'm trying to avoid doing something else), I do run it periodically to check what the program will look like on the iPhone.

Adding Graphics and the Rest of the Elements

All background color and text makes Jack a dull boy, so you'll definitely want to add some graphics to keep Jack's (or Jill's) interest. I created my own little iPhone graphic, and will show you how to get it safely into an application. (I'll admit that I didn't give up a promising career as a graphic artist to become a software developer, but it's the thought that counts, right?)

To get an image placed in your application, first you need (well, yeah) an image.

The preferred format for the image is .png. Although most common image formats will display correctly, Xcode automatically optimizes .png images at build time to make them the fastest and most efficient image type for use in iPhone applications.

After you have your image, do the following:

1. **Back in Xcode, drag the graphics file into the Resources folder in the Project window, as shown in Figure 5-8.**

   Xcode asks you whether you want to make a copy of the icon file. Otherwise, it will simply create a pointer to the file. The advantage of using a pointer is that if you modify the image later, Xcode will use that modified version. The disadvantage is that Xcode won't be able to find the image file if you move it.

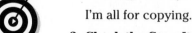

   I'm all for copying.

2. **Check the Copy Items into Destination Group's Folder checkbox to copy the file, as shown in Figure 5-9.**

   An alternative is to click the Resources folder in Xcode, choose Project ➪ Add to Project, and then navigate to the file you want to add.

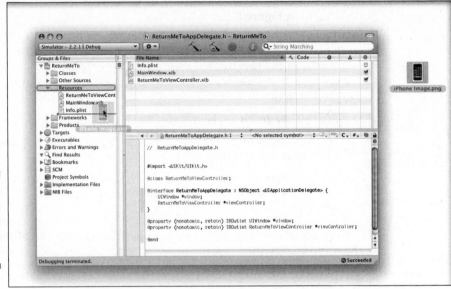

Figure 5-8:
Dragging a
file into the
resource
folder.

3. **Return to Interface Builder and then select the Data Views sub-sub-folder under the Cocoa Touch Plugin subfolder.**

You can do that by clicking in an Interface Builder Window or by clicking the Interface Builder icon in the dock. The Library window refreshes to show the various elements contained in the Data Views sub-subfolder.

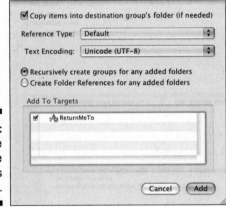

Figure 5-9:
Copying the
image to the
Resources
folder.

4. Drag the Image View element from the Library onto the View window, as shown in Figure 5-10.

Notice the blue lines displayed by Interface Builder. They're there to make it easy to center the image. Interface Builder also displays blue lines at the borders to help you conform to Apple User Interface Guidelines. If you jump ahead to Figure 5-14, you can see the borderlines as plain as day.

5. Select the Image View element in the View window.

Doing so changes what you see in the Attribute Inspector. It now displays the attributes for an Image view.

6. Using the inspector's Image drop-down menu, choose the image you want to use for the image view, as shown in Figure 5-11.

That inspector's a handy little critter, isn't it?

7. Choose Layout⇨Size to Fit and Layout⇨Alignment⇨Align Horizontal Center in Container to align and center the image.

Your image does what it's told, and your View screen ends up looking like Figure 5-12.

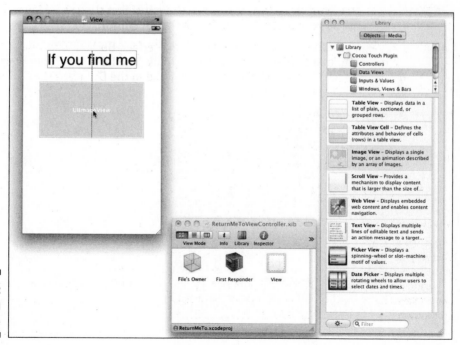

Figure 5-10:
Centering
the image.

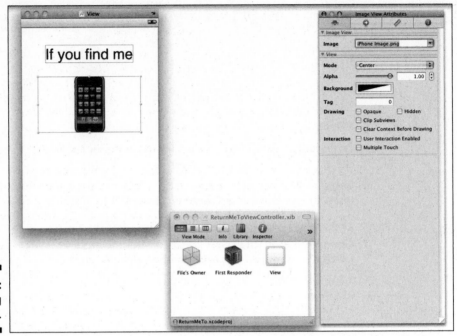

Figure 5-11:
Selecting
the image.

Figure 5-12:
The red
"Please
call" label.

8. **Using the steps included in the previous section for adding the "If you find me" text, add the "Please call" text.**

   You know the drill: Drag a label from the Library window, add the "Please call" text, increase the font size to 34, and then chose Layout⇨Size to Fit and Layout⇨Alignment⇨Align Horizontal Center in Container. Click the Color field in the Attributes Inspector to call up the little crayon box, but this time click the red (not the white) crayon to make the text red so it stands out more.

9. **Add yet another label to display the number to call.**

   This next label needs to hold the text of the number the user enters. (As you'll see later, I also use it to communicate some information to the user so it needs to be able to fit more text than just a phone number.) Just drag a label object from the Library into the view, but this time, since you don't know the size of the text you're going to display, widen it to almost the width of the view. To do that, use the selection points you see in Figure 5-13 to resize the label. (The blue lines shown in Figure 5-14 help you stay within the iPhone Human Interface Guidelines.)

   You want the text centered in the view, but since this time the text may be smaller than the view, you should make sure it's centered by clicking the Align Center icon in the Layout field of the Attributes Inspector, as shown in Figure 5-13.

Align Center

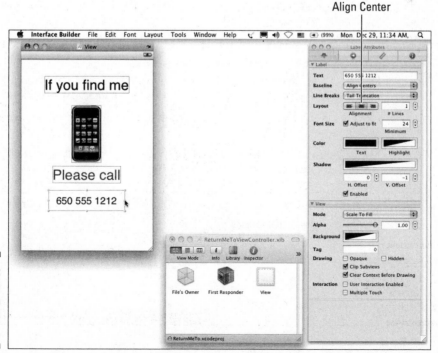

Figure 5-13:
Dragging the label's selection points.

Figure 5-14:
Formatting
the number-
to-call label.

You could leave the text field blank, or put in some default text for the user to see before they've entered a phone number the first time. I've done it both ways, and found (after some user testing) that people preferred that they see some text when they first launch the application, so I added "650 555 1212," No matter what you do, make sure the Align Center icon is chosen.

Label fields are not editable by the user, but you can change the text in your program.

10. **Drag a Text View element from the Library (refer to Figure 5-10) into the View window to add a text-entry field, as shown in Figure 5-15.**

    This is the field a user will use to enter his or her phone number. Go ahead and put it under the Phone Number label.

11. **Using the text field's selection points, extend both sides of the field so that it ends up matching the field above.**

    If you click into the text field, you'll see both a Text and Placeholder field in the Attributes Inspector. The Text field specifies what the user will see before he or she touches the text field to enter something. The Placeholder, on the other hand, is a "default" text that the users will see after they touch the text field to enter text. Personally, I find the default annoying, so I left it blank. I also prefer text entry to be aligned left, which is the default for the Text field.

12. **Set the Keyboard Type to Numbers & Punctuation, as shown in Figure 5-15.**

13. **Make your Xcode window the active window again, and then click the Build and Go icon in the Project Window toolbar. (Refer to Figure 5-2.).**

    You can also choose Build⇨Build and Go (Run) from the main menu or press ⌘+Return.

    I bet you've been waiting for this moment with bated breath and can hardly wait to see what it looks like. Your application should look like Figure 5-16, depending on which (if any) liberties you have taken.

Keyboard Type

Figure 5-15:
Adding the
text entry
field number
to call.

Figure 5-16:
The completed user interface in the Simulator.

Adding an Application Icon

One design goal for the ReturnMeTo application was to make it obvious to anyone who found my iPhone that he or she should touch the application icon.

But if you click the Simulator's home button — the black button with the white square at the very bottom of the window, — what you see in Figure 5-17 is an application icon that is noticeable only for what it is not. What I need is an icon that reaches out and says, "Touch me!"

An application icon is simply a 57-by-57-pixel .png file, just like the one I used for our image (albeit smaller) in the "Adding Graphics and the Rest of the Elements" section, earlier in the chapter. I created an icon matching those measurements in a graphics program, and then added it to the ReturnMeTo project in the same way I added the image file earlier — by dragging it into the Resources folder.

After I add the icon, I also need to specify that I want this icon used as the application's icon. I do that by using one of those other mysterious files you see in the `Resources` folder. Here's how:

Figure 5-17:
The stylish
ReturnMeTo
icon.

1. **In the Resources folder, click the** `info.plist` **file, as shown in Figure 5-18.**

   The contents of the `info.plist` file are displayed in the Editor pane. You're treated to some information about the application, including an item in the Key column labeled Icon file.

2. **Double-click in the empty space in the Value column next to Icon file.**

3. **Type in** ReturnMeTo icon.png **(or whatever name you chose to give your image) and then build the project as you normally would.**

   You know, clicking the Build and Go icon in the Project Window toolbar, choosing Build⇨Build and Go (Run) from the main menu or pressing ⌘+Return.

I'll be doing more with the `info.plist` and its various settings when I get ReturnMeTo ready for the App store in Chapter 13.

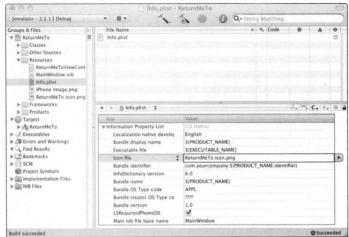

Click the Home button and you should be able to see your application icon.
(For a peek at mine, check out Figure 5-19.)

Figure 5-19:
The
ReturnMeTo
icon on the
iPhone.

A Lot Accomplished Very Quickly

In only a few pages, you've accomplished quite a bit. I want to emphasize, as you will see, that what I have done is not just a design. What you see here is the specification for "code" that will take what I have laid out in Interface Builder and create the objects that will implement it at runtime.

I do have to write code, however, if I want the application to actually do something. But before I get into that in detail, it is important that you understand how the application works at runtime — how the objects fit together and communicate. I explain what you need to know about that whole business in the next chapter.

Chapter 6

While Your Application Is Running

*T*aking a peek at the iPhone application architecture (Chapter 2) and working through the steps of creating the user interface for an application (Chapter 5) are all fine and dandy, but at some point you have to add some code — and to do that, you need an additional frame of reference: You need to know how all this stuff works at runtime.

Uncovering the mysteries of runtime is the goal of this chapter.

Okay, if you can't wait to code, then by all means skip to the next chapter. Honestly, if I were you (or me without benefit of hindsight), I'd be itching to do the same thing. But you'll probably run into trouble, just as I did, if you don't take some time beforehand to examine how the objects work together to deliver the user's experience of the application.

Application Anatomy 101 — The Life Cycle

The short-but-happy life of an application begins when a user launches it by tapping its icon on the Home screen. The system launches your application by calling its `main` function.

The main function does only three things:

✔ Sets up an autorelease pool.

✔ Calls the UIApplicationMain function.

✔ At termination, releases the autorelease pool.

To be honest, this whole main function thing is not something you even need to think about. What is important is what happens *after* the UIApplicationMain function is called. The whole ball of wax is shown in Figure 6-1. Here's the play-by-play:

1. **The main nib file is loaded.**

   A *nib file* is a resource file that contains the specifications for one or more objects. The main nib file usually contains a window object of some kind, the application delegate object, and any other key objects. When the file is loaded, the objects are reconstituted (think "instant application") in memory.

   For our ReturnMeTo example, this is the moment of truth when the ReturnMeToAppDelegate, ReturnMeToViewController, its view, and the main widow are created.

   For more on those objects and the role they play in applications, see Chapter 2.

2. **The UIApplicationMain calls your code in the *application delegate* (the applicationDidFinishLaunching: method).**

   This step is where you initialize and set up your application. You may display your main application window as if the user was starting from scratch, or the way the window looked when the user last exited the application. The application delegate object is a custom object that you code. It is responsible for some of the application-level behavior of your application. (Delegation is an extensively used design pattern that I explain in Chapter 2.)

3. **The UIKit framework sets up the event loop.**

   The *event loop* is the code responsible for polling input sources — the screen, for example. Events, such as touches on the screen, are sent to the object — say, a controller — that you have specified to handle that kind of event. These handling objects contain the code that implements what you want your application to do in response to that particular event. A touch in a control may result in a change in what the user sees in a view, a switch to a new view, or even the playing of *My Melancholy Baby*.

4. **When the user performs an action that would cause your application to quit, UIKit notifies your application and begins the termination process.**

Your application delegate's `applicationWillTerminate:` method is called, and you do what you need to do to terminate your application, including saving where the user was in the application. Saving is important, because then, when the application is launched again, (see Step 2 above) **and** the `UIApplicationMain` calls your code in the application delegate, `applicationDidFinishLaunching`, you can restore the application to where the user left off.

It all starts with the main nib file

When you create a new project using a template — quite the normal state of affairs, as I explain in Chapter 3 — the basic application environment is included. That means that when you launch your application, an application object is created, is connected to the window object, the run loop established, and so on — despite the fact that you haven't done a lick of coding. Most of this work is done by the `UIApplicationMain` function as illustrated in Figure 6-1.

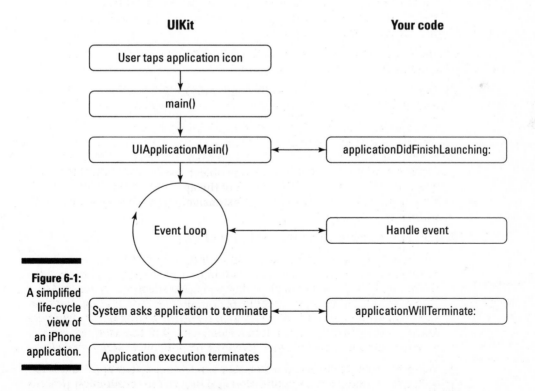

Figure 6-1: A simplified life-cycle view of an iPhone application.

But what does the `UIApplicationMain` function actually do? I'm glad you asked. When it goes through its paces, the process works more or less as follows, as illustrated in Figure 6-2.

1. **An instance of `UIApplication` is created.**

2. `UIApplication` **looks in the** `info.plist` **file, trying to find the main nib file.**

   It makes its way down the Key column until it finds the Main Nib File Base Name entry. Eureka! It peeks over at the Value column and sees that the value for the Main Nib File Base Name entry is `MainWindow.nib`.

3. `UIApplication` **loads** `MainWindow.xib`.

The file `MainWindow.xib` is what causes your application's delegate, main window, and view controller instances to get created at runtime. Remember, this file is provided as part of the project template. You don't need to change — or do — anything here. This is just a chance to see what's going on behind the scenes.

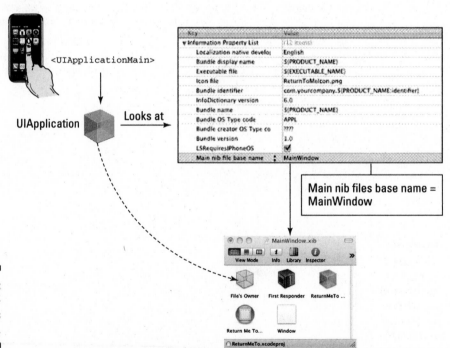

Figure 6-2:
The application is launched.

To take advantage of this once-in-a-lifetime opportunity, go back to your project window in Xcode, expand the Resources folder in the Groups & Files listing on the left and then double-click `MainWindow.xib`. (You do have a project, right? If not, check out Chapter 4.) When Interface Builder opens, take a look at the nib file's main window — the one labeled `MainWindow.xib`, which should look like the `MainWindow.xib` you see in Figure 6-2. Double-click the `ReturnMeToViewController` object as well as the Window object, if they are not already open. You should end up with three windows open, as shown in Figure 6-3.

Figure 6-3 shows `MainWindow.xib` contains five files. The objects you see are as follows:

- **A File's Owner proxy object:** The File's Owner object is actually the `UIApplication` instance. This object isn't created when the file is loaded as is the window and views. It's already created by the `UIApplicationMain` object before the nib file is loaded.

- **First Responder proxy object:** This object is the first entry in an application's responder chain, which is constantly updated while the application is running to (usually) point to the object with which the user is currently interacting. If, for example, the user taps a text field to enter some data, the first responder would become the text field object.

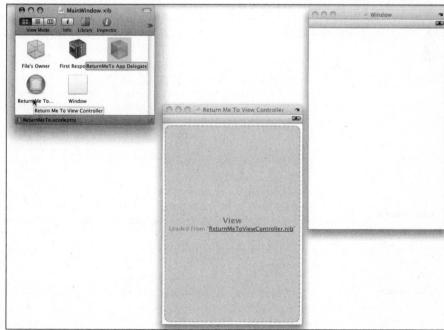

Figure 6-3: The application's Main Window. xib as it appears in Interface Builder.

✔ **An instance of** `ReturnMeToAppDelegate` **set to be the application's delegate.**

✔ **An instance of the** `ReturnMeToViewController`.

✔ **A window:** The window has its background set to white and is set to be visible at launch. This is the window you'll see when the application launches.

Okay, so all these disparate parts of the MainWindow.xib are loaded by `UIApplication`. What happens next is shown in Figure 6-4. The numbers in the figure correspond to the following steps:

1. **Create** `ReturnMeToAppDelegate`.

2. **Create** `Window`.

3. **Create** `ReturnMeToViewController`.

4. `ReturnMeToViewController:LoadView` **loads the view from the** `ReturnMeToViewController.xib` **file.**

   Wait a sec — how does the `ReturnMeToViewController` know that it's supposed to do that? If you double-click the `ReturnMeToView Controller` object in the `MainWindow.xib` window (refer back to Figure 6-3), you can see the `ReturnMeToViewController` window with its view. There, right In the middle of that view, it tells you that it will be "Loaded from `ReturnMeToViewController.nib`." (Remember how I said in Chapter 4 that a .nib file type used to be the term of choice? Here is a vestige of that. Don't worry; despite the .nib business, it really will be the .xib file). If you use the Inspector to look at the View Controller attributes (see Figure 6-5), you can see the NIB Name drop-down menu specifies said NIB name — the .nib file for the view controller. In this case, you see `ReturnMeToViewController` specified. This makes the connection explicit between the `MainWindow.xib` and the `ReturnMeToViewController.xib`. All done without any fuss or bother, I might add, by Xcode when you created the project from the template.

Initialization

The next step is for the `UIApplication` to call the `ReturnMeToApp Delegate applicationDidFinishLaunching:` method. Step 5 in Figure 6-6 represents what happens when the `applicationDidFinishLaunching:` method is called.

Okay, Figure 6-6 does look exactly like Figure 6-4, except I added a Step 5: Putting the view into the window and then making the window visible. At this point, you'd do any other application initialization as well — *and* return everything to what it was like when the user last used the application.

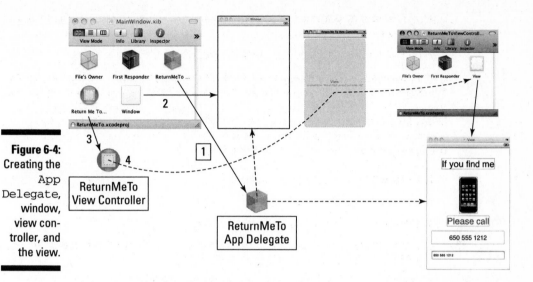

Figure 6-4:
Creating the
`App`
`Delegate`,
window,
view con-
troller, and
the view.

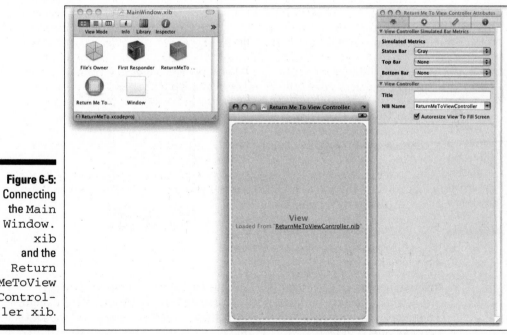

Figure 6-5:
Connecting
the `Main`
`Window.`
`xib`
and the
`Return`
`MeToView`
`Control-`
`ler xib.`

Figure 6-6 is more than just a conceptual diagram, as shown in Listing 6-1, where the code shows two instance variables, `window`, and `viewController`. These are automatically "filled in" for you when your application is launched. Then, in `the applicationDidFinishLaunching:` method, the view controller and its view are added to the window and the window becomes visible. Note that this was generated automatically by Xcode. (I'll get into what all those strange things like `IBOutlet` and `@property` mean in the next chapter.)

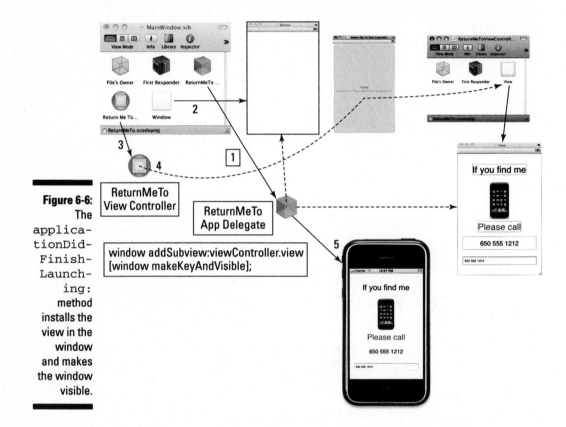

Figure 6-6: The `applicationDidFinishLaunching:` method installs the view in the window and makes the window visible.

What this does is quite a bit; what it doesn't do is connect objects added to the user interface with the objects that need to know about them. How does my application access the phone number that the user enters, for example? Of course, I could root around in the code, but it would be much easier to have Interface Builder do it at application launch. I show you how that is (easily) done in the next chapter.

Your goal during startup should be to present your application's user interface as quickly as possible — quick initialization = happy users. Don't load large data structures that your application won't use right away. If your application requires time to load data from the network (or perform other tasks that take noticeable time), get your interface up and running first — and then launch the slow task on a background thread. Then you can display a progress indicator or other feedback to the user to indicate that your application is loading the necessary data or doing something important.

The application delegate object is usually derived from NSObject, the root class (the very base class from which all iPhone application objects are derived), although it can be an instance of any class you like, as long as it adopts the UIApplicationDelegate protocol. The methods of this protocol correspond to behaviors that are needed during the application life cycle and are your way of implementing this custom behavior. Although you are not required to implement all of the methods of the UIApplicationDelegate protocol, every application should implement the following critical application tasks:

  ✔ Initialization, which I have just covered.

  ✔ Responding to interruptions

  ✔ Responding to low memory warnings

I show you what has to be done to carry out these tasks in the last two sections.

Listing 6-1

```
// ReturnMeToAppDelegate.h
#import <UIKit/UIKit.h>
@class ReturnMeToViewController;
@interface ReturnMeToAppDelegate : NSObject
           <UIApplicationDelegate> {
  UIWindow *window;
  ReturnMeToViewController *viewController;
}
@property (nonatomic, retain) IBOutlet UIWindow *window;
@property (nonatomic, retain) IBOutlet
ReturnMeToViewController *viewController;

@end
// ReturnMeToAppDelegate.m

#import "ReturnMeToAppDelegate.h"
#import "ReturnMeToViewController.h"

@implementation ReturnMeToAppDelegate
@synthesize window;
@synthesize viewController;

- (void)applicationDidFinishLaunching:(UIApplication *)
          application {

  [window addSubview:viewController.view];
  [window makeKeyAndVisible];
}
```

Event Processing

After a user launches your application, the functionality provided in UIKit framework manages most of the application's infrastructure. Part of the initialization process mentioned in the previous section involves setting up the main run loop and event handling code, which is the responsibility of the UIApplication object.

When the application is on-screen, it's driven by external events — say, stubby fingers touching sleek screens, as shown in Figure 6-7. Here's a rundown of how external events drive an application:

1. **You have an event — the user taps a button, for example.**

   The touch of a finger (or lifting it from the screen) adds a touch event to the application's event queue, where it's *encapsulated* in — placed into — a UIEvent object. There is UITouch object for each finger touching the screen so you can track individual touches. As the user manipulates the screen with his or her fingers, the system reports the changes for each finger in the corresponding UITouch object.

   My advice to you: Don't let your eyes glaze over here. This UIEvent and UITouch stuff is important, as you'll discover when I show you how to handle touch events while walking you through building the more advanced parts of the ReturnMeTo application.

2. **The run loop monitor dispatches the event.**

   When there is something to process, the event-handling code of the UIApplication processes touch events by dispatching them to the appropriate *responder* object — the object that has signed up to take responsibility for doing something when an event happens (when the user touches the screen for example). Responder objects can include instances of UIApplication, UIWindow, UIView, and its subclasses (all which inherit from UIResponder).

3. **A responder object decides how to handle the event.**

   For example, a touch event occurring in a button (view) would be delivered to the button object. The button handles the event by sending an action message to another object — in this case the UIViewController object. Setting it up this way enables you to use standard button objects without having to muck about in their innards — just tell the button what method you want called in your view controller and you're basically set.

   Processing the message may result in changes to a view, or a new view altogether, or some other kind of change in the user interface. When this happens, the view and graphics infrastructure takes over and processes the required drawing events.

4. **You're sent back to the event loop.**

   After an event is handled or discarded, control passes back to the run loop. The run loop then processes the next event or puts the thread to sleep if there's nothing more for it to do.

Termination

Getting stuff to (safely) shut down is another application delegate responsibility. To handle termination, the application delegate implements the delegate method `applicationWillTerminate:` to save any unsaved data or key application *state* (where the user is in the application — the current view and stuff like that) to disk. (Okay, I know, the disk in the iPhone is not really a disk, it's a solid-state drive that Apple *calls* a disk, but if they call it that, I probably should, too, just so I don't confuse too many people.). You can also use this method to perform additional cleanup operations, such as deleting temporary files.

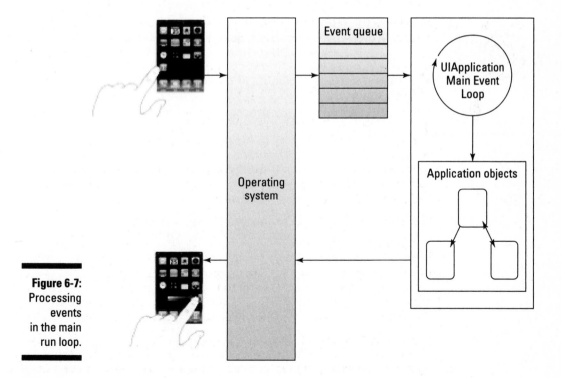

Figure 6-7:
Processing
events
in the main
run loop.

Other Runtime Considerations

Launch, initialize, process, terminate, launch, initialize, process, terminate . . . It has a nice rhythm to it, doesn't it? And those *are* the four major stages of the application's life cycle. But life isn't simple — and neither is runtime. To mix things up a bit, your application will also have to come to terms with interruptions and memory management.

Responding to interruptions

Various events besides termination can interrupt your application to allow the user to respond — for example, incoming phone calls, SMS messages, calendar alerts, or the user pressing the Sleep button on an iPhone. Such interruptions may only be temporary. If the user chooses to ignore an interruption, your application continues running as before. If the user decides to answer the phone or reply to an SMS message, however, your application will be terminated.

Figure 6-8 shows the sequence of events that occurs during the arrival of a phone call, SMS message, or calendar alert. Here's what that looks like step by step:

1. **The system detects an incoming phone call or SMS message, or a calendar event occurs.**

2. **The system calls your application delegate's** `applicationWill ResignActive:` **method.**

   Because these interruptions cause a temporary loss of control by your application — meaning that touch events are no longer sent to your applications — it is up to you to prevent what is known in the trade as a "negative user experience." For example, if your application is a game, you should pause the game.

3. **The system displays an alert panel with information about the event.**

   The user can choose to ignore the event or respond to it.

4. **If the user ignores the event, the system calls your application delegate's** `applicationDidBecomeActive:` **method and resumes the delivery of touch events to your application.**

   You can use this delegate method to restore the application to the state it was in before the interruption. What you do depends on your application.

In some applications, it makes sense to resume normal processing. In others — if you've paused a game for example — you could leave the game paused until the user decides to resume play.

5. **If the user responds to the event, instead of ignoring it, the system calls your application delegate's** `applicationWillTerminate:` **method.**

   Your application should do what it needs to do terminate gracefully.

The way the Sleep/Wake button is handled is a little differently. When the application enters or resumes from a sleep state, two of the application delegate's methods are called: its `applicationWillResignActive:` method and its `applicationDidBecomeActive:` method, respectively. In this case, your application always resumes, though the user might immediately launch a different application.

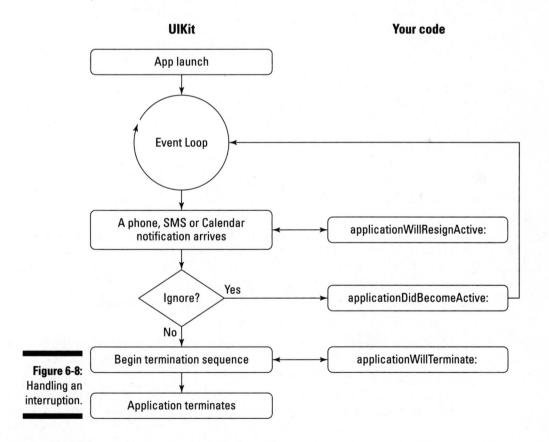

Figure 6-8:
Handling an
interruption.

Seeing how memory management works on the iPhone

One of the main responsibilities of all good little applications is to deal with low memory. So the first line of defense is (obviously) to understand how you as a programmer can help them *avoid* getting into that state.

In the iPhone OS, each program uses the virtual-memory mechanism found in all modern operating systems. But virtual memory is limited to the amount of physical memory available. This is because the iPhone OS doesn't store "changeable" memory (such as object data) on the disk to free up space, and then read it in later when it's needed. Instead, the iPhone OS tries to give the running application the memory it needs — using memory pages that contain read-only contents (such as code), where all it has to do is load the "originals" back into memory when they're needed. Of course, this may only be a temporary fix if those resources are needed again a short time later.

If memory continues to be limited, the system may also send notifications to the running application, asking it to free up additional memory. This is one of the critical events that all applications must respond to.

Observing low-memory warnings

When the system dispatches a low-memory notification to your application, it is something you must pay attention to. If you don't, it is a reliable recipe for disaster. (Think of your low-fuel light going on as you approach a sign that say "next services 100 miles.") UIKit provides several ways of setting up your application so that you receive timely low-memory notifications:

✔ Implement the `applicationDidReceiveMemoryWarning:` method of your application delegate. Your application delegate could then release any data structure or objects it owns — or notify the objects to release memory they own.

✔ Override the `didReceiveMemoryWarning:` method in your custom `UIViewController` subclass. The view controller could then release views — or even other view controllers — that are off-screen

✔ Register to receive the `UIApplicationDidReceiveMemoryWarning Notification:` notification. A model object could then release data structures or objects it owns that it doesn't need immediately and can re-create later

Each of these strategies gives a different part of your application a chance to free up the memory it no longer needs (or doesn't need right now). As for how you actually get these strategies working for you, while I will mention a strategy for implementing the view controller's `didReceiveMemory`

`Warning`: in Chapter 15, this is dependent on your application's architecture. That means you'll need to explore it on your own.

Not freeing up enough memory will result in the iPhone's OS calling your `applicationWillTerminate`: method and shutting you down. For many applications, though, the best defense is a good offense, and you need to manage your memory effectively and eliminate any memory leaks in your code. I cover how to do that in Chapter 12 when I show you how to evaluate your applications memory usage using the Instruments application.

Avoiding the warnings

When you create an object — a window or button for example — memory is allocated to hold that object's data. The more objects you create, the more memory you use, and the less there is available for additional objects you might need. Obviously, it's important to make available (deallocate) the memory that an object was using when the object is no longer needed. This is what is meant by memory management.

The Objective-C language — the application-programming language used to develop iPhone applications — uses reference counting to figure out when to release the memory allocated to an object. It's your responsibility (as a programmer) to keep the memory-management system informed when an object is no longer needed.

Reference counting is a pretty simple concept. When you create the object, it is given a reference count of 1. As other objects use this object, they use methods to increase the reference count, and decrease it when they are done. When the reference count reaches 0, the object is no longer needed, and the memory is de-allocated.

Some basic memory-management rules you shouldn't forget

For those who love Dos and Don'ts lists, here are the fundamental rules when it comes to memory management:

- ✔ Any object you create using `alloc` or `new`, any object that contains `copy`, and any object you send a `retain` message to is yours — you own it. That means you're responsible for telling the memory-management system when you no longer need the object and that its memory can now be used elsewhere.

- ✔ Within a given block of code, the number of times you use `new`, `copy`, `alloc` and `retain` should equal the number of times you use `release` and `autorelease`. You should think of memory management as consisting of pairs of messages. If you balance every `alloc` and every `retain` with a `release`, your object will eventually be freed up when you're done with it.

✔ When you assign an instance variable using an accessor with a property attribute of `retain`, `retain` is automatically invoked — that is, you now own the object. Implement a `dealloc` method to release the instance variables you own.

✔ Objects created any other way (through convenience constructors or other accessor methods) are not your problem.

If you have a solid background in Objective-C memory management (all three of you out there), this should be straightforward or even obvious. If you don't have that background, no sweat: I show you how to do this in practice, and point out the pitfalls as I present the code for the ReturnMeTo application.

Reread this section!

Okay, there are some aspects of programming that you can skate right past without understanding what's really going on, and still create a decent iPhone application. But memory management is *not* one of them!

There is a direct correlation between the amount of free memory available and your application's performance. If the memory available to your application dwindles far enough, the system will be forced to terminate your application. To avoid such a fate, keep a few words of wisdom in mind:

✔ Make *minimizing the amount of memory you use* a built-in feature of your implementation design.

✔ Be sure to use the memory-management functions I explain as I develop the ReturnMeTo application.

✔ In other words, *be sure to clean up after yourself,* or the system will do it for you, and it won't be a pretty picture.

Whew!

Congratulations — you have just gone through the Classic Comics version of another several hundred of pages of Apple documentation, reference manuals, and how-to guides.

Although there's a lot left unsaid (although less than you might suspect), what's in this chapter is enough not only to get you started, but also to keep you going as you develop your own iPhone applications. It provides a frame of reference on which you can hang the concepts I throw around with abandon in upcoming chapters — as well as the groundwork for a deep enough understanding of the application life cycle to give you a handle on the detailed documentation.

Time to move on to the really fun stuff.

Part III

From "Gee, That's a Good Idea" to the App Store

The 5th Wave   By Rich Tennant

"Stop working on the Priority Parking Spot Allocation program. They want to fast track the Coffee Pot/Cubicle Proximity program."

In this part . . .

Y ou're not the only one who dreams of the riches and glory an iPhone application can bring — your author has dreams, too. In this part, I will take you through the entire process of developing the small yet real and sort of functional application that you built the user interface for in Part II. Not far down the development trail, you get to see how to add all the features your app needs, and even what to do when you change your mind (whether because you found a better way to do something or your users demanded it). I end up showing you how to get your application running on the iPhone and then into the App Store. All this should keep you out of trouble for a while, but at the end, you can start thinking about a trip around the world by private jet, or something equally reasonable.

Chapter 7

Actually Writing Code

*I*f you've jumped right to this chapter, you're probably really itching to start writing some code. I understand the urge, and if you're up for it, this chapter — and the chapters that follow — will definitely scratch that code-writing itch for you. (If you start out here and then find some of this tough going, you may want to jump back a chapter or two so I can fill you in on some concepts you'll need under your belt in order to make your coding experience a bit more productive — and more fun!)

Buckle Up, It's Time to Code

Previous chapters talk about design principles in general, as well as about the specific iPhone developer tools (Xcode, Interface Builder) available to you. Chapter 5, for example, has you create the skeleton for a fully functioning iPhone application (my ReturnMeTo jewel) — and now you get to flesh it all out with the code necessary for transforming the ReturnMeTo application from something that just sits there and looks pretty to something that actually *does* something.

A quick refresher peek at Chapter 5 will show you that quite a bit of the ReturnMeTo application is already in place and ready to go. If you click the text field, for example, you *do* get the keyboard — though you can't do anything with it just yet. Both the text field and the label are automatically created from the nib file — which is great — but somehow you have to accomplish two tasks:

✔ Get what the user enters into the text field.

✔ Display the user input in the label you created.

In effect, you have to connect things up so the left hand knows what the right hand is doing.

Fortunately, the framework was designed to allow you to do this easily and gracefully. The view controller can refer to objects in the nib by using a special kind of *instance variable* (a variable defined as part of a class, with each object of that class having its own copy) referred to as an *outlet*. If I want (for example) to be able to access the text field object in my ReturnMeTo application, I take two steps:

1. Declare an outlet in my code.

2. Use Interface Builder to point the outlet to the text field I created earlier.

Then, when my application is initialized, the text field outlet is automatically initialized with a pointer to the text field. I can then use that outlet from within my code to get the text the user entered in the text field.

The fact that a connection between an object and its outlets exists is actually stored in a nib file. When the nib file is loaded, each connection is reconstituted and reestablished — thus enabling you to send messages to the object. IBOutlet is the keyword that tags an instance-variable declaration so the Interface Builder application knows that a particular instance variable *is* an outlet — and can then enable the connection to it with Xcode.

In my code, it turns out I need to create two outlets — one to point to the text field and one to point to the label where I will display the number the user enters. To get this outlet business started, I need to *declare* it, which I do with the help of the aforementioned IBOutlet keyword.

Okay, I'm guessing you realize that *declaring* something in programming doesn't involve standing on a soapbox in Hyde Park and saying something at the top of your lungs. Declaring something code-wise involves . . . writing code. (You knew that.) More specifically, in iPhone application development declaring something code-wise involves writing code using the Xcode editor — which leads us right to the next section.

The Xcode Code Editor

The main tool you use to write code for an iPhone application is the Xcode text editor. Apple has gone out of its way to make the text editor as user-friendly as possible, as evidenced by the following list of (quite convenient) features:

- **Header-File Lookup:** Headers are a big deal in code because they're the place where you'll find the *class declaration* — which includes all of its instance variables and method declarations. By ⌘+double-clicking a particular symbol, you can view the header file that declares the symbol.

- **API Reference Lookup:** You can use this feature to double-click a symbol to get access to an API reference — the go-to place for getting documentation about a method or more info about the methods and properties in a framework class. (Using the API reference is how I discovered that a view has a frame, which I'll use to determine how much to scroll the view to keep the text field visible in Chapter 8.)

- **Code Completion:** As you type code, you can have the editor help out by inserting text for you that completes the name of whatever Xcode thinks you're going to enter.

- **Code Folding:** With code folding, you can collapse code that you're not working on and display only the code that requires your attention. You do this by clicking in the column to the left of the code you want to hide.

- **Switching between header and implementation windows:** On the toolbar above the code editor, you click the last icon before the lock to switch from .h to .m (header and implementation) and vice versa. While the header lets you see the class's instance variables and method declarations, you find your actual code in the implementation file. If you look in the Groups & Files pane of the project window, you can see the separate .h and .m files for the four classes we have started with.

- **Launching a file in a separate window:** Double-click the file name to launch the file in a new window. This enables you folks with big monitors, or multiple monitors, to look at more than one file at a time. You could, for example, look at the method of one class *and* the method it calls in the same, or even a different class.

The next few sections will focus on the two features of the Xcode text editor I find most useful as a developer: code completion and API lookup.

Using Code Completion

Using Code Completion in Xcode means you'll be able to type code faster, no ifs, ands, or buts. When Code Completion is active, Xcode uses the text you typed, as well as the context into which you typed it, to provide suggestions for completing what it thinks you're *going to* type. It's not 100 percent accurate — what mind-reading software program ever is? — but it does a pretty good job of figuring out the code you need.

Code Completion is not active by default; you have to activate it manually. Here's how that's done:

1. **With Xcode open, choose Xcode⇨Preferences from the main menu.**

2. **Click the Code Sense in the toolbar, as shown in Figure 7-1.**

   The Xcode Preferences window refreshes to show the various Code Sense preferences.

3. **Choose Immediate from the Automatically Suggest pop-up menu.**

4. **Click OK to close the Xcode Preferences window.**

From now on (as long as Code Completion is active) whenever you start to type the name of a symbol — a method or an instance variable, for example — Xcode may recognize that symbol before you have finished typing it and offer to fill in the rest. You can accept suggestions by pressing Tab or Return. You may also display a list of completions by pressing Escape.

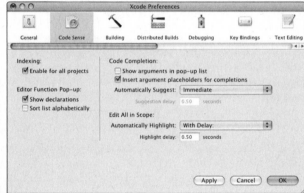

Figure 7-1:
Setting
Code
Completion
prefer-
ences.

Accessing API documentation

Like many developers, you may find yourself wanting to dig deeper when it comes to a particular bit of code. That's where Xcode's Research Assistant — as well as its Documentation window — can come to the rescue. With these tools, you can quickly access the API and/or other documentation for a particular class, method, or property.

Using the Documentation window, you can browse and search the developer documentation — the API references, guides, and article collections about particular tools or technologies — installed on your computer.

To see how this works, let's say I have the project window open with the code displayed in Figure 7-2. If I wanted to find out more about UIApplication Delegate, I'd simply right-click in `UIApplicationDelegate`. Xcode highlights it for me and displays the pop-up menu you see in Figure 7-2. The menu gives you several choices, including these:

✔ **Find Selected Text in API Reference:** Selecting this option brings up the protocol reference for the selected symbol — in this case, `UIApplicationDelegate` — in a new window.

✔ **Find Selected Text in Documentation:** Selecting this option, as I did in Figure 7-3, displays a new window with a list of all the documents in which UIApplicationDelegate appears, with the most relevant document first. (In this case, I get the `UIApplicationDelegate` Protocol Reference.)

The difference between Find Selected Text in Documentation and Find Selected Text in API Reference is that this selection lists *all* of the documents that contain the reference while the former lists only the API's (*application programming interface*) for a class — the methods, properties, etc. and some explanation about them.

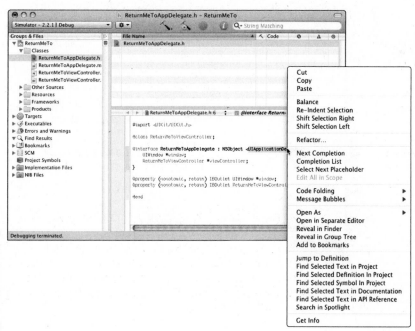

Figure 7-2:
Accessing
Docu-
mentation
window.

✔ **Find Selected Symbol in Project:** This is very useful in tracking down every single place you call a particular method or refer to a variable. If you click on `ReturnMeToViewController` in Figure 7-2 and then select Find Selected Symbol in Project, for example, you'd get the window with the top pane you see in Figure 7-4. The file you're searching on is underlined and the line of code that contains the symbol is listed below it.

Notice that, in the top pane, I clicked in one of the entries and it opened that file in the bottom pane and highlighted the line. If I had double-clicked the entry, Xcode would have opened the file up in a new window, and if it were in a `.xib` file, Xcode would have opened the nib file in which it occurred in Interface Builder.

You can also get this window by simply pressing shift+⌘+F, You can then type whatever you're looking for into the Find field and then select Find. In addition, the drop-down menu that is currently grayed out and displaying In Project in Figure 7-4 will be enabled, and you can specify in what sets of files (open project files, etc) you want to search. (A great feature for tracking down something in your code — you're sure to use it often.)

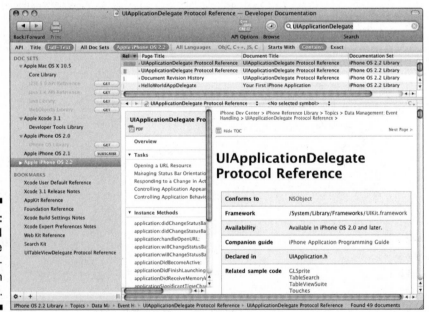

Figure 7-3: Viewing API reference in the Documentation window.

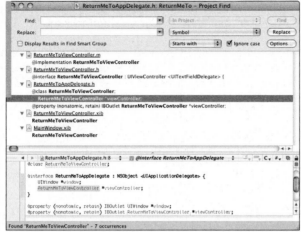

Figure 7-4:
Finding a
symbol in
the project.

Although the Documentation window is a great tool to use when browsing
the iPhone documentation library, the Research Assistant provides the
same information in condensed form in a smaller, less obtrusive window (as
shown in Figure 7-5). Basically, the Research Assistant follows along with the
cursor and when it recognizes a symbol that has an API reference, it displays
that reference. (Again, see Figure 7-5.) The Research Assistant is not visible
by default; you have to call it up. To do that, simply choose Help⇨Show
Research Assistant from the main menu.

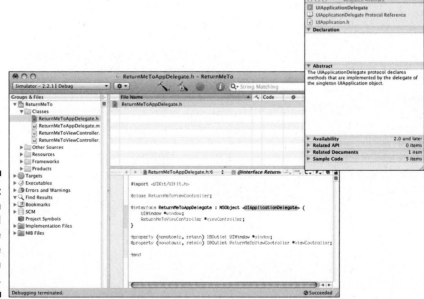

Figure 7-5:
Viewing an
API
reference
in the
Research
Assistant.

Adding Outlets to the View Controller

Now that you have some idea of how to use the Xcode editor, it's time to write some code. Before taking you on our editor tour, I mentioned that one of the things I needed to do was add outlets to my ReturnMeTo application. That's what you are going to do now — add outlets to the ReturnMeToViewController. Here's how:

1. **Go to the Xcode project window and, in the Groups & Files pane, click the triangle next to Classes to expand the folder.**

2. **From the Classes folder, select** ReturnMeToViewController.h **— the header file for** ReturnMeToViewController.

   The contents of the file appear in the main display pane of the Xcode editor, as shown in Figure 7-6.

3. **Look for the following lines of code in the header:**

   ```
   #import <UIKit/UIKit.h>

   @interface ReturnMeToViewController: UIViewController{


   }
   @end
   ```

   Got it? Great.

4. **Type the following four lines of code between** UIViewController {and @end: **(the curly brace you see below the last IBOutlet and first @property statements will already be there)**

   ```
   IBOutlet UITextField *textField;
   IBOutlet UILabel *label;
   }
   @property (nonatomic, retain) UITextField *textField;
   @property (nonatomic, retain) UILabel *label;
   ```

   When you're done typing, your code should look exactly like Figure 7-6.

   The first two lines of code here declare the outlets, which will automatically be initialized with a pointer to the text field (textField), and label objects (label) when the application is launched. But while this will happen automatically, it won't *automatically* happen automatically. I have to help it out a bit.

   In procedural programming, variables are generally fair game for all. But in object-oriented programming, a class's instance variables are tucked away inside an object and shouldn't be accessed directly. The only way for them to be initialized is for you to create what are called *accessor methods*, which allow the specific instance variable of an object to be read and (if you want) updated. Creating accessor methods is a two-step process that begins with an @property declaration which tells the compiler that there are accessor methods.

And that is what I have done above; I coded corresponding @property declarations for each IBOutlet declaration. You'll notice there are some arguments to the @property declaration. These specify how the accessor methods are to behave — I explain exactly what that means in the next section. For now, just know that you need to add them.

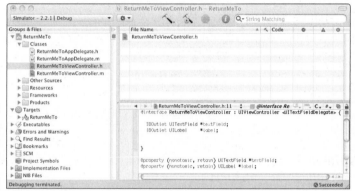

Figure 7-6:
ReturnMe
ToView
Controller.h.

5. **Go back to the Classes folder in the Groups & Files listing and select** ReturnMeToViewController.m — **the implementation file for** ReturnMeToViewController.

6. **Look for the following lines of code in the implementation file:**

```
#import "ReturnMeToViewController.h"

@implementation ReturnMeToViewController
```

They're pretty much right at the top.

7. **Type the following two lines of code after** @implementation ReturnMeToViewController **and before anything else.**

```
@synthesize textField;
@synthesize label;
```

When you're done, your code should like what you see in Figure 7-7.

While the @property declaration tells the compiler that there are accessor methods, they still have to be created. In the good old days, you had to code these accessor methods yourself and, in a large program, it got to be very tedious. Fortunately, Objective-C will create these accessor methods for you whenever you include an @synthesize statement for a property.

That is what you did above. The two @synthesize statements tells the compiler to create two accessor methods for you — one for each @ property declaration.

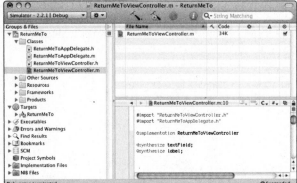

8. **Scroll down the code for** ReturnMeToViewController.m **until you reach the following lines:**

```
- (void)dealloc {

    [super dealloc];
}
```

You can use cmd@+F to find something in a single file, as opposed to shift+⌘@+F, which finds it in all project files

9. **Enter the following two lines of code between the –** (void)dealloc { **and** [super dealloc]; **lines:**

```
[textField release];
[label release];
```

The new code should look like what you see in Figure 7-8.

Those of you who remember my obsession with memory management from previous chapters will recognize release as a tool for freeing up no-longer-needed memory commitments. (Those of you who have not yet heard my memory-management stump speech will get a chance to hear it later in this chapter.)

That's it. You've added outlets to your view controller. Step back and admire your handiwork. Then move on to the next section and see how the little snippets of code you added above to your ReturnMeToViewController.m and ReturnMeToViewController.h files tie in with the basic principles of programming using the Objective-C language.

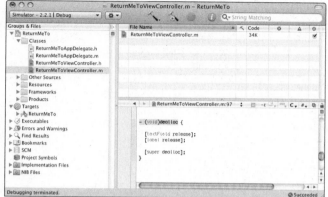

Figure 7-8:
Doing a little
memory
manage-
ment.

Objective-C properties

As you'll soon discover, you're going to use properties *a lot.* In the previous section, I had you blindly follow me and add the properties. But by now you've probably figured out that I don't believe you should be doing things blindly, so in this section I get to explain what you need to know about properties.

Now, you may remember that, in object-oriented programming, a class's instance variables are tucked away inside an object and shouldn't be accessed directly. If you need to have an instance variable accessible by other objects in your program, you need to create accessor methods for that particular instance variable. (This will sound familiar from the previous section.)

For example, in Chapter 9, you're going to add an instance variable `saved Number`, to the `ReturnMeToAppDelegate`. You'll do that because you need something to hold the telephone number someone's supposed to use to call you when they find your lost iPhone. The `ReturnMeToAppDelegate` saves that number when the application terminates, and loads it when it launches. But the `ReturnMeToViewController` needs access to that number to display it in the view, and needs to update it when the user enters a new number.

The methods that provide access to the instance variables of an object are called *accessor methods*, and they effectively get (using a *getter method*) and set (using a *setter method*) the values for an instance variable. Although you could code those methods yourself, it can be rather tedious. This is where properties come in. The Objective-C Declared Properties feature provides a simple way to declare and implement an object's accessor methods. The compiler can synthesize accessor methods for you, according to the way you told it to in the property declaration.

Objective-C creates the getter and setter methods for you by using an `@property` declaration in the interface file, combined with the `@synthesize` declaration in the implementation file. The default names for the getter and setter methods associated with a property are *whateverTheProperty NameIs:* for the getter and *setWhateverThePropertyNameIs:* for the setter. (You replace what is in italics with the actual property name.) For example, the accessors generated in our ReturnMeTo application are `textField:` as the getter, and `setTextField:` as the setter. Similarly, the names for the label accessors are `label:` and `setLabel:` for the getter and setter respectively.

All that being said, at the end of the day you need to do three things in your code to have the compiler create accessors for you:

1. **Declare an instance variable in the interface file.**

2. **Add an** `@property` **declaration of that instance variable in the same interface file (usually with attributes** nonatomic **and** retain**).**

   This is what you did in Step 4 in the previous section. The declaration specifies the name and type of the property and some attributes that provide the compiler with information about how exactly you want the accessor methods to be implemented.

   For example, the declaration

   ```
   @property (nonatomic, retain) UITextField *textField;
   ```

   declares a property named `textField`, which is a pointer to a `UIText Field` object. As for the two attributes — `nonatomic` and `retain` — `nonatomic` tells the compiler to create an accessor to return the value directly, which is another way of saying that the accessors can be interrupted while in use. (This works fine for applications like this one.)

   The second value, *retain*, tells the compiler to create an access method that sends a `retain` message to any object that is assigned to this property. This will keep it from being *deallocated* — having its memory taken back by the iPhone OS to use elsewhere — while you are still using it. (I go into that a bit more when I explain the `dealloc` method that Xcode created for us.)

3. **Use** `@synthesize` **in the implementation file so that Objective-C generates the accessors for you.**

   The `@property` declaration (like the two you placed in the interface file in Step 4 in the previous section) only declares that there are accessors. It is the `@synthesize` statement (like the two you placed in the implementation file in Step 7 in the previous section) that tells the compiler to create them for you. Using @synthesize results in four new methods.

```
textField:
setTextField:
label:
setLabel:
```

If I didn't use @synthesize it would be up to me to implement the methods myself, using the attributes in the @property statement. So if I were to write my own accessors, I would be responsible for sending a retain message to the textField or label when it was assigned to the instance variables. While there are circumstances when you do want to do that, I'll not get into them in this book.

Memory Management

In Chapter 6, I spend a lot of time berating you about memory management — and I promised there that I would make sure to show you how to do this memory-management thing, using a real-world example. I'll start to keep that promise by explaining the dealloc method created for me by the Xcode template when I created the ReturnMeTo application. Now, if you can remember back to the steps list from two sections ago (Step 9, to be precise), I asked you to add the following two lines of code:

```
[textField release];
[label release];
```

to the dealloc method, so the end product would look like the following:

```
- (void)dealloc {

        [textField release];
        [label release];

        [super dealloc];
}
```

Well, here's why: Adding these bits of code *releases* textField and label.

Chapter 6 gave you some handy memory-management rules. Here's one of them:

You own an object you create with `alloc` or `new` or if it contains `copy`, or if you send it a `retain` message. That means you are responsible for telling the memory-management system you are done with it.

In other words, you have to release it when you are done.

So why, then, you might ask, do I have to release `textField` and `label`? If I had created the `textField` and `label` using `alloc` or `new`, obviously it would be my job to release them. But I didn't do that — or did I?

No, you didn't, but what you *did* do was send a `retain` message to both `textField` and `label`.

"Oh, yeah?" you might say, "where?"

Check out the `@property` declarations you made earlier:

```
@property (nonatomic, retain) UITextField *textField;
@property (nonatomic, retain) UILabel *label;
```

You see, lo and behold, `retain`.

The impact of adding that simple two-syllable word `retain` is that any time I assign to that instance variable — assigning a phone number to a label, for example — a `retain` message would be sent to it — and that is precisely what happens at runtime for the outlets.

Notice that while the `dealloc` method generated by Xcode for the `ReturnMe ToViewController` only called `[super dealloc]`, the one generated for me in `ReturnMeToAppDelegate` did more than that

```
- (void)dealloc {
        [viewController release];
        [window release];
        [super dealloc];
}
```

This is because while Xcode didn't know about the `label` and `textField` I was going to create (it can't read my mind after all), it did know about the window and view controller it created for me, and created the code to release them in the `dealloc` method.

Connecting the Pieces in Interface Builder

Earlier in this chapter, I told you if you want to be able to access the label and text field objects in my ReturnMeTo application, you had to take two steps:

1. Declare an outlet in your code.

2. Use Interface Builder to point the outlet to the label and text fields you created earlier in Interface Builder.

You've created the outlets and their accessor methods in your code — I saw you do it in the previous section Now I'm going to show you how to create the connection in Interface Builder so that when the nib file is loaded, the nib loading code will create these connections automatically, using the *accessors you had the compiler create for the* `label` *and* `textField`. (aha!) With these connections established, you'll be able to send messages to your interface objects. (I'll show you how to *receive* messages from interface objects a bit later.)

So, its connection time.

1. **For your ReturnMeTo project, be sure to add the instance variables, @property declaration, and @synthesize statement to your code as spelled out in the Steps 4 and 7 in the "Adding Outlets to the View Controller" section, earlier in this chapter, and then choose File⇨Save or press ⌘+S to save what you have done.**

   You have to save your code, otherwise Interface Builder won't be able to find it.

2. **In the project window, double-click** `ReturnMeToViewController. xib` **to launch Interface Builder.**

   Interface Builder duly makes an appearance on-screen, with the main nib window and the View window open for inspection. (For more on the mechanics of Interface Builder, see Chapter 5.)

3. **Holding down the control key, click the File's Owner icon in the main nib window and drag it to the label field in the View window, as shown in Figure 7-9.**

   You need to use the control key here or you will just end up dragging the File's Owner icon, rather than initiating a connection.

You should see the `label` value (650 555 1212) appear when you are over the label field. (If you remember, that was the value you set when you created the label in Chapter 5.)

4. **With the cursor still over the label field, let go of the mouse button.**

   A pop-up menu appears, looking like the one in Figure 7-10.

Figure 7-9:
Dragging
from the
File's Owner
to the label.

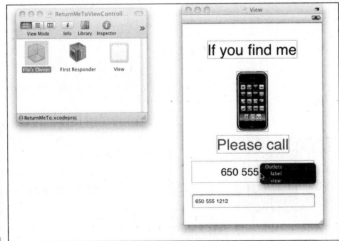

Figure 7-10:
Releasing
the mouse
button and
selecting
label.

5. **Choose label from the pop-up menu.**

   Interface Builder now knows that one of the File Owner's outlets (in this case, the `label` value I selected in the pop-up menu, which is one of the `ReturnMeToViewController` outlets) should point to the label at runtime.

   There's another way to do this, however, one that's a little more obvious. To see how that method works, check out how I connect the other outlet — the `textField` outlet — to its text field.

6. **Right-click the File's Owner icon in the main nib window to call up a dialog displaying a list of connections.**

   This particular dialog can also be accessed by choosing the Connections tab in the Interface Builder Inspector.

7. **Drag from the `textField` outlet item in the dialog onto the text field in the View window, as shown in Figure 7-11.**

   Interface Builder now knows that the `textField` outlet should point to the text field at run time. All is right with the world.

8. **Go back to the Xcode project window and click the Build and Go button to compile and build the application.**

   Figure 7-12 shows what happens if you click in the text field. Neat, huh?

Figure 7-11:
Connecting
the text field
in another
way.

The only problem, of course, is that after the keyboard comes up, you can't dismiss it and therefore can't see anything behind it. A bit of a problem, I admit, but it's easily fixable — as the next chapter makes clear.

Chapter 8

Entering and Managing Data

. . . .

. . . .

*T*hings aren't perfect with our ReturnMeTo application yet. The iPhone on the left in Figure 8-1 shows what happens when you select the text field to enter a phone number.

Not very useful, is it? Reminds me of the time I sat behind Yao Ming in the movie theater. (Can you say, "Down in front!"?)

The iPhone on the right in Figure 8-1 does it the way it should be — as in, the keyboard ducks down so you can see what you're typing.

Okay, maybe the movie-theater metaphor isn't that appropriate (I was kidding about famous basketball players anyway). It's not that the keyboard ducks down so you can better see the content view; rather, the idea is to *scroll the content view up* when the keyboard appears so you can see the phone number you're entering as you continue to develop the application.

Incidentally, implementing this little scrolling business is probably the most complicated thing you'll be doing with this application. It involves a number of different objects and methods that are called over the life of the application.

Figure 8-1:
Well, you
do get a
keyboard,
but not
much else.

I have an ulterior motive here: As I take you through implementing the scrolling of the content view, I also show you the dynamic flow of the application. Keeping a close eye on this flow will give you a good working sense of how and where to insert your own code to handle such tasks as these:

✔ initialization and termination of your application

✔ initialization and termination of views

✔ processing user touches on the screen

Developing this knack is vital for your own applications. Fortunately, even the simple example in this chapter provides a structure that you'll be sure to use in much more sophisticated applications.

Scrolling the View

On iPhone applications, when a user touches a text field used for data entry, the keyboard scrolls up from the bottom of the screen. That's all fine and dandy. The problem is that, by default, if the text field you've specified as the User Entry field is toward the bottom of the content view, that magically-appearing keyboard is going to scroll up and cover every inch of the text field so the user can't see what he or she is entering. The solution (as mentioned in the previous section and displayed on the right in Figure 8-1) is to scroll the content view — which includes the text field — up so the text field will still be visible.

Simple enough concept. Getting to it requires a number of steps:

1. **Registering to be notified when the keyboard appears.**

    This involves asking the iPhone OS to call a method I specify whenever the keyboard is about to scroll into view.

2. **Deciding whether the text field will in fact end up being covered by the keyboard.**

3. **Moving the content view up so the text field will not be covered by the keyboard.**

4. **After the user is done editing, dismissing the keyboard and restoring the content view back to where it was.**

5. **Unregistering for keyboard notifications when the view is dismissed or not visible.**

This is the scenario at runtime — although, as you'll see, this is not the order in which I necessarily want to implement the code. I'll deal with the registering and unregistering for keyboard notifications first, since they are mirror images of each other, and then get on with the code that does all of the work.

But before I get into any of that, you have to know where to put your code so it gets called at the right time.

Where Does My Code Go?

One of the biggest challenges facing a developer working with a new framework is understanding where in the *control flow* — the sequence in which methods are called during execution — he or she needs to add the code to get something done. I discuss some of these more traffic-cop-ish aspects of application development in Chapter 6 ("okay, your turn — now you over there, yield — now you in the right lane, go"), but I want to expand upon that discussion here, using the scrolling of a view in response to user action as a concrete example.

Figure 8-3 illustrates the higher-level control flow within our ReturnMeTo application. Look closely and you'll see two objects — `ReturnMeToAppDelegate` and `ReturnMeToViewController` — that you'd find at runtime if you went behind the screen and sifted through memory. (I bolded the two objects in the figure to make them stand out.) The next two sections look at what these two objects do for you as part of the ReturnMeTo application.

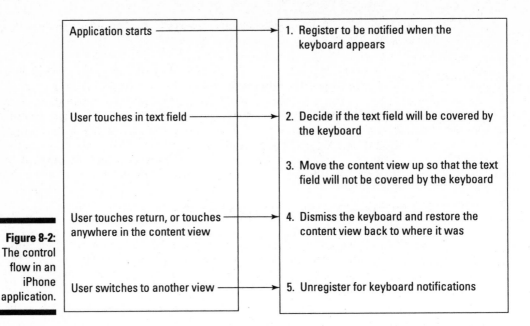

Figure 8-2:
The control
flow in an
iPhone
application.

The Delegate object

The first, ReturnMeToAppDelegate, has two methods I want to call your attention to:

- ✔ applicationDidFinishLaunching:
- ✔ applicationWillTerminate:

applicationDidFinishLaunching: is called at the very beginning of the application, before the user can even see anything on the screen. Here's where you'd insert your code to initialize your application — where you'd load data, for example, or restore the state of the application to where it was the last time the user exited.

In the case of the ReturnMeTo application, there really is only one state we need to concern ourselves with, so you don't have to worry about saving any state. (I wouldn't count the keyboard scrolled up in full view as a state I would want to leave the application in.) In more complex applications, you would have to work a bit in the applicationDidFinishLaunching: method to set things up correctly. I *do* show you how to both save and restore the state in Chapter 16, but even for a simple application like this, saving and restoring data is important.

applicationWillTerminate: is called right before your application terminates. It's the mirror image of applicationDidFinishLaunching: — and it's also the place where you would store any unsaved data, and save the current state of the application. If you check out Chapter 9, you can see how

I use `applicationWillTerminate` to save the phone number the user has entered.

The `applicationDidFinishLaunching:` method and the `application-WillTerminate:` method are in the `UIApplicationDelegate` protocol. As I explain in Chapter 2, protocols are simply rules that spell out methods that can be implemented by any class. My `ReturnMeToAppDelegate` (for example) has adopted the `UIApplicationDelegate` protocol, so if I implement `applicationDidFinishLaunching:` and `applicationWillTerminate:` in the `ReturnMeToAppDelegate` implementation, they will be automatically called.

The Controller object

`ReturnMeToViewController` is the controller responsible for managing the application's *view* — what the user sees and interacts with, including text editing. There are three methods here I want to call your attention to:

- ✔ `viewDidLoad`
- ✔ `viewWillAppear:`
- ✔ `viewWillDisappear:`

`viewDidLoad` is called right after the view has been loaded from the nib file — check out Chapter 6 for a complete explanation of that loading process. This is the place where you insert your code for *view initialization*, which in this case means updating the text in the label to show the phone number.

`viewWillAppear:` is called right before the view will appear. This is the place to insert your code to do anything needed before the view becomes visible.

Finally, `viewWillDisappear:` is called right before a view is dismissed or covered up. This is the place to insert your code to do anything you need to do before a view may be released or freed.

These three methods are declared in the `UIViewController` class and are called at the appropriate times by the framework. In this case, since `ReturnMeToViewController` is derived from the `UIViewController` class, I will *override* those methods. To do that, I simply implement a new method with the same name as one defined in the `UIViewController` class in the `ReturnMeToViewController` implementation.

Most of the time, you do your initialization at the application level using the `applicationDidFinishLaunching` method in your application delegate. As for your initialization of the view level, you'd normally take care of that using the `viewDidLoad` and `viewWillAppear` methods in your `UIViewController` derived class — `ReturnMeToViewController`, in our example. When it comes to shutting down your app, you'd use the applicationWillTerminate method in your application delegate to handle all the chores of terminating your application — and the viewWillDisappear method in your UIViewController to take care of dismissing the view.

Knowing the control flow I outline above — how and where to insert your code in order to add your specific application functionality — will make developing your own application much easier. Trust me on that one.

Where I Am Starting From

Time to get your hands dirty again. Listings 8-1 and 8-2 show the code pulled together in Chapter 7 as the foundation for our ReturnMeTo application. (The bolded code is the code you actually had to type in, whereas the unbolded code was already put in place for you by the UIKit framework.)

Listing 8-1:   ReturnMeToViewController.h

```
#import <UIKit/UIKit.h>

@interface ReturnMeToViewController: UIViewController {

  IBOutlet UITextField *textField;
  IBOutlet UILabel     *label;

}

@property (nonatomic, retain) UITextField *textField;
@property (nonatomic, retain) UILabel *label;

@end
```

Listing 8-2:   ReturnMeToViewController.m

```
#import "ReturnMeToViewController.h"

@implementation ReturnMeToViewController

@synthesize textField;
@synthesize label;


- (void)didReceiveMemoryWarning {

  [super didReceiveMemoryWarning];
```

```
}

- (void)dealloc {

  [textField release];
  [label release];
  [super dealloc];
}

@end
```

In order to enable scrolling of the content so that all content will be accessible at all times, you'll need to make a few changes to both the `ReturnMeToViewController.h` file — the file containing interface stuff, as spelled out in Listing 8-1 — and the `ReturnMeToViewController.m` — the file containing implementation stuff as well as a few other things whose purpose will become abundantly clear over the course of this chapter. (Listing 8-2 shows the `ReturnMeToViewController.m` file as it stands right now.)

Building on a Foundation

The code put together in Chapter 7 for the ReturnMeTo application is a great start, but you'll still have to address the My Keyboard is Hiding Crucial Parts of My View problem I mention at the beginning of this chapter. Now, the solution clearly is to move things around so that the iPhone keyboard no longer hogs the view, but getting to that point is a bit tricky. For example, if I am going to scroll the content view when the keyboard appears, I need to know *when* the keyboard is going to appear. Luckily for me, the iPhone OS has something in place that fits my needs exactly. It is a *Notification* system.

Notification

Notification is a system that allows objects within an application to learn about changes that occur elsewhere in that application. Usually, objects get information by messages that come to them. But that means the object that sends the message must know what objects it needs to update whenever it does something that those objects care about. And let's face it, the `UIWindow` object, being as it is in the keyboard displaying business, has no clue about my `ReturnMeToViewController` object.

That's where notification comes in. Notification is a broadcast model where I can register my objects to be notified of a particular event. I can even post a notification, although I am not interested in doing that here. Notifications are managed by a single object, NSNotificationCenter which is accessed using the class method defaultCenter:.

For our ReturnMeTo application, we want to be notified when a UIKeyboard WillShowNotification is posted. That notification is posted by the UIWindow class.

Registering a notification

If I want to be notified of an event that occurs in response to a user's action in a view — the user touching the text field and the keyboard appearing, to take the most obvious example — that notification has to reach me before the user has a chance to do anything else.

At this point, take a look at Figure 8-3; it shows (among other things) that the best place to put your request for notification — that is, the best place to *register* to be notified — is *after* view initialization but *before* the view becomes visible.

The iPhone icons on the left side of Figure 8-3 show that the view will appear after the viewWillAppear: method is called. That is the ideal place to insert the code that registers the fact that you want to be notified before the keyboard appears. All I need to do to override viewWillAppear: is add this method to my implementation, as spelled out in Listing 8-3. (For all the dirty details about adding your own code to that handy bunch of code provided by the frameworks, check out Chapter 7.)

Now, if you were to look in the ReturnMeToViewController code, guess what? You are not going to find viewWillAppear:, not as a stub, or even commented out. You're going to have to add it yourself. Rather than adding things at random, though, you may want to group similar code together, and I'll talk about how to do that later in this chapter. For right now, I'd put it right after the commented out viewDidLoad, which we will use shortly. You can find that bit of code in the ReturnMeToViewController.m file by pressing ⌘+F, which opens up a Find dialog that you can then use to find whatever you want in a particular file. Handy tool that one is.

Listing 8-3:   Override viewWillAppear:

```
- (void)viewWillAppear:(BOOL)animated {

  [[NSNotificationCenter defaultCenter] addObserver:self
    selector:@selector(keyboardWillShow:)
    name:UIKeyboardWillShowNotification
    object:self.view.window];

  [super viewWillAppear:animated];
}
```

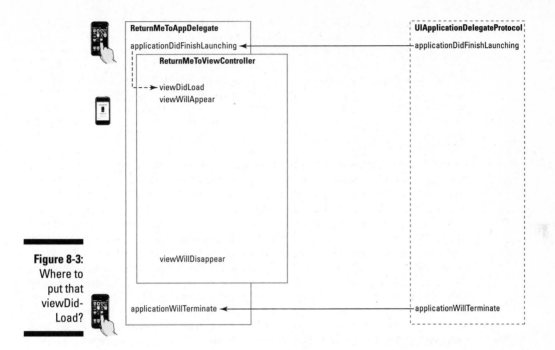

Listing 8-3 shows the code necessary to receive the UIKeyboardWill
ShowNotification. Here's the blow-by-blow account:

1. **I send the** NSNotificationCenter **the** defaultCenter: **message,
   passing it the following items:**

   - addObserver: The object you want to send the message to. It's
     going to be either self or the object making the request; in this
     case, it's ReturnMeToViewController.

   - selector: The method within the object you want to call. For our
     example, the method I want to code is keyboardWillShow. The
     selector must have one, and *only* one, argument.

   - name: This specifies the notification you're registering for — in this
     case, UIKeyboardWillShowNotification.

   - object: The particular object whose notification I am registering
     for — in this case, window.

2. **I then call the super class's** (UIViewController) **method** [super
   viewWillAppear:animated];.

   This is important because there may be some things UIViewController
   needs to do on its own before the view appears.

Unregistering a notification

While I'm at it, I should also write the code for *un*registering for the notification. That's because I don't want the notification center to send a notification to an object that has been *freed* (that is, deallocated). Again, a quick peek back at Figure 8-3 shows that the framework supplies a convenient place to put an appropriate call — `viewWillDisappear` — when the user decides to switch to another view or terminate the application. (Listing 8-4 shows the code you need for unregistering the application.)

If you skip this unregistering step, you'll generate a runtime error if the center sends a message to a freed object.

At the beginning of this chapter, I laid out the five-step plan for how we want to deal with scrolling up the view. That plan had "unregister the notification" as Step # 5 — so why am I talking about unregistering *now*? Well, I *did* say that the five-step plan was meant to describe *what happens at runtime*, and that sequence of events isn't necessarily the best order to follow in implementing the code. Here's proof of that fact — my advice to you is to take care of registering and unregistering notifications as part of the same step in your coding.

Although the ReturnMeTo application has only one view, other applications you create could very well have other views — or you may even come back later and enhance *this* application with another view. So it's always good form to do this kind of unregistering cleanup *before* a view is either freed or is no longer visible. Here (again) you use a `defaultCenter:` message, passing the following items to it:

✔ `removeObserver:` The object you want to send the message to. It's either going to be `self` or the object making the request, in this case the `ReturnMeToViewController`.

✔ `name:` This specifies the notification you're *un*registering for — in this case, the `UIKeyboardWillShowNotification`.

✔ `object:` Since I am unregistering, I use a `nil` for `object` here because that will remove all `UIKeyboardWillShowNotification` notifications (if there were more than one).

Here's another method you need to add. I suggest you add it right after `viewWillAppear:`.

Listing 8-4: Override `viewWillDisappear:`

```
- (void)viewWillDisappear:(BOOL)animated {

[[NSNotificationCenter defaultCenter] removeObserver:self
        name:UIKeyboardWillShowNotification object:nil];

[super viewWillDisappear:animated];
}
```

Keeping the text field visible

It's often a challenge to implement the scrolling of your content in a view because sometimes it's hard to determine how much scrolling you need to do — or whether you should do any scrolling at all. For example, when the keyboard appears, it may not even cover the text field you've added to the view — which means you shouldn't scroll the content view. In fact, if the text field won't be covered by the keyboard, scrolling the content might be a bad thing to do; you may end up scrolling the content out of sight.

Things are starting to get a little complicated, so I'm going to pull out the good old illustrative line drawing (Figure 8-4) on the theory that a picture is worth a thousand words.

The concept

Because you thought ahead and signed up to receive a notification when the keyboard in my ReturnMeTo application is about to scroll up — you did that in the previous section — the `keyboardWillShow` method will be called right after the user touches in the text field, but before the keyboard appears. (All this is beautifully illustrated in Figure 8-4.)

Using that method, first you determine whether the keyboard is going to cover the text field; if you see that it will, then you set the method's instance variable `moveViewUp` to `YES`. This variable will be used after the user is done editing, to see whether the content view has been scrolled and needs to be restored.

As part of this process, you have to compute the actual amount you need to scroll. You only want to scroll the content view enough for the text field — plus a little margin — to be visible above the top of the keyboard. After computing that value, you'll save it in an instance variable so the method that actually scrolls the content view knows how much "scroll" to use.

That's the concept. The actual mechanics of coding this scroll business get ironed out in the next section.

The mechanics of scrolling the view

When `keyboardWillShow:` is called, it is passed an `NSDictionary` that contains, among other things, the height of the keyboard.

Dictionaries manage pairs of keys and values. Each of these key-and-value pairs is an *entry*. Each entry has two objects; one object represents the key, and a second object is that key's value. An `NSDictionary` object manages a *static array* — an array whose keys and values cannot be added to or deleted (although individual elements can be modified).

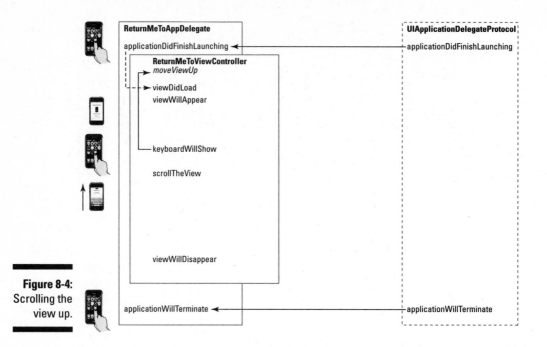

Figure 8-4:
Scrolling the
view up.

The dictionary has the three entries, as shown in Figure 8-5:

✔ The key `UIKeyboardCenterBeginUserInfoKey` has as its value the center of the keyboard in screen coordinates before animation, that is, before it is scrolled in.

✔ The key `UIKeyboardCenterEndUserInfoKey` has as its value the center of the keyboard in screen coordinates after animation, that is, after it is scrolled in.

✔ The key `UIKeyboardBoundsUserInfoKey` has as its value the bounds rectangle of the keyboard — in other words, the size of the keyboard.

You want to scroll the content view only enough so that the text field, plus a small margin, is sitting just above the top of the keyboard. Now, Figure 8-5 shows you that you can get the size of the keyboard from the `NSDictionary`. Basically, you can calculate the size of the view as well as the origin of the text field and its size. With this figure in hand, you can compute the `bottomPoint`, which you can see on the right side of the figure. You can then determine the number of pixels between the bottom of the view itself and the calculated `bottomPoint`. And if you use that pixel value (you will in the computation), you can then determine the amount to scroll the content view.

Listing 8-5 shows the implementation of `keyboardWillShow`. The handy steps list that follows Listing 8-5 gives the color commentary on what all this code is actually doing. (Again, if you need a refresher on how one actually modifies a given method by messing with its code, check out Chapter 7.)

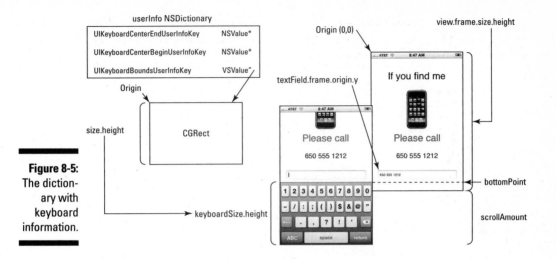

Figure 8-5:
The diction-
ary with
keyboard
information.

This is another method you will be adding. I suggest you add it right after `viewWillDisappear:`.

Listing 8-5: Add keyboardWillShow

```
- (void)keyboardWillShow:(NSNotification *)notif {

  NSDictionary* info = [notif userInfo];

  NSValue* aValue = [info objectForKey:UIKeyboardBoundsUse
         rInfoKey];
  CGSize keyboardSize = [aValue CGRectValue].size;
  float bottomPoint = (textField.frame.origin.y+
                textField.frame.size.height+10);
  scrollAmount = keyboardSize.height -
         (self.view.frame.size.height-  bottomPoint);

  if (scrollAmount >0)  {
    moveViewUp =YES;
    [self scrollTheView:YES];
    }
  else
    moveViewUp =NO;
}
```

1. **Send a message to the notification center to return a reference to the dictionary that has the information.**

   ```
   NSDictionary* info = [notif userInfo];
   ```

2. Use the key to have the method extract the keyboard size for you.

```
NSValue* aValue = [info objectForKey:
                        UIKeyboardBoundsUserInfoKey];
CGSize keyboardSize = [aValue CGRectValue].size;
```

The NSValue object is a simple container for a single C or Objective-C data item. It can hold any of the scalar types (variables that hold values) such as int, float, and char, as well as pointers, structures, and object IDs. In this case, as you can see in this code snippet — as well as in Figure 8-5 — it points to a CGRect.

A CGRect is a structure that contains the location (origin) and dimensions (size) of a rectangle. [aValue CGRectValue] calls a method that extracts the size of the rectangle at which aValue is pointing. CGSize is a structure that contains width and height values.

3. Compute the bottomPoint.

```
float bottomPoint = (textField.frame.origin.y+
                        textField.frame.size.height+10);
```

textField.frame.origin.y in Figure 8-5 tells me the top-left point of the text field. To find the bottom point, I'm adding both the height of the text field and a 10-pixel margin to make it look nice. That's because the coordinate system on the iPhone starts at (0,0) in the top left corner of the screen and increases as you go down the screen. (Forget what you learned in Algebra I, because it won't help you deal with iPhone coordinates.)

4. Compute the amount to scroll.

```
scrollAmount = keyboardSize.height -
        (self.view.frame.size.height - bottomPoint);
```

As you can see in Figure 8-5, subtracting the bottomPoint from the height of the content view gives you the amount of the content view that I want covered by the keyboard. I get the height of the content view by using the view controller's pointer to the view — the aptly named view pointer. The view has an instance variable, frame, which is a CGRect that has a size, just as the CGRect for keyboard did. Subtracting that result from the keyboard height gives me the amount to scroll.

5. Check to see whether the view should be moved up.

```
if (scrollAmount >0) {
```

If the scroll amount is greater than zero, I set moveViewUp to YES. This will be used by the methods called when the user is done editing the text field to see whether the content view has been scrolled and needs to be restored. If not, I set it to NO. Finally, I call scrollTheView :YES to move the view up.

Of course, if the scroll amount is not greater than zero, I set moveViewUp to NO and forget about the whole thing.

A CGGeometry Reference

A CGRect is a structure that contains the location and dimensions of a rectangle.

```
struct CGRect {
    CGPoint origin;
    CGSize size;
};
typedef struct CGRect CGRect;
```

A CGPoint is a structure that contains a point in a two-dimensional coordinate system.

```
struct CGPoint {
    CGFloat x;
    CGFloat y;
};
typedef struct CGPoint
    CGPoint;
```

And finally, a CGSize is structure that contains width and height values.

```
struct CGSize {
    CGFloat width;
    CGFloat height;
};
typedef struct CGSize CGSize;
```

You may think this whole computing-and-calculating business is overkill. After all, I only have the one text field, and I *know* it's going to covered. But there's method in the madness: I did this to introduce you to some view geometry so you can see how to compute where things are in the view and where to find the values. I could have also hard-coded the size of the keyboard, but sizes, depending on the type of the keyboard you have chosen, may be different, and keyboard sizes may also change between different releases of the iPhone OS. In addition, the keyboard size can change according to whether the device is in portrait or landscape mode (if your iPhone supports that).

It wouldn't be the first time that a "quick and dirty" method came back to haunt you, or the last for that matter.

Remember what your parents said after they made you do something that was difficult? "I'm doing it for your own good."

Fortunately, this is as hard as it gets.

Moving the view

After you determine how much to scroll the content view for your ReturnMeTo application (see the previous section), you can then put the code in place for actually moving the view. Listing 8-6 shows the scrollTheView method, yet another one that must be added to the ReturnMeToViewController.m file.

Place this one right after `keyBoardWillShow:`. The steps list that follows highlights the major points along the way. (As always, if you need a refresher on code writing, check out Chapter 7.)

Listing 8-6: Add `scrollTheView:`

```
- (void)scrollTheView:(BOOL)movedUp {

  [UIView beginAnimations:nil context:NULL];
  [UIView setAnimationDuration:0.3];
  CGRect rect = self.view.frame;
  if (movedUp){
    rect.origin.y -= scrollAmount;
    }
  else {
    rect.origin.y += scrollAmount;
    }
  self.view.frame = rect;
  [UIView commitAnimations];
}
```

The first step has to do with *animating* the move — programming-speak for that nice smooth sliding up and down of views you see on the iPhone. I could just simply move it, but instead I want to move it in synch with the keyboard moving up. This is called *animating the transition*. The UIView framework that we have been working with has several class methods I can call to deal with the whole animation ball of wax:

✔ Methods to indicate that the transition should be animated in the first place

✔ Methods to indicate the type of transition that should be used

✔ Methods to specify how long the transition should take

Okay, here goes, one step at a time:

1. **Create an animation block.**

   To invoke a view's built-in animation behavior, you create an animation block and set the duration of the move.

   `beginAnimations` has arguments to pass information to animation delegates. Since you're not going to be using any such delegates in the ReturnMeTo application, you should set the arguments to `nil` and `NULL`.

   ```
   [UIView beginAnimations:nil context:NULL];
   ```

   `nil` is used when there is a null pointer to an object — `beginAnimations`, for example.

   `NULL` is used when there is a null pointer to anything else.

As for animation duration, I set that to .3 seconds, which matches the keyboard's animation.

```
[UIView setAnimationDuration:0.3];
```

2. **Get (access) the view's *frame*.**

   I did the very same thing in the keyboardWillShow method back in Listing 8-5.

   ```
   CGRect rect = self.view.frame;
   ```

3. **If the view should be moved up, subtract the keyboard height from the frame.**

   The CGRect also contains the view's origin in *x, y* coordinates, with the upper-left part of the screen being 0,0.

   ```
   if (movedUp){
       rect.origin.y -= scrollAmount;
   ```

4. **If the view shouldn't be moved up, restore it by adding the keyboard height back to the origin.**

   ```
   else {
       rect.origin.y += scrollAmount;
   ```

   If I move the content view up when the keyboard appears, then I must also restore the view to its original position when the keyboard disappears. This code allows me to call scrollTheView with NO, which will scroll the view down.

5. **Assign the new frame to the view.**

   ```
   self.view.frame = rect;
   ```

6. **Tell the view that you're all done with setting the animation parameters, and it should start the animation.**

   ```
   [UIView commitAnimations];
   ```

Changing the frame rectangle automatically redisplays the view! You don't have to lift a finger! Remember, though, that since you set the new frame inside an animation block, the view doesn't instantly move to the new position, but is instead animated over time (.3 seconds in this case) to the new frame position.

Updating the interface

Time for a bit of cleanup. So far in this chapter, you've made quite a few changes to the original code, so it's probably time to bring the interface up to speed on what you've been mucking about with. Listing 8-7 shows what you need to add to the interface to let it know what's been happening on its watch. (Note that the changes are in bold.) I have to make to the interface. You'll see right off the bat that you need to declare the two new instance variables, `moveViewUp` and `scrollAmount` — as well as the new method `scrollTheView` — in the interface.

As to where to put them, the two instance variables go in the `ReturnMeTo ViewController.h` file, right after the two outlets we added in the last chapter. The new method declaration should follow the property declarations we added in the last chapter.

Listing 8-7:   Add changes to the interface

```
@interface ReturnMeToViewController : UIViewController {

  IBOutlet UITextField *textField;
  IBOutlet UILabel     *label;
          BOOL          moveViewUp;
          CGFloat       scrollAmount;
}

@property (nonatomic, retain) UITextField *textField;
@property (nonatomic, retain) UILabel *label;

- (void)scrollTheView:(BOOL)movedUp;
@end
```

To inform the interface of what you've been up to, follow these steps:

1. **Add the** `moveViewUp` **and** `scrollAmount` **instance variables.**

   `moveViewUp` will be used to determine whether the content view needs to be — or has been — scrolled. `scrollAmount` is the amount the content view needs to be scrolled.

2. **Declare the** `scrollTheView` **method.**

Lowering the view when all is said and done

The way we've set up the ReturnMeTo application is that, after the user is done entering the necessary text into the text field — in this case, a telephone number — the keyboard is supposed to disappear and the view is meant to move back down to its original position. (If you remember, you added the capability to do this in Listing 8-6, and more specifically in Step 4 above.) As it happens, the UITextViewDelegate textFieldShould Return: method is called when the user taps the Return key on the keyboard, giving me the opportunity to add any functionality needed when the user is done entering text. As you can see in Figure 8-6, this is the perfect place to add code that restores the view to its original position. The user is done editing, so all you have to do is dismiss the keyboard and restore the view to its original position You do that by adding the code shown in Listing 8-8 to the ReturnMeToViewController.m file, right after the dealloc method, but before the @end statement.

Listing 8-8: Implement textFieldShouldReturn

```
- (BOOL) textFieldShouldReturn: (UITextField *) theTextField {

    [theTextField resignFirstResponder];
    if (moveViewUp) [self scrollTheView:NO];

    return YES;
}
```

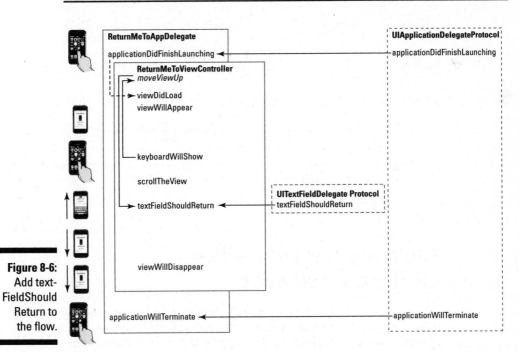

Figure 8-6:
Add text-
FieldShould
Return to
the flow.

The method `textFieldShouldReturn` is passed the current text field that is being edited — namely, `theTextField`.

1. **Call** `[theTextField resignFirstResponder]`.

   If you were wondering how to dismiss the keyboard, this does the trick:

   ```
   [theTextField resignFirstResponder];
   ```

2. **At times when the view has been scrolled up (yes, this is one of those situations), call** `scrollTheView`, **with the argument of** NO, **to restore the view to its original position:**

   ```
   if (moveViewUp) [self scrollTheView:NO];
   ```

   `moveViewUp` lets the `textFieldShouldReturn` method know that the view has been scrolled and it needs to be restored.

3. **Return YES.**

   This tells the text field to implement its default behavior for the Return key.

Now the keyboard has been dismissed and the view restored to its original position. All's right with the world. And because you already took care of the code for unregistering the notification earlier in the chapter, you've completed the five-step plan that puts in place a system for efficiently scrolling your content view up and down as needed. Now all you have to do is tie up a few loose (code) strings and you're set — except for the compiling and testing, of course.

Managing the keyboard

When the user taps a view, that view becomes the *first responder* — the first object in the responder chain given the opportunity to respond to an event. (For more on first responders and responder chains and events, see Chapter 6.) If the view is a text field (or any other object that has editable text), then an editing session starts and the keyboard is displayed automatically — you don't have to lift a finger to make the keyboard appear.

But just because the keyboard is *displayed* automatically doesn't mean that the keyboard will be *dismissed* automatically. In fact, it is your responsibility to dismiss the keyboard at the appropriate time, when the user taps the Return or Done button on the keyboard or, in this case, when the user touches in the view.

To dismiss the keyboard, you call the `resignFirstResponder:` method of the text field — the initial first responder. When the text field resigns, it is no longer the first responder — just like Nixon was no longer President of the United States after he resigned.

This may sound a bit convoluted but it's the only way to dismiss the keyboard. You can't send a message to the keyboard directly — as in, "Hey, you're fired. Pack your things and go!" You can only make the keyboard disappear by having it resign its first-responder status of the text field.

Polishing the Chrome and Adding the Vinyl Pinstriping

It should come as no surprise to you that the star of the last section — the aptly named `textFieldShouldReturn:` method — is a method within a particular protocol, just like the `applicationDidFinishLaunching:` and `applicationWillTerminate:` methods were also methods within a protocol. In this case, the `textFieldShouldReturn:` method is a member of the `UITextFieldDelegate` protocol — the protocol which sets the rules for messages sent to a text field delegate as part of the editing sequence.

Now, protocols simply declare methods that can be implemented by any class. In response to certain events, the framework checks to see whether there's a delegate that implements a certain method — and if there is, it will call that method. That means if I have my `ReturnMeToViewController` class adopt the `UITextFieldDelegate` protocol and then implement the `textFieldShouldReturn` method, the `UITextFieldDelegate` protocol kicks into action and the `textFieldShouldReturn` method is called automatically.

Sounds great! But you do have to jump through a few hoops to have your `ReturnMeToViewController` class adopt the `UITextFieldDelegate` protocol. Here's the birds-eye view in two easy steps:

1. **Signal to the complier that the** `TextFieldDelegate` **protocol has been adopted by the delegate — in this case,** `ReturnMeToView Controller`.

2. **Connect the** `ReturnMeToViewController` **to the** `textField` **to let** `textField` **know in no uncertain terms that** `ReturnMeToView Controller` **is its delegate.**

That's the bird's-eye view. The next few sections show what the process looks like down on the ground.

Adopting a protocol

Adopting a protocol is a pretty straightforward process. You'll be working with the header file for your class — `ReturnMeToViewController.h`, in this case. The idea here is to update the `@interface` declaration so the left hand knows what the right hand is doing.

The change is in bold in Listing 8-9.

Listing 8-9:   Add a protocol declaration to the interface

```
@interface ReturnMeToViewController : UIViewController
        <UITextFieldDelegate> {

  IBOutlet UITextField *textField;
  IBOutlet UILabel     *label;
           BOOL        moveViewUp;
           CGFloat     scrollAmount;
}

@property (nonatomic, retain) UITextField *textField;
@property (nonatomic, retain) UILabel *label;

- (void)scrollTheView:(BOOL)movedUp;
@end
```

Here's the blow-by-blow account:

1. **Add** <UITextFieldDelegate>.

   Listing a protocol within angle brackets after the superclass name — UIViewController, in this case, the Big Papa class of your ReturnMeToViewController class — specifies that your class has adopted the UITextFieldDelegate protocol.

   Classes can adopt several protocols. To add more than one protocol, you just put them all in the angle brackets, separated by commas.

2. **Save the file. You're done.**

Not too many blows there, as you can see. On to the next section.

Connecting things up with Interface Builder

Back in Chapter 7, you worked a bit with Interface Builder to connect outlet values to their corresponding view elements. You're now going to have to trundle out Interface Builder again in order to connect ReturnMeToView Controller with the appropriate text field so that the connections are set up for you at run time. Here's how the process works:

1. **Back in Xcode, open the Resources folder for your ReturnMeTo project in the Groups & Files listing on the left and then double-click the** ReturnMeToViewController.xib **file.**

   Interface Builder opens onscreen, displaying the main nib window and the View window open for inspection.

2. **Right-click the File's Owner icon in the main nib window.**

   A dialog appears, listing the various connections for File's Owner.

3. **Select the text field and right click on it.**

   A pop-up menu appears, listing the text field's connections. Under the first section, Outlets (expand it if it is not expanded) you will see delegate.

4. **Drag from the little circle next to the text field's Delegate item listed under Outlets in the pop-up menu to the File's Owner icon in the main nib window, as shown in Figure 8-7.**

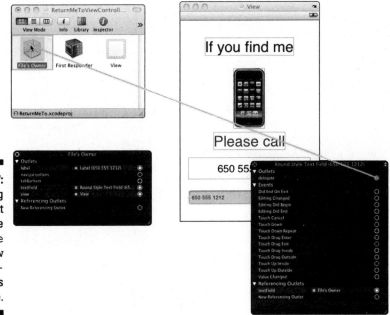

Figure 8-7: Connecting the text field to the `ReturnMe ToView Controller` as its delegate.

The File's Owner (`ReturnMeToViewController`) is now the delegate for the text field. (Want proof? Check out the pop-up menu for the the text field in Figure 8-8, which lists File's Owner as the delegate under Outlets.)

This completes what you need to do to implement scrolling, but there are still a couple of more things I recommend that you do to make everything shiny and bright. My detailing list includes the following:

- ✔ Adding a Clear button to make it more convenient for the user.

- ✔ Adding a feature for the user so that touching anywhere in the view does the same thing as tapping Return on the keyboard.

✔ Saving the phone number the user enters for future reference and then displaying it in the label.

Because adding these extras will enable you to delve even deeper into the mechanics of Objective-C, I strongly recommend you finish up with these details.

Adding a Clear button

I mention earlier in the chapter (and even give visual proof in Figure 8-3) that the `viewDidLoad` method — one of the methods generated (albeit commented out) by Xcode when you chose the View-Based Application template in Chapter 4 — is the place to do your view initialization tasks, including adding functionality not specified in the nib file. As you might have guessed, this is the perfect place to add a Clear button to the text field, which I do in Listing 8-10.

Find `viewDidLoad` in the `ReturnMeToViewController.m` file by pressing ⌘+F and entering `viewDidLoad` in the Find field. Uncomment it out and add the code in Listing 8-10.

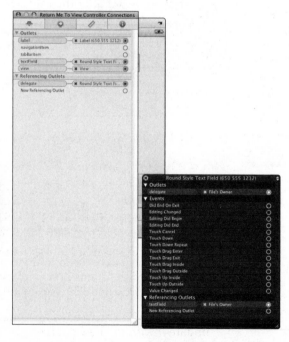

Figure 8-8:
The File's owner is now a delegate.

Listing 8-10: Override viewDidLoad

```
- (void)viewDidLoad {
textField.clearButtonMode =
        UITextFieldViewModeWhileEditing;
}
```

`clearButtonMode` controls when the standard clear button appears in the text field. This particular mode indicates only while editing, although there are other choices including never, and always.

That was easy!

Saving the phone number for future reference

To save the phone number the user entered, you have to add a new method — the `updateCallNumber` method — to `ReturnMeToViewController.m`. Place it after `textFieldShouldReturn:`. This method — shown in Listing 8-11 — simply saves the text and assigns the text to the label. We use it here to keep track of the number the user has entered.

Listing 8-11: Add updateCallNumber

```
- (void)updateCallNumber {
        self.callNumber = textField.text;
        label.text = self.callNumber;
}
```

Here's what's up with Listing 8-11:

1. **Store the text of the text field in the** `callNumber` **instance variable.**

   ```
   self.callNumber = textField.text;
   ```

   That's why you added an `IBOutlet` for the text field back in Chapter 7. It enables you to get the text the user enters.

2. **Set the text of the label to the value of the** `callNumber` **instance variable.**

   ```
   label.text = self.callNumber;
   ```

   And that's why you needed an `IBOutlet` for the label — to be able to update it with the new number.

updateCallNumber saves the number data. But even though it's imple-mented in the view controller, updateCallNumber is really, in part, a model function. In this sample program, though, there is no separate model. In reality, there isn't that much for the model to do, except save and return the saved phone number. Rather than adding complexity to the ReturnMeTo application, I decided that it was far easier and less complex to simply put the code in the view controller. (Of course, I *do* use a model when I develop the iPhoneTravel411 application; I discuss model design and use when I talk about the MobileTravel411 and iPhoneTravel411 design in Chapter 14 and imple-ment a model in Chapter 17.)

At this point you also will need to add the callNumber instance variable and the corresponding @property and @synthesize statements. Read on to find out how:

1. **In the** ReturnMeToViewController.h **file, add the following instance variable**

   ```
   NSString      *callNumber;
   ```

2. **and the property declaration**

   ```
   @property (nonatomic, retain) NSString *callNumber;
   ```

   as shown in Listing 8-12.

3. **Still in the** ReturnMeToViewController.h **add the** @synthesize **statement after the** @synthesize label **statement you added in Chapter 7, as you can see in Listing 8-13.**

Listing 8-12:   Add callNumber to the interface

```
@interface ReturnMeToViewController : UIViewController
        <UITextFieldDelegate> {

        IBOutlet UITextField *textField;
        IBOutlet UILabel     *label;
                 BOOL            moveViewUp;
                 CGFloat         scrollAmount;
                 NSString        *callNumber;

}

@property (nonatomic, retain) UITextField *textField;
@property (nonatomic, retain) UILabel *label;
@property (nonatomic, retain) NSString *callNumber;
```

Listing 8-13: Add the property declaration

```
#import "ReturnMeToViewController.h"
#import "ReturnMeToAppDelegate.h"

@implementation ReturnMeToViewController

@synthesize textField;
@synthesize label;
@synthesize callNumber;
```

You've added the updateCallNumber method. That's great — but to actually save the number and display it in the label someone is going to have to call updateCallNumber when the user is actually done entering the number. (Duh.) One of the places you need to do that is in the textFieldShouldReturn: method. At that point in the process, the user has finished entering the phone number and has tapped Return on the keyboard. In Figure 8-9, I have added the updateCallNumber method and shown textFieldShouldReturn: calling it. Note that I've placed the method off to the side in the diagram, in an area labeled *Model*. This is to let you know that while the method is being implemented in the ReturnMeToViewController class, it is — conceptually, at least — a model method. Listing 8-14 shows the modifications I made to textFieldShouldReturn: in bold.

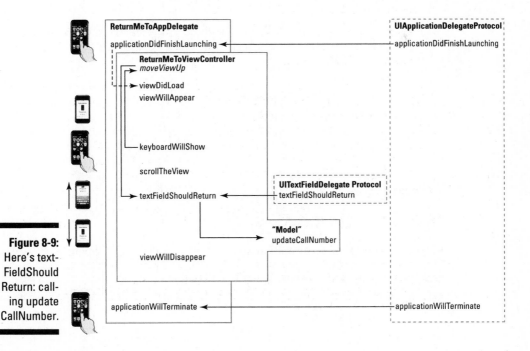

Figure 8-9: Here's text-FieldShould Return: calling update CallNumber.

Listing 8-14: Modify `textFieldShouldReturn:`

```
-(BOOL)textFieldShouldReturn:(UITextField *)theTextField {

    [theTextField resignFirstResponder];
    if (moveViewUp) [self scrollTheView:NO];
    [self updateCallNumber];

    return YES;
}
```

Adding a method here means I need to add the method declaration to the interface as well. Listing 8-15 shows how to code that addition.

Listing 8-15: Add changes to the interface

```
@interface ReturnMeToViewController : UIViewController
        <UITextFieldDelegate> {

    IBOutlet UITextField *textField;
    IBOutlet UILabel     *label;
            BOOL          moveViewUp;
            CGFloat       scrollAmount;
        NSString     *callNumber;
}

@property (nonatomic, retain) UITextField *textField;
@property (nonatomic, retain) UILabel *label;
@property (nonatomic, retain) NSString *callNumber;


- (void)scrollTheView:(BOOL)movedUp;
- (void)updateCallNumber;

@end
```

Dismissing the keyboard when the user touches in the view

I want the keyboard to disappear when one of two things happens:

✔ The user taps the Return button on the keyboard.

✔ The user touches anywhere else in the view.

This lets you know the user is done entering text and doesn't need the keyboard any longer.

I have already implemented the first requirement in `textFieldShould Return`. Figure 8-10 shows the method `touchesBegan`. I am overriding a method of the `ReturnMeToViewController`'s super class, `UIResponder` from which the view controller is derived. `touchesBegan:` is a method called when one or more fingers touches down in a view. The implementation of that is shown in Listing 8-16. Notice `touchesBegan:` also references `moveViewUp` to determine whether it should call `scrollTheView:` to restore the content view.

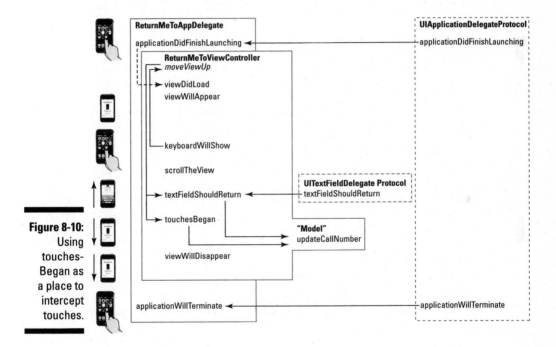

Figure 8-10:
Using touches-Began as a place to intercept touches.

Listing 8-16: Override `touchesBegan:`

```
- (void)touchesBegan:(NSSet *)touches withEvent:
                                            (UIEvent
          *)event {
  if( textField.editing) {
    [textField resignFirstResponder];
    [self updateCallNumber];
    if (moveViewUp) [self scrollTheView:NO];
  }
  [super touchesBegan:touches withEvent:event];
}
```

The following steps list breaks down Listing 8-14 into its constituent parts:

1. **See whether the text field is currently being edited.**

```
if( textField.editing) {
```

The user may touch the view any time, not just when he or she is done entering a phone number. Every time the user touches in the view, `touchesBegan` is called, and I shouldn't go through the code to resign as first responder and update the call number if the user hasn't really finished the editing job yet.

`textField.editing` is a Boolean value that indicates whether the text field is currently in edit mode. I only process the touch then — when I am in editing mode.

2. **Call** `resignFirstResponder:`.

That will cause the keyboard to disappear.

3. **Call** `updateCallNumber:`.

This method updates the text in the label with the text that the user typed, and then saves the text in an instance variable.

4. **Call** `[super touchesBegan:touches withEvent:event];`.

This passes the event to the super class if it needs to do anything more.

Because you used an accessor method to assign a value to `callNumber` — remember the @property and @synthesize statements you added? — it was sent a `retain:` message. That makes you responsible for releasing it (freeing up the memory), just as you were for the outlets in Chapter 7. Listing 8-17 shows you how.

Listing 8-17:   Releasing the callNumber

```
- (void)dealloc {
  [textField release];
  [label release];
  [callNumber release];
  [super dealloc];
}
```

Finding Your Way Around the Code

When you look in Listing 8-18 (it's on my Web site), you'll see several `#pragma` statements. For example, this one:

```
#pragma mark - UIViewController methods
```

Any statement that begins with #pragma is actually a compiler directive — meaning that it has nothing to do with code, it just passes information to the compiler or, in this case, code editor. It tells Xcode's editor to put a "heading" in the pop-up menu at the top of the Editor Pane that stores a running list of methods and functions used in the project. You get this pop-up list by selecting the up and down arrows highlighted in Figure 8-11. The field to the right displays the last method you were in, in this case viewDidLoad. Choose a method or function from the pop-up menu and you're brought to the implementation of that method in the code.

Up and Down Arrows

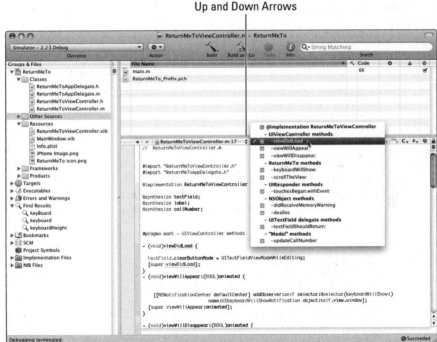

Figure 8-11:
Finding the
pop-up list.

Some of your classes, especially some of your controller classes, are likely to have a lot of code. If you make it a habit to use this gem of a pop-up menu, you'll find it much easier to find things.

When You're Done

If you head over to my Web site at www.nealgoldstein.com, you'll find Listings 8-18 and 8-19, which show the changes I have made to the original code in Listing 8-1 — the whole kit and caboodle. Changes are in bold.

When you compile and run this code in Xcode, using the handy Build and Go button on the toolbar, you end up with the obediently-scrolling iPhone view highlighted back in Figure 8-1 on the right. You still have some work to do, though. (No rest for the weary.) For starters, you need to set up a way to save the data entered by your user — and when you're done with that, I have a few surprises for you.

More on that in the next chapter.

Chapter 9

Saving Data and Creating a Secret Button

In This Chapter

▶ Setting and accessing user preferences

▶ Saving data in user preferences

▶ Disabling and enabling text fields

▶ Responding to user touches

*I*n putting together a great iPhone application, a big part of the whole process involves getting your application to work well from the user interface perspective. Your potential user should be able to scroll the keyboard, work with text fields, enter stuff, delete stuff, admire your fashion sense when it comes to images and background color, and generally have a grand old time exploring the corners of your app.

Interfaces are important — so important, in fact, that most of the chapters so far in this part deal explicitly with how to set up a user-friendly interface — but interfaces are not the only thing in the iPhone app universe. For your application to function as an application, it has to do application-like stuff. For example, it has to be able to save data entered by a user for the next time he or she fires up that app. In this chapter, I tackle how to get your app to save data entered by the user. Again, I'm going to trot out my ReturnMeTo application as a means of imparting this little lesson in data saving.

Wait! That's not all! It occurred to me while I was showing people my handy ReturnMeTo application that whoever found my iPhone could accidently enter a number in the text field — corrupting the crime scene, as it were — and then wouldn't know where to call me. So I decided that after the user saved a number for the first time, I would make it a little more of a challenge to write over that data. If there's a saved number, I'm going to disable the text field — and require the user to know where to tap in the content view to enable it.

Saving user entry and then controlling the editing process are two good skills to master when you're developing iPhone applications. By the end of this chapter, you should be an old hand at both skills.

Saving User-Entry Data

The iPhone is, first and foremost, a *phone*; as such you would expect it to be able to deal with numbers — phone numbers, especially. So it is quite reasonable for the user to expect the ReturnMeTo application to save phone numbers entered into the user-entry text field. (And quite frankly, what would the point of the application be if it didn't?)

The iPhone gives us three ways to save a phone number:

- **Save the number in a file:** A perfectly respectable option, which I discuss in greater detail in Chapter 17.

- **Save the number in a database:** iPhone has a built-in SQL database that's efficient at storing and retrieving large amounts of (structured) data.

- **Save the number as an application preference:** The iPhone provides support for user preferences — allowing users to customize applications or keep track of configuration settings from launch to launch. (Hmm, the phone number to call if you lose your iPhone comes to mind here.)

So many choices. But we're definitely going with Door # 3. Let me explain why.

Preferences

Most people these days have spent enough time around computers that they know what we mean when we throw the term "preferences" around. On your desktop, for example, you can set preferences at the system level for things like security, screen savers, printing, and file sharing . . . just to name a few. But keep in mind that preferences aren't just a system-level thing; you can just as easily set preferences at the application level. You could, for example, set all sorts of preferences in Xcode — not to mention all those preferences in your browser and word-processing programs.

The latter are application-specific settings used to configure the behavior or appearance of an application. On the iPhone, application preferences are supported as well, but instead of having to (re-) create a user interface for each separate application, the iPhone displays all application-level preferences through the system-supplied Settings application (its icon looks like a bunch of gears on your iPhone's home screen). Okay, you don't have to forego creating a separate settings feature in your application — but keep this in mind: Whatever separate settings feature you come up with has to function within the framework of iPhone's Settings application; in effect, the Settings application makes you color within the lines.

What (guide)lines does the iPhone impose? Here's a short summary:

- ✔ **If you have preference values that are typically configured once and then rarely changed:** Leave the task of setting preferences to the system Settings application. On an iPhone, this would apply to things like enabling/disabling Wi-Fi access, setting wallpaper displays, setting up mail accounts, and any other preference you would set and then leave in place for a while.

- ✔ **If you have preference values that the user might want to change regularly:** In this situation, you should consider having users set the options themselves in your application.

The iPhone's weather app is a good example: Let's say I have this thing for Dubrovnik — where it happens to be 48° F as I am writing this — and I'd like to add it to my list of preferred cities that I want the weather app to keep tabs on. To load Dubrovnik into the weather app, all I have to do is tap the info button at the bottom of the screen, the view will flip around, and I can add it to my list of cities. That's a lot easier than going back to the home screen, launching the Settings application, adding the new city, and then launching the Weather application again.

The reason I'm leading you down this path is not because I'm about to show you how to use the Settings application to set user preferences — that actually comes in Chapter 16, in due time — but because the iPhone has a built-in, easy to use class that lets you read and set user preferences — NSUserDefaults. It is even used by Settings application itself, which has graciously consented to let us peons use it as well — and I'm going to show you how to put that power to work so that your application can both read and set user preferences.

The NSUserDefaults class

You use NSUserDefaults to read and store preference data to a defaults data base, using a key value, just as you'd access keyed data from an NS Dictionary. (For more on key-value pairs in general and NSDictionary in particular, see Chapter 8.) The difference here is that NSUserDefaults data is stored in the file system rather than in an object in memory — objects, after all, go away when the application terminates.

By the way, don't ask me why they stick `Defaults` in the name rather than something to do with preferences — fewer letters, maybe — but that's the way it is. Just don't let their naming idiosyncrasies confuse you.

Storing the data in the file system rather than in memory gives me an easy way to store application-specific information. With the help of `NSUserDefaults`, you can easily store the state the user was in when he or she quit the application — or store something simple like a phone number — which just so happens to be precisely what we need for our ReturnMeTo application.

Saving data using NSUserDefaults

Enough background information, it's time to actually save some data to `NSUserDefaults`.

The first thing you need to decide is where in your application you plan on loading and then saving your data. As Figure 9-1 makes clear, the obvious places to do that are in `applicationDidFinishLaunching:` and `applicationWillTerminate:` — the very same methods I use in Chapter 8 to perform initialization and termination at the application level.

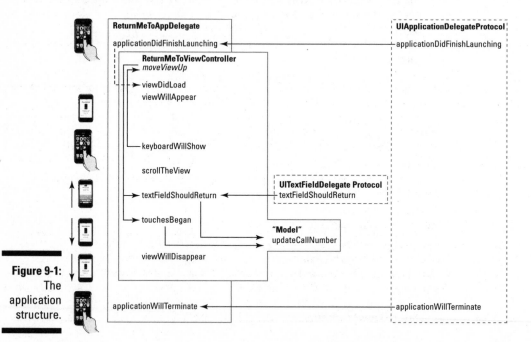

Figure 9-1:
The application structure.

I am going to start by showing you how to save the phone number. After all, being able to read the phone number from the defaults database is not all that useful if there is nothing there to read.

(Although it turns out the first time we start the application there is nothing to load, but I'll show you how to deal with it shortly.)

Setting it up

Since I'm going to be doing all the work in the ReturnMeToAppDelegate, I'm going to first declare an instance variable that will hold the number that needs to be saved.

1. **Add a new instance variable called savedNumber and declare @property in the** ReturnMeToAppDelegate.h **file.**

   Property declarations tell the compiler that there are going to be accessors for an instance variable, making it available to other objects. Since the ReturnMeToViewController object is going to have to be able to read and write the savedNumber value, the accessors have to be there.

   This is shown in Listing 9-1. (Again, the new stuff is bold.)

2. **Add the** @synthesize **statement to the** ReturnMeToAppDelegate.m. **file to let the compiler know that you want it to do all the work and create the accessors for you.**

   This is shown in Listing 9-2. (You guessed it — new is bold.)

Listing 9-1:   Add the instance variable to the interface

```
@class ReturnMeToViewController;

@interface ReturnMeToAppDelegate : NSObject
          <UIApplicationDelegate> {

UIWindow*window;
ReturnMeToViewController*viewController;
NSString    *savedNumber ;
}

@property (nonatomic, retain) IBOutlet UIWindow *window;
@property (nonatomic, retain) IBOutlet
          ReturnMeToViewController *viewController;
@property (nonatomic, retain) NSString *savedNumber ;


@end
```

Listing 9-2: Add the synthesize to the implementation

```
@implementation ReturnMeToAppDelegate

@synthesize window;
@synthesize viewController;
@synthesize savedNumber;
```

Once the instance variable is there, to make it feel useful I'm going to have to update it with the phone number. If you recall back in Chapter 8, you added the `updateCallNumber` method to keep track of the number the user entered. Well, there was method to the madness because I now have a handy place to update the `ReturnMeToAppDelegate`'s `savedNumber` whenever it is changed by the user.

When the user enters a new phone number, you need to update the `saved-Number` instance variable (which in turn will be saved in the `applica-tionWillTerminate:` method.) You do this by adding some code to the `updateCallNumber` method, which you had earlier placed in the `ReturnMeToViewController.m` file. This is done in Listing 9-3.

Listing 9-3: Update updateCallNumber

```
- (void)updateCallNumber {
  self.callNumber = textField.text;
  label.text = self.callNumber;

  ReturnMeToAppDelegate *appDelegate =
            [[UIApplication sharedApplication] delegate];
  appDelegate.savedNumber = self.callNumber;
}
```

Now, here's the big question: If the `savedNumber` is in the `ReturnMeToApp Delegate` object, how do you get to it? Here's how:

1. **Get a reference to the `ReturnMeToAppDelegate`.**

   It turns out that this is done so often that there's a really easy way to do it. All you do is send a message to the `UIApplication`, and ask for the delegate

   ```
   [[UIApplication  sharedApplication] delegate]
   ```

   This returns back the delegate object — in this case `ReturnMeToApp Delegate` — which I assign to local variable `appDelegate`.

Now you can access the application delegate and assign the number the user entered (callNumber) to the ReturnMeToAppDelegate's instance variable (savedNumber) (which will then be saved in applicationWillTerminate:). The changes the user made are kept safe and sound, ready to appear again the next time the application is launched.

Saving the phone number

It's down hill from here. When the application terminates, you'll save the number in the standardUserDefaults database. As you identified for Figure 9-1, the place to do that is the applicationWillTerminate: method. You'll need to add to the ReturnMeToAppDelegate.m file, right after the applicationDidFinishLaunching: method. The code to use is shown in Listing 9-4.

Listing 9-4: Override applicationWillTerminate:

```
- (void)applicationWillTerminate:
                            (UIApplication *)application {

   [[NSUserDefaults standardUserDefaults]
           setObject:savedNumber
     forKey:kNumberLocationKey];
}
```

While it's true that it's just a single statement, it is pretty complex, so let me take you through it.

It's really easy to both access and update a preference — as long as you have NSUserDefaults by your side. The trick here is to use the NSUserDefaults class to read and update whatever the user enters as the phone number. NSUserDefaults is implemented as a *singleton,* meaning there's only one instance of NSUserDefaults running in your application. To get access to that one instance, I call the class method standardUserDefaults:

```
[NSUserDefaults   standardUserDefaults]
```

standardUserDefaults: returns back the NSUserDefaults object. As soon as I have access to the standard user defaults, I can store data there, and then get it back when I need it. To store data, I simply give it a key and tell it to save the data using that key.

The way I tell it to save something is by using the setObject;forKey: method. In case your knowledge of Objective-C is a little rusty (or not there at all), that's the way any method call that takes two arguments is referred to.

The first argument, `setObject:`, is the object I want `NSUSerDefaults` to save. This object must be `NSData`, `NSString`, `NSNumber`, `NSDate`, `NSArray`, or `NSDictionary`. In our case `savedData` is an `NSString`, so we are in good shape.

The second argument is `forKey:`. In order to get the data back, and in order for `NSUserDefaults` to know where to save it, I have to be able to identify it to `NSUserDefaults`. I can, after all, have a number of preferences stored in the `NSUserDefaults` data base, and the key tells `NSUserDefaults` which one I am interested in. The particular key I am using is `kNumberLocation-Key`, which I am going to add to the to `ReturnMeToAppDelegate.m` file, right after the last `#import` statement, as you can see in Listing 9-5.

Listing 9-5: Add the key to ReturnMeToAppDelegate.m

```
#import "ReturnMeToAppDelegate.h"
#import "ReturnMeToViewController.h"

NSString *kNumberLocationKey = @"NumberLocation";
```

When I save the phone number, as I did above I tell `NSUserDefaults` to save it with a key of `kNumberLocationKey`. The key needs to be a string (`NSString`) (and so do keys in `NSDictionary`, by the way, which this is very similar to). Then when I want the data back, (which I'll show you in a second) I just ask for it with that key.

Loading the preference entry to get the data

To get the phone number back, now that it's out there when the application is launched, all I need to do is ask for it with the key.

Whoops, what about the very first time the application is launched, when there is no data out there yet? Let me show you how to take care of that. In the `applicationDidFinishLaunching:` method you're going to need to do two things:

- ✔ First check to see whether the preference entry exists. If one doesn't exist, you have to create one.
- ✔ If the preference does exist, you're home free and you can read it.

Listing 9-6 shows the code necessary for accomplishing these two tasks. `applicationDidFinishLaunching:` is in the `ReturnMeToApp Delegate.m` file — you'll have to add the code in bold.

I am working now the `ReturnMeToAppDelegate` interface and implementation.

Listing 9-6:   Update applicationDidFinshLaunching:

```
- (void)applicationDidFinishLaunching:(UIApplication *)
        application {

self.savedNumber  = [[NSUserDefaults
    standardUserDefaults]objectForKey:kNumberLocationKey];
if (savedNumber == nil) {
    savedNumber = @"650 555 1212";
    NSDictionary *savedNumberDict = [NSDictionary d
            ictionaryWithObject:savedNumber
            forKey:kNumberLocationKey];
    [[NSUserDefaults standardUserDefaults] registerDefault
            s:savedNumberDict];
}

[window addSubview:viewController.view];
[window makeKeyAndVisible];
}
```

Here's the blow-by-blow:

1. **Access the preference entry and save it in an instance variable.**

```
self.savedNumber = [[NSUserDefaults
standardUserDefaults]objectForKey:kNumberLocationKey];
```

We did something similar when we saved the number. Here, we're using a NSUserDefaults object as well, but this time we call the object-ForKey: method. Reading is a little easier than saving, because you only have to give it one argument — the key that you used to save the data in the first place. objectForKey: will return an Objective-C object like an NSString, NSDate, NSNumber, or any of the other types I mentioned above (again, savedNumber is an NSString so we're okay). I'm going to assign what I get back to savedNumber, which is the instance variable I originally saved.

2. **Check to see whether the entry exists:**

```
if (savedNumber == nil)
```

objectForKey either returns the object associated with the specified key or, if the NSUserDefaults can't find data for the key or doesn't find the key at all, it returns nil. That's precisely what's going to happen the first time I run the program — there is nothing stored because I didn't store anything yet.

3. **If there is no data there, create a new entry in the NSUserDefaults database.**

I know that's easy for me to say. Let me show you how.

a. *Create a new dictionary.*

```
savedNumber = @"650 555 1212";
NSDictionary *savedNumberDict = [NSDictionary
            dictionaryWithObject:savedNumber
            forKey:kNumberLocationKey];
```

In order to use `objectForKey` (to read preference data) or `setObject` (to update preference data), you have to create an entry for the item you want to read or update in `standardUser Defaults`. (For `NSUserDefaults` to know anything about my preferences, you have to *tell* it about them first, right?) To let `NSUserDefaults` know what's going on, you have to create a dictionary listing of all the key-value pairs you plan on using here — all *one* of them, since all you need is the `savedNumberforKey`/ `kNumberLocationKey` value pair.

`dictionaryWithObject:forKey:` creates and returns a dictionary containing the key and value you give it. You pass it `saved-Number`, which you initialized with 650 555 1212 (the value), and `kNumberLocationKey` (the key) Notice I had you use the same value — 650 555 1212 — to initialize the preference that you used for the text field in Interface Builder back in Chapter 7, so as not to confuse the user.

b. *Register the defaults using* `registerDefaults:`.

```
[[NSUserDefaults standardUserDefaults]
            registerDefaults:savedNumberDict];
```

`RegisterDefaults:` simply tells the `NSUserDefaults` object to add this key and this value to its database for this application. You only have to do that once and then you can simply access it (using `objectForKey`) or update it (using `setObject`).

4. If there is a saved number, I'm fine, and I can go along my merry way.

Dictionaries manage pairs of keys and values. A key-value pair within a dictionary is called an *entry*. Each entry consists of one object that represents the key and a second object that is that key's value.

If you had more than one preference, you could have used `dictionary-WithObjectsAndKeys:`. That method creates and returns a dictionary containing entries constructed from the specified set of values and keys:

```
NSDictionary *dict = [NSDictionary
            dictionaryWithObjectsAndKeys:
savedNumber, kNumberLocationKey, @"another value", @"
            another key", nil];
```

As you implement and experiment with this code, you need to be aware of the fact that you should delete the application from the simulator if you change anything of significance — the key for example. The consequences of not doing so will become obvious when things don't work like you would expect them to. Deleting the application will delete any preferences for the app saved in `NSUserDefaults`.

Using Saved Data

There's only one thing left to do. The object that really cares about the number is the view, and it's the view controller's job to get it to the view. To put that saved data to use in an application's view, you have to link it up with a view controller — in our case, `ReturnMeToViewController`. If you look back at Figure 9-1, you'll see that the best place to do that is `viewDidLoad` which is called right after the view has been loaded from the nib file. `viewDidLoad` is found in the `ReturnMeToViewController.m` file, so that's where you'd go to insert your code to do view initialization.

If you're ever lost in the file and need to find your next destination fast, use ⌘+F to open a Find dialog to find it, or use the drop-down menu I showed you at the end of the Chapter 8. (Refer to Figure 8-11.)

Listing 9-7 shows the stuff you need to add to the `viewDidLoad` method in the `ReturnMeToViewController.m file`.

Listing 9-7:   Update `viewDidLoad`

```
(void)viewDidLoad {

   textField.clearButtonMode =
           UITextFieldViewModeWhileEditing;

   ReturnMeToAppDelegate *appDelegate =[[UIApplication
           sharedApplication] delegate];
   label.text = appDelegate.savedNumber;
   textField.text =appDelegate.savedNumber;

   [super viewDidLoad];
}
```

Here's what all the boldfaced stuff does:

1. **Gets the pointer to the application delegate object:**

   ```
   ReturnMeToAppDelegate *appDelegate =[[UIApplication
           sharedApplication] delegate];
   ```

   `sharedApplication` is a class method of `UIApplication` and returns the application delegate.

2. Assigns the saved number to the label and text field:

```
label.text = appDelegate.savedNumber;
textField.text =appDelegate.savedNumber;
```

`appDelegate` allows me to access the `ReturnMeToAppDelegate`'s instance variable, `savedNumber`. As you know (because I've mentioned it several times) one of the fundamental principles of object oriented programming is *encapsulation* — tucking an object's instance variable behind a wall so you can't access it directly.

But you did make it a property and told the compiler to generate the necessary accessors in Listing 9-1 and 9-2 above, so accessors are available for you to use. Now, I could access `savedNumber` by using the getter:

```
[appDelegate savedNumber]
```

But as I mentioned in Chapter 7, I could also invoke an accessor method using dot notation (which refugees from other object-oriented languages will recognize):

```
appDelegate.savedNumber
```

Being one of those refugees myself, I'll use the dot notation.

For a method in `ReturnMeToViewController` be able to access the `saved-Number` instance variable, it needs to know where it is. That information is in the class declaration, in the `ReturnMeToAppDelegate.h` (header) file. So I'll need to `#import` the `ReturnMeToAppDelegate.h` file in the `ReturnMeToViewController.m` (implementation) file. This is shown in Listing 9-8.

Listing 9-8: Include the ReturnMeToAppDelegate header file

```
#import "ReturnMeToViewController.h"
#import "ReturnMeToAppDelegate.h"
```

Finally, I need to clean up and deallocate the memory. This is shown in Listing 9-9.

Listing 9-9: dealloc the new variables

```
- (void)dealloc {
  [viewController release];
  [window release];
  [savedNumber release];
  [kNumberLocationKey release];

  [super dealloc];
}
```

Disabling Editing

I started out this chapter by mentioning that I wanted to create a way that kept someone other than the main user from entering a new phone number after it had been initially entered. I can easily do that by changing an instance variable in the text field. In Figure 9-2, you can see that the UIControl class, from which the UITextField class is derived, has a property instance variable enabled. If I set the enabled property of the UITextField to NO, the user can't enter any text; if the user taps the text field, nothing happens.

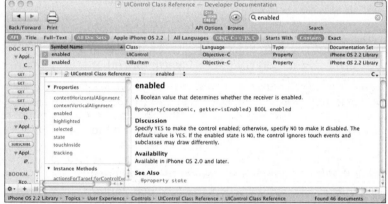

Figure 9-2:
How to
disable text
entry.

"But aren't you forgetting something?" you might ask. "Don't you have to allow the app's owner to be able change the number?"

I'm two steps ahead of you. To allow for just such a situation, I've decided to create a hidden "button." I thought it would be clever to make the label that displays the current number the hidden button, and to show you how flexible the framework is.

So how could I do that? To start with, labels are disabled for editing by default; they ignore touches. My first thought was simply to set the enabled property for the label (the same one I used for the text field) to YES. And lo and behold — it didn't work. So when all else fails, read the documentation, and Figure 9-3 shows what I found.

As you can see, the UILabel class changes the default for the property it inherits from UIView, userInteractionEnabled, to NO. Before I can receive touches in the label, I need to change it to YES. As you might surmise, the enabled property, which I tried setting earlier, has to do with temporarily enabling or disabling a control, while the overall ability to handle events is determined by userInteractionEnabled.

Figure 9-3:
How to
enable user
interaction
in the label
view.

Again, the place to disable editing in the text field — and enable user interaction in the label — is in `viewDidLoad` (notice a pattern here?) in the `ReturnMeToViewController.m` file. The code for doing all this is shown in Listing 9-10, with the updates in bold.

Listing 9-10:   Update `viewDidLoad`

```
- (void)viewDidLoad {

textField.clearButtonMode =
        UITextFieldViewModeWhileEditing;

ReturnMeToAppDelegate *appDelegate =
        (ReturnMeToAppDelegate *)[[UIApplication
        sharedApplication] delegate];
label.text = appDelegate.savedNumber;
textField.text =appDelegate.savedNumber;

if (![appDelegate.savedNumber isEqualToString:
                            @"650 555 1212"]) {
  textField.enabled=NO;
  label.enabled=YES;
  label.userInteractionEnabled = YES;
  }
[super viewDidLoad];
}
```

Here the code checks to see whether the user has ever entered a phone number — by determining whether the number is equal to the default value that you set in Interface Builder.

What you are doing in the code is checking to see if the savedNumber is *not* equal to the default number — which is why you see the negation operator ! used here. If it is not equal, then the user has entered a number and you need to disable the text field and enable the label.

Notice the method call:

```
[appDelegate.savedNumber isEqualToString:@"650 555 1212"])
```

savedNumber is an NSString object, and one of NSString's handy methods is isEqualToString:. This will return YES if the text values of two string objects are equal. Now, I can see where you might be tempted to do the compare as savedNumber== :@"650 555 1212". Unfortunately, what you would be doing here is comparing the string pointers, not the actual text values of the objects.

Letting the User Use the Secret Button

I mentioned in the previous section that we want to put a mechanism in place for the owner of our ReturnMeTo application to allow him or her to unlock a text entry field for editing. That mechanism is going to rely on the Old Secret Button trick, where the label field gets transformed into a trigger mechanism for changing the text-entry field from read-only to read/write. As you might expect, this is going to require some coding. The place to do this coding turns out to be the same method I used to process touches on the screen so the user could dismiss the keyboard — namely, the touchesBegan: method.

touchesBegan: is a method called when one or more fingers touches down in a view. The touch of a finger (or lifting it from the screen) adds a touch event to the application's event queue, where it's *encapsulated* — placed into — a UIEvent object. There is UITouch object for each finger touching the screen, which enables you to track individual touches. As the user manipulates the screen with his or her fingers, the system reports the changes for each finger in the corresponding UITouch object.

Listing 9-11 shows how to determine whether the user has touched the label; if so, the text field is enabled so the user can enter a new number.

Listing 9-11:   Is the touch in the label?

```
- (void)touchesBegan:(NSSet *)touches withEvent:(UIEvent
        *)event {

  if (!textField.enabled) {
    UITouch *touch = [touches anyObject];
    if (CGRectContainsPoint([label frame], [touch
            locationInView:self.view])) {
      textField.enabled = YES;
      label.text = @"You found it, touch below";
      textField.placeholder = @"You may now enter the
          number";
    }
  }
  else {

  if( textField.editing) {
    [textField resignFirstResponder];
    [self updateCallNumber];
    if (moveViewUp) [self scrollTheView:NO];
    }
  }
  [super touchesBegan:touches withEvent:event];
}
```

Here's how the code builds its magic button, step by step:

1. **If the text field is not enabled, get the touch object.**

   ```
   if (!textField.enabled) {
     UITouch *touch = [touches anyObject];
   ```

   Touches are passed in an NSSet object — an "unordered collection of distinct elements," for those of you not up on the intricacies of NSSet objects. To access an object in the NSSet, you use the anyObject method. This returns one of the objects in the set, or nil if the receiver contains no objects. Bear in mind that the object returned is chosen by some magic formula developed in secret by a cabal of Apple developers — the only thing *I* know about it is that the selection is not guaranteed to be random.

2. **Check to see whether the touch was in the label.**

   ```
   if (CGRectContainsPoint([label frame],
                   [touch    locationInView:self.view])) {
   ```

CGRectContainsPoint is a function that returns YES when a rectangle contains a specified point. You use the label frame here, which is a rectangle in the coordinates of the view. — that thing on the screen that you, I, and the user see.

Well, if I know where the view label is in the view's coordinate system, then I better know where the fingers are in the view's coordinate system as well. The problem is that if the user touches in a label, the OS could report back the touch's location in terms of the view, or in terms of the label. Fortunately, I can specify the terms — the coordinate system, to be precise — I want.

```
[touch locationInView:self.view]
```

This method returns *the current location of the touch* in the coordinate system of a given view — in this case, self.view specifies that you want the location of the touch in the content view's coordinate system. That means I am comparing apples to apples. (Do you believe I actually said that?)

3. **If the touch is in the label frame, display a clever message, enable the text field, and set the placeholder to give the user more guidance.**

   The placeholder is what the user sees when he or she touches the text field to start editing.

```
textField.enabled = YES;
label.text = @"You found it, touch below";
textField.placeholder = @"You may now enter the
       number";
```

What You Have Now — At Long Last

So it looks like you have all the pieces in place for your ReturnMeTo application. You can now enter and save numbers, and keep someone from changing the number if he or she doesn't know how.

Appearances can be deceiving, though.

Reality check: Some how-to books on software development should really be housed in the Fiction section of your local bookstore — because all their examples work flawlessly. In the real world — the non-fictional world — everything does not always go as planned; occasionally your software program blows up on you. That's why an essential part of software development is the *debugging* phase — teasing as many flaws out of your app as possible so you can squash 'em. In the next chapter, I show you how to work through the debugging phase of your project and introduce you to the SDK's very own debugging tool, a gizmo that is sure to make your software-development life a lot easier.

For a nice retrospective of the work you've done so far for the ReturnMeTo application, move on over to my Web site (www.nealgoldstein.com) and check out Listings 9-12 through 9-15. There, in all their glory, you'll find your app's completed code listings, from soup to nuts.

Chapter 10

Using the Debugger

*L*et's face it: When you're developing an application, sometimes things don't work out quite the way you planned — especially when you knock over a can of Jolt Cola on the keyboard and fry it out of existence.

"Stuff happens," in the immortal words of a famous ex-U.S. Secretary of Defense. When it comes to developing your own programs, that "stuff" comes in three categories:

✔ **Syntax errors:** Compilers — the Objective-C compiler in Xcode is a case in point — expect you to use a certain set of instructions in your code; those instructions make up the language it understands. When you type in `If` instead of `if`, or the subtler `[view release}` instead of `[view release]`, the compiler suddenly has no idea what you're talking about and generates a syntax error.

Syntax errors are the most obvious of errors out there, simply because your program won't compile (be able to run) until all of these are fixed. Generally, syntax errors spring from typographical errors like those mentioned here. (And yes, the errors can by pretty penny-ante stuff — an *I* for an *i*, for goodness sake — but it doesn't take much to stump a compiler.)

In Figure 10-1, you can see an example of a syntax error. This one was kindly pointed out to me by Xcode's friendly little Debugger feature (more on him later). I'd forgotten to put a ";" after `UITextFieldView ModeWhileEditing` in this line. It looked like this:

```
textField.clearButtonMode =
    UITextFieldViewModeWhileEditing
```

As a result, I got a number of errors because the compiler couldn't quite figure out what I was doing.

TIP

It's generally better to ignore the subsequent errors after the first syntax error because they may be the result of that first error. In this case, because of the first error, that line and the next one were treated as a single instruction and the line that declared `appDelegate` wasn't processed by the compiler as a separate instruction.

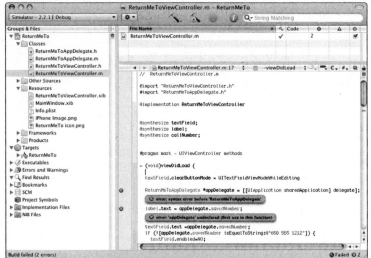

Figure 10-1:
A syntax
error. Oops.

✔ **Runtime errors:** *Runtime errors* cause your program to stop executing — it "crashes," in other words, as in "crash and burn to much wailing and gnashing of teeth." Something might have come up in the data that you hadn't expected (a division-by-zero error, for example) or the result of a method call dealt a nasty surprise to your logic, or you sent a message to an object that doesn't have that message implemented. Sometimes you even get some build warnings for these errors; often the application simply stops working or "hangs" (stops and does nothing). Or it shuts down and you get the (not particularly helpful) message in Figure 10-2.

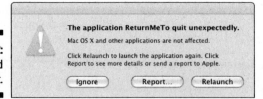

Figure 10-2:
Unexpected
quit.

✔ **Logic errors:** Your literal-minded application does exactly what you tell it to, but sometimes you unintentionally tell it the wrong thing, and it coughs up a *logic error*. In Figure 10-3, everything looks fine — not an error sign in sight — except when I try to enter a number into the text field, I discover that the field is disabled. Ironically, if I fool around and touch the label, I find that *then* I can enter text — which is the opposite of what I want.

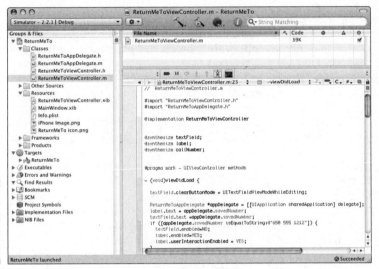

Figure 10-3:
Oh, great — it works backwards.

Look a bit more closely at this chunk of code, though:

```
if ([appDelegate.savedNumber
        isEqualToString:@"650 555 1212"]) {
    textField.enabled=NO;
    label.enabled=YES;
    label.userInteractionEnabled = YES;
}
```

See how I tell it to disable the text field if the saved number is `"650 555 1212"` but not to disable if the saved number is *not* equal to that value? I had mistakenly left out the `!` before the method call to the app delegate. Here's how it should have looked (note how it begins):

```
![appDelegate.savedNumber isEqualToString:@"650 555
1212"]
```

Not being able to guess what it was that I *really* wanted, it did what I *told* it to; the program worked, but not the way I intended it to.

Syntax errors, runtime errors, and logic errors can all be pains in the behind, but there's no need to think of them as insurmountable roadblocks. You're still on your way to a cool iPhone app. In this chapter, I am going to show you how to use the Debugger to remove at least some of these obstacles. The Debugger works best for Case 2 (the runtime errors), but as I point out later on, it can also help you track down the logic errors in Case 3.

Using the Debugger

In Figure 10-4, I have deliberately created a situation that will give me a runtime error: I am going to divide by zero — a mathematical no-no that any able-bodied fifth-grader would berate me for — which will enable me to show you how to approach runtime errors in general.

Here's the drill: After introducing my boneheaded error while writing my code in Xcode, I chose Build⇨Build and Go (Run) from Xcode's main menu.

You see the results in Figure 10-4. I get my favorite The Application ReturnMeTo Quit Unexpectedly message and the compiler was even kind enough to tell me what I was doing wrong.

Before you scoff and say that I should have caught such a basic error, okay, you're right to scoff — but I want to point out some things:

- ✔ First, in the middle of development, I may have been pelted with compiler's warnings that I didn't really need to take care of because they had no impact on the execution of the program. As a result, I might not have noticed *one more compiler warning* that actually *did* have an impact — a big one.

- ✔ Second, if my app were a bit more complicated, I could conceivably have ended up dividing by zero without realizing it. (Remember, stuff happens.)

- ✔ Finally, if you happen to save this code and then build it again, you wouldn't get the compiler warning because there were no changes to that file — so it wouldn't be recompiled. (This is definitely something to remember.)

How can the Debugger help me determine the source of a runtime error like this one? The next section gives you the details.

Prepping your project for debugging

To use the Debugger, I need to start by building the application in another way. With my project open in Xcode, I choose Build ⇨ Build and Debug from the main menu.

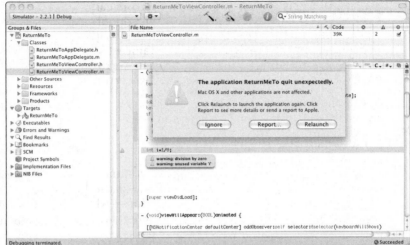

Figure 10-4:
Results of
division by
zero. Ack.

This is *not* the Build ➪Build and Run command I've trotted out before.

Turn your attention to Xcode's Editor pane in Figure 10-5. Notice the red arrow that shows you the instruction that caused the program to crash. That's the Debugger pointing out the problem to you.

There is even more information available, though — it comes to you in the Debugger window. Figure 10-6 shows what happens when I choose Run➪ Debugger from Xcode's main menu (or press Shift+⌘+Y). The next section goes into all the jewels the Debugger window contains.

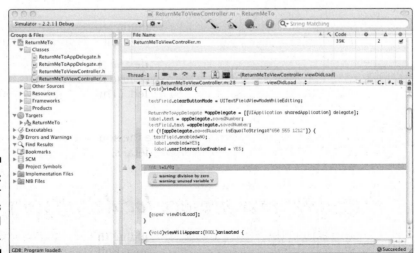

Figure 10-5:
The editor
highlights
the bad
instruction.

Using the Debugger window

Even though the Debugger is officially running, you have to open the Debugger window explicitly the first time you choose Run➪Debugger.

Figure 10-6 shows the Debugger window — the centerpiece of iPhone debugging. In the upper-left pane, you can see the *stack* — a trace of the objects and methods that got you to where you are now.

For example, `main` called `UIApplicationMain` — which called a number of framework methods, got eventually to `ReturnMeToAppDelegate: DidFinishLaunching`, and then finally to `ReturnMeToViewController viewDidLoad`. And that's where our little problem reared its ugly head.

Okay, the stack isn't really all that useful in this particular context of dealing with my boneheaded attempt to divide by 0. But it *can* be very useful in other contexts. In a more complex application, the stack can help you understand the path that you took to get where you are. Seeing how one object sent a message to another object — which sent a message to a third object — can be really helpful, especially if you didn't expect the program flow to work that way.

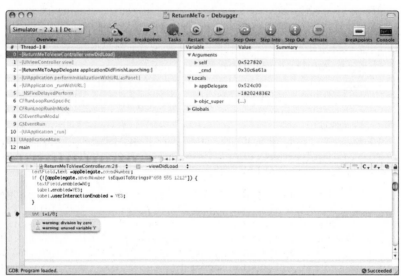

Figure 10-6:
The
Debugger
window.

Getting a look at the stack can also be useful if you're trying to understand how the framework does its job, and in what order the calls may happen. As you'll see later in this chapter, using something called a *breakpoint* can stop the execution of my program at any point and trace the calls made up to that point. So don't despair; you have options. For the moment, however, take another look at the Debugger window in Figure 10-6: The bottom pane not only shows the source code but also highlights the instruction that caused the problem; the top-right pane shows you the program's variables. (I'll show you how that can be useful shortly.)

Okay, your window may not look exactly like mine. That's because Xcode gives you lots of different ways to customize the look of the Debugger window. You could, for example, have chosen Run➪Debugger Display from the main menu and tweaked the way you want your Debugger window to look. The option I chose (Source Only, also shown in Figure 10-6), is checked — so that only the source code appears in the bottom pane. You could, of course, have checked the Source and Disassembly option if you had a hankering for checking both the source code *and* the assembly language (if you really care about assembly language); in that case, the bottom pane would divide down the center into two panes, with the source code on the left and the assembly code in the right.

It's not that I would actually expect you to use the Source and Disassembly option — at this point, I don't. But sometimes, as you explore interfaces, things end up not looking the way they used to. In my experience, this usually occurs because a different display option has been chosen — either by accident or on purpose.

Examine the top-right pane in the Debugger window. There you'll see a display of the program object's variables. If you click the little triangle next to appDelegate (as I have in Figure 10-7), you see its instance variables — including savedNumber, which is 650 555 1212, which is what you would expect. This is useful for a couple of reasons:

- ✔ **Checking variables:** If the view was not displaying the correct number, I would look here in the Variable pane to see what the value of the variable actually was. If the value were correct here, then I could conclude that either it gets changed by mistake later, or I'm displaying something other than what I intended to display.

- ✔ **Checking messages sent:** Some logic errors you may encounter are the result of what some people call a "feature" and others call a "bug" in Objective-C: For reasons which are not particularly important here, Objective-C, unlike some other languages, allows you to send a message to a nil object *without* generating a runtime error. If you do that, you should expect to subsequently see some sort of logic error, since a message to a nil object simply does nothing.

    So, when things don't happen the way you expect, you might have a real logic error in your code. But there's one other possibility: Maybe an object reference has not been set, and you're sending the message into the ether.

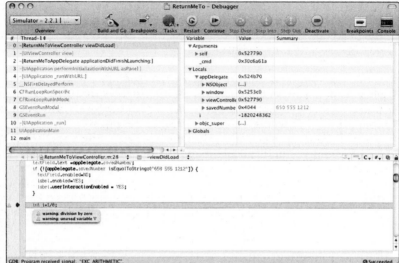

Figure 10-7:
The Return
MeTo
Application
Delegate's
instance
variables.

Now how can I use the variable pane to help me with that? Simple. In Figure 10-8, I clicked on the triangle next to self in the Variable pane. Doing so shows me the ReturnMeToViewController's instance variables this time, rather than appDelegate's. I then see that I added a new object reference instance variable called intoTheEther and never initialized it. You can see its value is 0x0. If I were to send a message to intoTheEther, that's exactly where it would go — into the ether. So when I get a logic error, the first thing I'm going to check is whether any of the object references I am using have 0x0 as their value, informing me that the reference was never initialized.

✔ **Checking for initialization:** Finally, notice the value of i in Figure 10-7. That long, seemingly random number is the way it is because it hasn't been initialized yet. The instruction that was going to initialize it was the one that generated a runtime error — because I tried to initialize i with the result of a divide-by-zero operation.

Take a look at Figure 10-9. I want to point out that when I choose the Build menu, the menu entry is Build and Go (Debug). Notice the Build and Go button in the toolbar; it stays the same regardless of whether I'm in debug mode. When you use the Build and Go button on the toolbar, you're simply telling Xcode to run the build the same way you did it the last time. If that's not what I want — say I don't want it to run in Debug mode — then I have to choose Build and

Run from the menu. And when I do that, the next time I look at the menu it says *Build and Go (Run)* instead of *Build and Go (Debug)*.

The Build and Go button in the toolbar always repeats the last build task.

As you can see, the debugger can be really useful when your program isn't doing what you expect. For the blatant errors, the debugger can show you exactly what is going on when the error occurred. It provides you with a trail of how you got to where you are, highlights the problem instruction, and shows you your application's variables and their values at that point. Had the cause of the error in this case been more subtle, looking at the value of the variable would have given me a good hint about what was going on.

What's just as valuable is how the debugger can help you with logic errors. Sending a message to `nil` is not uncommon, especially when you are making changes to the user interface and forget to set up an outlet, for example. In such situations, the ability to look at the object references can really help. And what can really help you with that is the ability to set breakpoints, which is the subject of the next section.

Figure 10-8:
The Return MeToView Controller's instance variables.

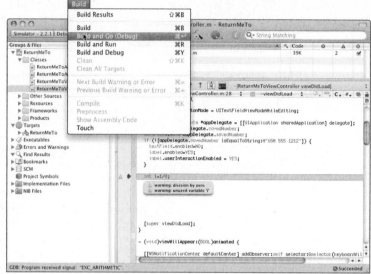

Figure 10-9:
Build and
Go (Debug).

Using Breakpoints

Xcode's Debugger feature is a great tool for tracking down runtime errors, as earlier sections in this chapter make clear. I want to highlight another useful feature of the Debugger — its capability of setting breakpoints. If you're stymied by a logic error, setting breakpoints is a great way to break that logjam.

A *breakpoint* is an instruction to the Debugger to stop execution at that instruction and wait for further instructions (no pun intended). By setting breakpoints at various methods in my program, I can step through its execution, at the instruction level, to see exactly what it is doing. I can also examine the variables the program is setting and using, which will allow me to determine if that is where the problem is lies.

In Figure 10-10, I've set a breakpoint simply by clicking in the far-left column of the Editor window. When I build and run the program again (as you can see in the Project Editor window in Figure 10-11), the program has stopped executing right at the breakpoint I set. (Figure 10-12 shows you the same Source Code view in the Debugger window.)

In Figure 10-13, I've expanded the window and clicked the triangle next to the appDelegate. That shows the appDelegate's variables, one of which is the viewController. If you notice the value under appDelegate for the `viewController`, it is 0x5277a0. If you notice the value at the very top for `self`, you see it is also 0x5277a0. This makes sense because the `viewController` variable is pointing to the `viewController`, which is in the object we are now in, and which is the value for `self`.

I've also clicked the triangle next to `self`, which shows me the view controller's variables. If I had clicked on `viewController` under `appDelegate`, I would have obviously seen the same thing.

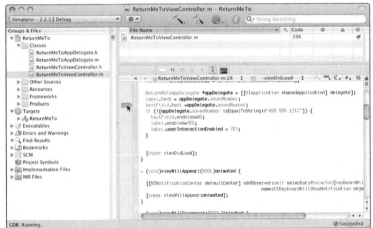

Figure 10-10: Setting a breakpoint.

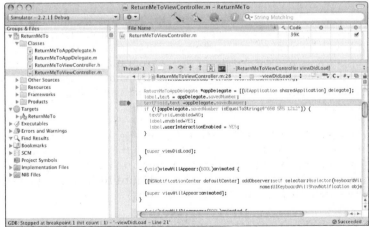

Figure 10-11: What the Editor window shows at the breakpoint.

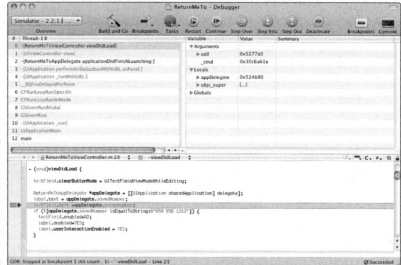

Figure 10-12:
What the Debugger window shows at the breakpoint.

Looking under the `appDelegate` variables, you can see the `callNumber` and its value, which is `nil`. If I'd been trying to do something using `call Number` at this point, that click would have shown me that I was trying to do something with a variable that hadn't been initialized with the value I needed. In other words, this would not have been a good time in the program flow to display the `callNumber` variable.

Figure 10-13:
A mug shot of the view-Controller variables.

Let's say I wanted to see precisely when that variable was set. I could execute the program instruction by instruction, simply by clicking on the Step Into button on the debugger toolbar. I would have executed `textField.text =appDelegate.savedNumber;` and then gone on to the next instruction, as you can see in Figure 10-14. I'd keep on clicking that Step Into button at every instruction until I got to where I wanted to be. (Which, by the way, can be a long and winding road.)

The Debugger window gives you a number of other options for making your way through your program in addition to Step Into. For example, you could try one of the following:

- ✔ **Step Over** gives you the opportunity to skip over an instruction.
- ✔ **Step Out** would take you out of the current method.
- ✔ **Continue** tells the program to keep on with its execution.
- ✔ **Restart** restarts the program. (You were hoping maybe if you tried it again it would work?)

To get rid of the breakpoint, simply drag it off to the side. You can also right-click the breakpoint and choose Remove Breakpoint from the pop-up menu that appears.

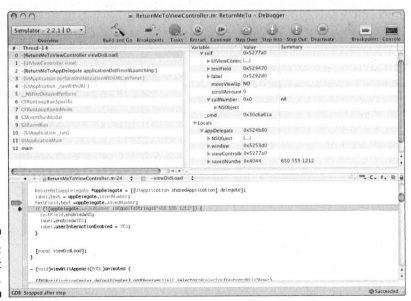

Figure 10-14:
The next
step.

One More Step

Obviously, the Debugger is a very valuable tool — even more so because it's so easy to use. You can use the Debugger to figure out how your code and the framework are interacting at breakpoint, examine the stack, and figure out where the bug is hiding.

So where am I?

At this point, you can enter and save the number — and after the first time you do that, you can only enter a new number if you touch the number displayed in the label, which enables editing. (The code for doing that is in Chapter 9, Listing 9-10.)

Originally I was planning to stop here in the development of the ReturnMeTo application. But as I showed it on my iPhone to prospective users (okay, my friends with iPhones), they had a couple of suggestions that made me realize (after first arguing that it was okay the way it was) that I wasn't done:

✔ One suggestion was that you should be able to touch the phone number and have it dial automatically for you.

✔ The second was that touching the label display was kind of hokey, and a better way to do what I wanted to do was to change the iPhone image into a button. (I show you how to do that in the next chapter.)

Chapter 11

Buttoning It Down and Calling Home

· ·

In This Chapter

▶ Adding a button in Interface Builder

▶ Using the Target-Action design pattern to implement a button touch in your code

▶ Finding out what Web views do

▶ Using the phone-number-detect feature of Web views to initiate a call

▶ Admiring the final ReturnMeTo listing

· ·

Developers tend to be optimistic when they put what they hope will be the finishing touches to their latest application. You've expended a certain amount of time and effort making your dream app a reality okay, maybe not blood, sweat, and tears, but a lot of work nevertheless — and you tend to think that your efforts will be greeted with great praise.

The reality, more often than not, is that when you take your spanking new application around to a few friends and colleagues it isn't always instantly welcomed as the newest, most advanced thing since sliced bread! Sure, it gets some praise, but there are some criticisms as well — "helpful suggestions" is how your friends put it.

To take a concrete example, when I started showing around the ReturnMeTo application the way it worked at the end of Chapter 9, I got the good-news-bad-news routine.

The good news was that everyone liked it. The bad news was, they almost all made the same two comments:

✔ Disabling editing was a good idea, but they also all thought that having to touch the label to enable it was pretty hokey. "Make the iPhone image a button" was suggested by more than one person.

✔ The second comment was, "Why can't I just touch the phone number to make a call?" ("It *is* a phone, right?" was usually the capstone to that comment.)

So be prepared for comments from the peanut gallery about how "this and this" and "such and such" is what your app needs to make it better/faster/ stronger. And be confident enough in your own skills as a developer to actually take such suggestions seriously, dispassionately evaluate each one, and incorporate the better ones into your work. I thought both comments about the ReturnMeTo application made a lot of sense, so I put my coder's cap back on and retooled the ReturnMeTo application so that the iPhone image acted as the enabling trigger for updating the phone number (as requested) and the iPhone "phoned home" when somebody touched the displayed phone number (as requested). This chapter shows the steps I had to go through in order to incorporate these suggestions.

Adding a Button to Your iPhone Interface

If you've made your way through enough of the coding in this book to get to this point (Chapter 11), more than likely you won't have trouble adding a measly button to the interface. If you just remember that buttons use the Target-Action design pattern I talk about in Chapter 2, you'll get your head around the whole button concept pretty quickly.

Ready? Let's get started.

The Target-Action pattern

You use the Target-Action pattern (see Chapter 2) to let your application know that a user has done something. When he or she taps a button for example, your application is supposed to respond — which usually happens in due course because the button calls some method that you specified in your code. The method that gets called is (usually) in the view controller that manages the view in which the particular button resides. In the case of our ReturnMeTo application, that view controller would be `ReturnMeToViewController`.

In Figure 11-1, I've added a new piece to the user interface — a `UIControl` (a button). As you can see, whenever the user taps that button, it calls the `buttonPressed:` method in the `ReturnMeToViewController`.

End of story — well, at least for what happens when the button is tapped. Here, I'm only replacing one control (the label) with another control (the button). It really comes down to a plumbing issue, and makes the point that when you use the Model-View-Controller design pattern, making a user interface change is almost trivial — it just requires a little replumbing in the controller. And, oh yes, a little bit of replumbing in Interface Builder as well.

Working through your button code

If you add a button to your interface, you need to add a method to your code to handle those times when somebody decides to actually tap the button — the button *action*, in other words.

Okay, it's time to start. First, you'll need to add the action method to the interface (as shown in Listing 11-1). You'll do this in the ReturnMeToView Controller.h file.

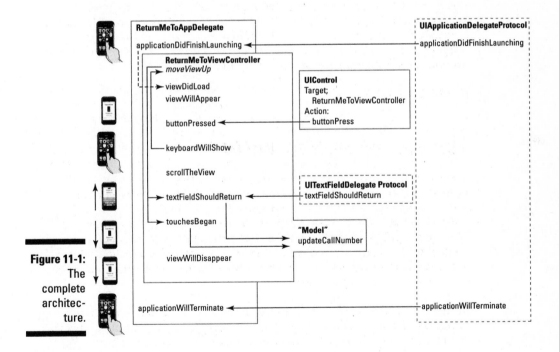

Figure 11-1: The complete architecture.

Listing 11-1: Add the action

```
@interface ReturnMeToViewController : UIViewController
            <UITextFieldDelegate> {

  IBOutlet UITextField *textField;
  IBOutlet UILabel      *label;
  BOOL                   moveViewUp;
  CGFloat                scrollAmount;
  NSString              *callNumber;

}

@property (nonatomic, retain) UITextField *textField;
@property (nonatomic, retain) UILabel *label;
@property (nonatomic, retain) NSString *callNumber;

-(void)scrollTheView:(BOOL)movedUp;
-(void)updateCallNumber;
-(IBAction)buttonPressed:(id)sender;

@end
```

Here I've declared a new method — buttonPressed — with a new keyword
right smack in front of it — IBAction.

IBAction is one of those cool little techniques, like IBOutlet, that does nothing in the code but provides a way to inform Interface Builder (hence the IB
in both of them) that this method can be used as an action for Target-Action
connections. All IBAction "does" is act as a tag for Interface Builder — identifying this method (action) as one you can connect to an object (namely the
button) in a nib file. In this respect, this whole IBAction trick is similar to the
IBOutlet mechanism I discuss in Chapter 7. In that case, however, you were
tagging instance variables; in this case, methods. Same difference.

You will use IBAction later when you launch Interface Builder and connect
the new button with the ReturnMeToViewController method. IBAction is
actually defined as a void, so if you think about it, all you've done is declare
a new method with a return type of void.

```
IBAction) buttonPressed:(id)sender; = (void)
          buttonPressed:(id)sender;
```

Which simply means that you've declared a method that doesn't return anything to whoever called it.

The actual name you give the method can be anything you want, but it must
have a return type of IBAction. Usually the action method takes one
argument — typically defined as id, a pointer to the instance variables of

an object — which is given the name `sender`. The control that triggers your action will use the `sender` argument to pass a reference to itself. So, for example, if your action method was called as the result of a button tap, the argument `sender` would contain a reference to the specific button that was tapped.

A word to the wise — having the `sender` argument contain a reference to the specific button that was tapped is a very handy mechanism, even if we're not going to take advantage of that in our ReturnMeTo application. With that reference in hand, you can access the variables of the control that was tapped.

Okay, you've declared the method; the next thing on your To-Do list is to actually add the `buttonPressed` method to the implementation file, `ReturnMeToViewController.m`. You can see the code that does this deed in Listing 11-2. I added a new `#pragma` here, and I added the method after that.

```
#pragma mark - Target Action methods
```

Just to keep things in the order I like, I added it right before

```
#pragma mark - "Model" methods

- (void)updateCallNumber {
```

I do that because I like to keep my "model" methods separated out from overridden and delegate methods.

Listing 11-2:   Add buttonPressed:

```
-(IBAction)buttonPressed:(id)sender{
    textField.enabled = YES;
    label.text = @"You found it, touch below";

    textField.placeholder = @"You may now enter the number";
}
```

If this code looks familiar to you, you get extra points for paying attention. None of this code is new; I just moved it from the `touchesBegan:` method I put together back in Chapter 9, where I tied this code to the label. Remember I said that user interface changes were mostly going to be a matter of plumbing? Which reminds me — as long as you're going the button route rather than the label route, you'd best remove the code from the `touchesBegan:` method. To see what code needs to be excised, check out Listing 11-3, where I've commented out (and used ~~double strikethrough~~) to show the code to be removed.

Listing 11-3: Remove code from touchesBegan:

```
- (void)touchesBegan:(NSSet *)touches withEvent:(UIEvent
             *)event {

//   if (!textField.enabled) {
//     UITouch *touch = [touches anyObject];
//     if (CGRectContainsPoint([label frame], [touch
//               locationInView:self.view])) {
//       textField.enabled = YES;
//       label.text = @"You found it, touch below";
//       textField.placeholder = @"You may now enter the
//               number";
//     }
//   }
//   else {

  if( textField.editing) {
    [textField resignFirstResponder];
    [self updateCallNumber];
    if (moveViewUp) [self scrollTheView:NO];
  }
//}

    [super touchesBegan:touches withEvent:event];
}
```

One last bit of cleanup and you're through with this chore: Because we no longer want the label to act as a trigger for enabling editing in the ReturnMeTo application, we have to remove the code for enabling the label that you added to viewDidLoad back in Chapter 9. Listing 11-4 shows what needs to go. (Again, look for the lines that have been commented out and have double strikethrough.)

Listing 11-4: Remove the label enabling code from viewDidLoad

```
- (void)viewDidLoad {

  textField.clearButtonMode =
          UITextFieldViewModeWhileEditing;

  ReturnMeToAppDelegate *appDelegate = [[UIApplication
          sharedApplication] delegate];
  label.text = appDelegate.savedNumber;
  textField.text =appDelegate.savedNumber;
```

```
   if (![appDelegate.savedNumber isEqualToString:@"650 555
      1212"]) {
     textField.enabled=NO;
// label.enabled=YES;
// label.userInteractionEnabled = YES;
   }

   super viewDidLoad];
}
```

Adding a button to your interface really takes no more code than that. Getting the button to actually *do* something for you takes a bit more work, but (fortunately) Interface Builder makes that task pretty much a snap. But before you go there, be sure to save your work. You know the drill ⌘+S.

Connecting the Button in Interface Builder

So far, you've implemented the method you want to have called when the user taps the iPhone image button. Now, you need to do two things to make that work:

1. Create the button.

2. Give the button a method to call and tell it the object that method is in.

Doing this is really easy thanks to our (now) old buddy Interface Builder. If you think about it, you are doing the same thing you did when you connected the outlets in Chapter 7. Now you'll connect the action.

Launch Xcode and open the ReturnMeTo project:

1. **In the Groups & Files listing on the left, double-click the ReturnMeTo ViewController.xib file.**

   You'll find the file in the Resources folder of the ReturnMeTo project's main folder.

   Double-clicking the file launches Interface Builder, which should display the three windows you see in Figure 11-2.

Note: If the Library window isn't open for some reason, open it by choosing Tools⇨Library from the main menu. And (weirder still) if the View window isn't visible, open it by double-clicking the View icon in the `ReturnMeToViewController.xib` window. (Where there's a will there's a way . . . .)

2. **In the upper pane of the Library window, navigate to the Cocoa Touch Plugin folder.**

   It's the first folder inside the main Library folder.

3. **From within the Cocoa Touch Plugin folder, select the Inputs & Values subfolder.**

   The items contained in the Inputs & Values subfolder are displayed in the bottom pane of the Library window

4. **Drag the Round Rect Button item from the Library window to the View window, placing the item right next to your iPhone image.**

   If you use the blue guide lines that Interface Builder provides, you can resize and position the button so it's the same size as your iPhone image, as I do in Figure 11-2.

5. **Delete the Image View by selecting it and pressing the delete key and then drag the Round Rect Button item to where the Image View used to be.**

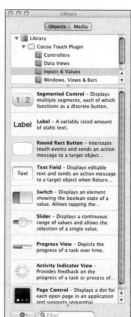

Figure 11-2:
Dragging a button.

6. **Click to select your Round Rect button and then choose Tools⇨ Attribute Inspector to bring up the Attribute Inspector**

   Make sure you have the button selected.

   You're going to use the Attribute inspector to add an image to the button.

7. **Choose iPhone Image.png from the Image drop down menu in the Attribute inspector, as shown in Figure 11-3.**

   That's it — that's all it takes to create a button using an image! Now to connect things up.

8. **Right-click the button to display a list of connections.**

9. **Drag from the little circle to the right of the Touch Up Inside item and drop it on the File's Owner icon in the** `ReturnMeToViewController.` `xib` **window, as shown in Figure 11-4.**

The Touch Up Inside connection is a good choice in this situation because Touch Up Inside is the event that is generated when the last place the user touched before lifting his or her finger was inside the button. This allows a user to change his or her mind about touching the button by moving his or her finger off the button before lifting it up.

The blue guide line you see here when dragging is the same blue line you see when connecting Outlets, as you did in Chapter 7.

Figure 11-3:
Adding an image to the button.

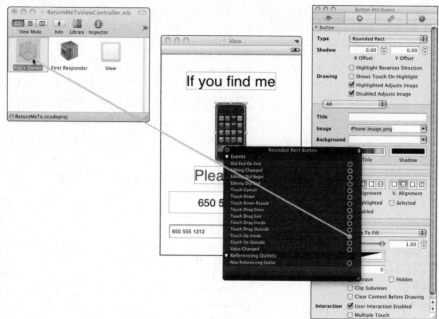

Figure 11-4:
Connecting
the button
with the
view
controller.

10. **With the cursor still over the File's Owner icon, let go of the mouse button and then choose** `buttonPressed` **from the pop-up menu that appears, as shown in Figure 11-5.**

    Doing so makes your connection.

    As you can see, Interface Builder found the `IBAction` tag you declared in the previous section and displays it for you as a choice. You can now rest easy.

If you save your work and then compile and run the application in the Simulator, you'll discover that the iPhone image is now a fully functioning button that works the same as touching the label had previously. And it's so much prettier.

Figure 11-5:
Finishing the
connection.

Phoning Home

Why push 10 buttons when you can push just one? I had originally designed my ReturnMeTo application so that any Good Samaritan who found my lost iPhone could see the right contact phone number and give me a call so we could arrange a handover. When I showed this application to my friends, one in particular looked at me a bit incredulously when I told him he couldn't just press the displayed phone number to make the call. "Why not?" he said. "Lots of applications do that."

I realized he was right, and it's pretty easy to do that using a *Web view* (UIWebView), a view class that is part of the UIKit. It already has the ability to automatically recognize a phone number and initiate a call.

You use the UIWebView class to not only embed Web content in your application, but to display anything coded with HTML — making it the number one choice for displaying formatted text in your app. To do so, you simply create a UIWebView object. You can have the view take up the whole window (as I will in the iPhoneTravel411 application in Chapter 17) or you can also treat it like a control and make it a subview of your content view (which is functionally equivalent to how you used the label), as I will do here. In either case, all you need to do is tell it to display some HTML content, and presto chango, you are done. That HTML content can be virtually (no pun intended) anywhere — on the Internet, stored locally, or in a string you create in your program. I show you how to deal with HTML content from the Internet and stored locally when I walk you through the iPhoneTravel411 application later on (in Chapters 14 through 17), but for now, I'm just interested in a loading an HTML string — our beloved phone number.

The thing for you to remember is that, by default, a Web view recognizes a phone number and converts that number to a Phone Link. When the user taps a Phone Link, the Phone application launches and dials the number — which is precisely what you want.

Tweaking the code

Our ReturnMeTo application has managed so far with just a label view, simply because you only wanted the label to display a telephone number. Now that you want the number dialed when it is touched, you are going to replace the label view you're currently using with a Web view. To do that successfully, you need to tackle the following three tasks:

1. Identify and modify all the places that assign the telephone number to the label. Right now, to display the number in the label, all you have to do is assign it to label.text, and it gets displayed. It will now take

a little more work to display it (but worth it) because you'll have to replace each assignment with a call to a UIWebView method that will load the HTML string into webView.

2. Create the HTML string you want displayed.

3. Replace the UILabel with a UIWebView in Interface Builder and then connect everything up.

Listing 11-5 shows the code you'll need. I start out by making the necessary changes to the interface in the ReturnMeToViewController.h file. I replaced the label outlet with a webView outlet and I also added an instance variable htmlString to compose the text I load into the Web view. The changes are in bold; I have commented out (and marked with ~~double strikethrough~~) the deletions.

Listing 11-5: Update the interface

```
@interface ReturnMeToViewController : UIViewController
        <UITextFieldDelegate> {

        IBOutlet UITextField *textField;
//      IBOutlet UILabel      *label;
        IBOutlet UIWebView    *webView;
        BOOL                  moveViewUp;
        CGFloat               scrollAmount;
        NSString              *callNumber;
        NSString              *htmlString;


}

@property (nonatomic, retain) UITextField *textField;
// @property (nonatomic, retain) UILabel *label;
@property (nonatomic, retain) UIWebView *webView;
@property (nonatomic, retain) NSString *callNumber;

- (void)scrollTheView:(BOOL)movedUp;
- (void)updateCallNumber;
- (IBAction)buttonPressed:(id)sender;
@end
```

You'll also have to add

```
@synthesize webView;
```

You should do that right after @synthesize textField; in the ReturnMe ToViewController.m file. And since you have deleted the label, you're also going to have to delete

```
@synthesize label;
```

Dealing with this @synthesize business is shown in Listing 11-6.

Listing 11-6

```
#import "ReturnMeToViewController.h"
#import "ReturnMeToAppDelegate.h"

@implementation ReturnMeToViewController


@synthesize textField;
// @synthesize label;
@synthesize webView;
@synthesize callNumber;
```

Implementing the Web view

Implementing the Web view itself is fairly simple.

In our first version of the ReturnMeTo application, you simply assigned the savedNumber instance variable (the instance variable you added in Chapter 9 to hold the phone number you wanted to save) to the label.text field.

```
label.text = appDelegate.savedNumber;
```

As promised, moving to a Web view means you're going to have to do a little more work. In fact, you'll need to replace the label.text assignment with comparable code to create an HTML string and then have the Web view load and display it. The changes are in bold and I have commented out (and marked with ~~double strikethrough~~) the deletions.

There are two lines in Listing 11-7 below

```
// label.enabled=YES;
// label.userInteractionEnabled = YES;
```

that you previously deleted in listing 11-4. I have left them in here so you wouldn't wonder where they disappeared to.

All of this involves existing methods in the ReturnMeToViewCont roller.m file.

Listing 11-7: Change viewDidLoad

```
- (void)viewDidLoad {


  textField.clearButtonMode =
          UITextFieldViewModeWhileEditing;

  ReturnMeToAppDelegate *appDelegate =
          [[UIApplication sharedApplication] delegate];
// label.text = appDelegate.savedNumber;
  textField.text =appDelegate.savedNumber;
  htmlString = @"<div style=\"font-family:Helvetica,
             Arial, sans-serif; font-size:48pt;\"
             align=\"center\">";
  htmlString = [htmlString stringByAppendingString:
             appDelegate.savedNumber];
  htmlString = [htmlString stringByAppendingString:
             @"</span>"];

 [webView loadHTMLString:htmlString baseURL:nil];


  if (![appDelegate.savedNumber isEqualToString:@"650 555
          1212"]) {
    textField.enabled=NO;
// label.enabled=YES;
// label.userInteractionEnabled = YES;
  }
  [super viewDidLoad];
}
```

All we are doing here is getting rid of the label assignment, the one that assigns the savedNumber "vanilla" string:

```
label.text = appDelegate.savedNumber;
```

And replacing it with code that creates an HTML formatted string.

To start, you need to create a formatted HTML string, which surrounds the same appDelegate.savedNumber with the formatting information. Notice the appDelegate.savedNumber buried in there:

```
htmlString = @"<div style=\"font-family:Helvetica,
           Arial, sans-serif; font-size:48pt;\"
           align=\"center\">";
htmlString = [htmlString stringByAppendingString:
           appDelegate.savedNumber];
htmlString = [htmlString stringByAppendingString:
           @"</span>"];
```

To create the HTML string with the saved number in it, I use the `stringBy-AppendingString:` method — which creates a string by adding one string after another. The only tricky thing here is that I had to use the backslash character before the embedded quotes in the HTML string.

I won't go into the HTML here. If you want to delve further into HTML, feel free to check out *HTML, XHTML & CSS For Dummies* by Ed Tittel and Jeff Noble.

Then I simply tell the Web view to load the HTML string:

```
[webView loadHTMLString:htmlString baseURL:nil];
```

Here the `loadHTMLString` method does exactly what I need it to do — it takes a string (with HTML formatting information embedded) and loads it into the Web view. Here's a closer look at the method's arguments:

- ✔ The first argument, `htmlString`, is the string I just formatted. Nothing surprising there.
- ✔ The second argument, `BaseURL` is an `NSURL` object, An `NSURL` object, to no one's surprise, is an object that contains a URL. It can reference either a Web site or a local file. (It is not necessary here since you are not telling the Web view to access a URL.)

In effect, Listings 11-6, 11-7, and 11-8 all show you doing the same thing — in three different places.

Even though the HTML strings in the listings in this book span multiple lines, you can't do that in Xcode. You will get errors such as

```
error: syntax error before'@' token
```

and

```
error: syntax error at 'OTHER' token
```

unless, of course, you use the escape character (\) as the last character on the line, right before the carriage return.

Listing 11-8:   Change buttonPressed:

```
#pragma mark - Target Action methods

-(IBAction)buttonPressed:(id)sender{

  textField.enabled = YES;

  // label.text = @"You found it, touch below";
```

(continued)

Listing 11-8 *(continued)*

```
    htmlString =  @"<div style=\"font-family:Helvetica,
            Arial, sans-serif; font-size:48pt;\"
            align=\"center\">";
    htmlString =  [ htmlString stringByAppendingString:
            @"You found it, touch below"];
    htmlString =  [ htmlString stringByAppendingString: @"</
            span>"];
    [webView loadHTMLString:htmlString baseURL:nil];


    textField.placeholder = @"You may now enter the number";
}
```

Listing 11-9:   Change updateCallNumber

```
    - (void)updateCallNumber {

    self.callNumber = textField.text;
//  label.text = self.callNumber;
    htmlString =  @"<div style=\"font-family:Helvetica,
            Arial, sans-serif; font-size:48pt;\"
            align=\"center\">";
    htmlString =  [ htmlString stringByAppendingString:
            callNumber];
    htmlString =  [ htmlString stringByAppendingString: @"</
            span>"];
    [webView loadHTMLString:htmlString baseURL:nil];


    ReturnMeToAppDelegate *appDelegate = [[UIApplication
            sharedApplication] delegate];
    appDelegate.savedNumber = self.callNumber;
}
```

And don't forget that wonderful sentiment, "if you love somebody, set them free." In programming terms, that means you always have to release all the objects you own. (If this "release" stuff doesn't ring a bell, check out Chapters 6 and 7, where I cover the idea in greater detail.)

Listing 11-10:   Last but not least — dellaoc:

```
    - (void)dealloc {

    [textField release];
//  label release];
```

```
[webView release];
[callNumber release];
[htmlString release];

[super dealloc];
}
```

Adding and connecting the Web view in Interface Builder

As was the case when we replaced the Image View with the Round Rect Button (earlier in the chapter), we have to tell Interface Builder about our decision to replace the Label with a Web View. To get that ball rolling, do the following:

1. **Launch Xcode and open the ReturnMeTo project.**

2. **In the Groups & Files listing on the left, double-click the** ReturnMeTo ViewController.xib **file.**

   Interface Builder launches and you end up with the windows you see in Figure 11-6.

   Note: Again, if the Library window is not open for some reason, go ahead and open it by choosing Tools⇨Library from the main menu. And (weirder still) if the View window isn't visible, open it by double-clicking the View icon in the ReturnMeToViewController.xib window.

3. **From within the Cocoa Touch Plugin folder, select the Data Views sub-folder.**

   The items contained in the Data Views subfolder are displayed in the bottom pane of the Library window.

4. **Drag a Web View item from the Library window to the View window.**

   Use the blue lines to resize and position the Web View so it is the same size (and in the same place) as the label, as shown in Figure 11-6.

5. **Delete the (old) label by selecting it and pressing delete.**

6. **Right click the File's Owner icon in the** ReturnMeToView Controller.xib **window to display a list of connections.**

   Notice that this method of making a connection is different from the one I showed you earlier in the chapter, when you had to deal with the Round Rect Button. I felt it would be a good idea to show you both ways of making the connection.

Figure 11-6:
Dragging a
Web view.

7. **Click** webView **in the list of connections — it's there under the Outlets heading — and drag the little circle over to the View window and onto the Web View itself, as shown in Figure 11-7.**

Figure 11-7:
Connecting
the Web
view to its
controller.

8. Make sure that the Detects Phone Numbers check box is checked in the Attributes Inspector.

What you've done here is you've replaced the label with a Web view and connected the new `webView` outlet to the Web view in the same way that the label outlet had been connected to the label previously. (Not bad for a day's work.)

A Bug

In the spirit of making this a real world exercise and not some piece of theory, I have to confess that when I was testing this application out for the final time, three days before the final final chapters were due, I found a bug. It doesn't get much more real world than that, does it?

When I replaced the label with the Web view, there was an unintended consequence (the polite way of saying I introduced a logic error in my code).

The way that I handled dismissing the keyboard and restoring the view when the user touched the screen (see Chapter 8) was by capturing the touches that were passed to the view controller in `touchesBegan:`.

That even worked if the user touched the label, because the label passed the touches on. But while the label didn't care about touches, the Web view does. (It captures touches so it can detect when you touch a Web or Phone Link and load the URL or initiate the dialing of the number.) That meant that if the user happened to touch the screen in the Web view I just added — say, to indicate that he or she was done entering the number — `touchesBegan:` in the controller would never be called.

Ironically, the keyboard was dismissed because the Web view becomes the first responder when the user touches in it. (You can find out more about that in Chapter 8). But since `touchesBegan:` was never called, the view was never restored to its pre scrolled state.

Incidentally, I figured all this out using a breakpoint in the handy dandy debugger — like I show you in Chapter 10. Talk about eating your own dog food.

Fixing it was simple. All I had to do was keep the Web view from handling touches during the period from when the user started using the keyboard until after the user dismissed it. I did that by setting the Web view's `user InteractionEnabled` property to `NO` as soon as the keyboard appeared. The place to do that was in `keyboardWillShow:` which is called right before the keyboard appears (as you recall from Figure 11-1). All I had to do was add one line of code (in bold in Listing 11-11) to `keyboardWillShow:`.

```
webView.userInteractionEnabled=NO;
```

Of course once I disabled the Web view, I had to enable it again if I wanted the Web view to be able to initiate the call when the Phone Link was tapped. As you recall, `textFieldShouldReturn:` is called after the user has finished entering the phone number and taps return, and `touchesBegan:` is called after the user has finished entering the phone number and taps the screen. So I added the following code (in bold in Listing 11-11) to both of those methods after the keyboard is dismissed.

```
webView.userInteractionEnabled=YES;
```

Piece of cake.

Listing 11-11:   Disabling and re-enabling the web view

```
- (void)keyboardWillShow:(NSNotification *)notif {

  NSDictionary* info = [notif userInfo];

  NSValue* aValue = [info objectForKey:UIKeyboardBoundsUse
          rInfoKey];
  CGSize keyboardSize = [aValue CGRectValue].size;
  float bottomPoint = (textField.frame.origin.y+
          textField.frame.size.height+10);
  scrollAmount = keyboardSize.height - (self.view.frame.
          size.height-  bottomPoint) ;

  if (scrollAmount >0)   {
    moveViewUp =YES;
    [self scrollTheView:YES];
  }
  else
    moveViewUp =NO;
    webView.userInteractionEnabled=NO;
}
- (void)touchesBegan:(NSSet *)touches withEvent:(UIEvent
          *)event {

// if (!textField.enabled) {
//    UITouch *touch = [touches anyObject];
//    if (CGRectContainsPoint([label frame], [touch
//        locationInView:self.view])) {
//      textField.enabled = YES;
//      label.text = @"You found it, touch below";
//      textField.placeholder = @"You may now enter the
//        number";
//    }
// }
```

```
//  else {

  if( textField.editing) {
  [textField resignFirstResponder];
  [self updateCallNumber];
    if (moveViewUp) [self scrollTheView:NO];
    webView.userInteractionEnabled=YES;
  }
//  }

  [super touchesBegan:touches withEvent:event];
}

-(BOOL)textFieldShouldReturn:(UITextField *)theTextField {

  [textField resignFirstResponder];
  webView.userInteractionEnabled=YES;
  if (moveViewUp) [self scrollTheView:NO];
  [self updateCallNumber];
  webView.userInteractionEnabled=YES;

  return YES;
}
```

We Are Finally Done

With this last change, I am putting the ReturnMeTo application to bed. But before I submit it to the App Store — a process I describe in Chapter 13 — I'd better make sure that it's a lean, mean application machine — that it has no memory leaks or other object-allocation issues, in other words. (This chapter has gone on long enough, so I'll reserve that discussion for the next chapter.)

Chapter 13 — my All-Things-Having-to-Do-with-Provisioning-And-App-Store — will be the capstone to Part III. After that, we still have Part IV to deal with, where you get to look at some of the more advanced application-development techniques. There, I concentrate on explaining the ins and outs of designing my MobileTravel411 and iPhoneTravel411 applications. Drilling down a bit, I go through how to develop the iPhoneTravel411 app. Now, that's a more complex application — incorporating some techniques and tools you'll likely end up using in your own application — stuff like saving files, using table views (to navigate, among other things), forming an alliance with the Settings application, figuring out internationalization, and accessing data on the Internet.

The Final Code

Behold: Listings 11-12 through 11-15 are the final code for the ReturnMeTo application. I've bolded any changes from the listing posted at the end of the last chapter and have commented out (and marked with ~~double striketh-rough~~) all deletions.

Even though the HTML strings in the listings span multiple lines, you can't do that in Xcode unless you use the escape character (\) right before the carriage return.

Listing 11-12: ReturnMeToAppDelegate.h

```
#import <UIKit/UIKit.h>

@class ReturnMeToViewController;

@interface ReturnMeToAppDelegate : NSObject
          <UIApplicationDelegate> {
  UIWindow                    *window;
  ReturnMeToViewController    *viewController;
  NSString                    *savedNumber ;
}

@property (nonatomic, retain) IBOutlet UIWindow *window;
@property (nonatomic, retain) IBOutlet
          ReturnMeToViewController *viewController;
@property (nonatomic, retain) NSString *savedNumber ;

@end
```

Listing 11-13: ReturnMeToAppDelegate.m

```
#import "ReturnMeToAppDelegate.h"
#import "ReturnMeToViewController.h"
NSString *kNumberLocationKey = @"NumberLocation";

@implementation ReturnMeToAppDelegate

@synthesize window;
@synthesize viewController;
@synthesize savedNumber;


#pragma mark - UIApplicationDelegate methods
```

```objc
- (void)applicationDidFinishLaunching:
          (UIApplication*) application {

  self.savedNumber = [[NSUserDefaults
  standardUserDefaults]objectForKey:kNumberLocationKey];
  if (savedNumber == nil) {
    savedNumber = @"650 555 1212";
    NSDictionary *savedNumberDict  = [NSDictionary
          dictionaryWithObject:savedNumber
          forKey:kNumberLocationKey];
    [[NSUserDefaults standardUserDefaults] registerDefault
          s:savedNumberDict ];
  }

  [window addSubview:viewController.view];
  [window makeKeyAndVisible];
}

- (void)applicationWillTerminate:(UIApplication *)
        application {

        [[NSUserDefaults standardUserDefaults]
        setObject:savedNumber
        forKey:kNumberLocationKey];
}

- (void)dealloc {
    [viewController release];
    [window release];
    [savedNumber release];
    [kNumberLocationKey release];
    [super dealloc];
}

@end
```

Listing 11-14:   ReturnMeToViewController.h

```objc
@interface ReturnMeToViewController : UIViewController
        <UITextFieldDelegate> {

  IBOutlet UITextField *textField;
  //      IBOutlet UILabel *label;
  IBOutlet UIWebView *webView;
  BOOL moveViewUp;
  CGFloat scrollAmount;
  NSString *callNumber;
```

(continued)

Listing 11-14 *(continued)*

```
   NSString *htmlString;
}
@property (nonatomic, retain) UITextField *textField;
// @property (nonatomic, retain) UILabel *label;
@property (nonatomic, retain) UIWebView *webView;
@property (nonatomic, retain) NSString *callNumber;

- (void)scrollTheView:(BOOL)movedUp;
- (void)updateCallNumber;
-(IBAction)buttonPressed:(id)sender;

@end
```

Listing 11-15:   ReturnMeToViewController.m

```
#import "ReturnMeToViewController.h"
#import "ReturnMeToAppDelegate.h"

@implementation ReturnMeToViewController


@synthesize textField;
// @synthesize label;
@synthesize webView;
@synthesize callNumber;


#pragma mark - UIViewController methods
- (void)viewDidLoad {

  textField.clearButtonMode =
          UITextFieldViewModeWhileEditing;

  ReturnMeToAppDelegate *appDelegate =
          [[UIApplication sharedApplication] delegate];
// label.text = appDelegate.savedNumber;
  textField.text =appDelegate.savedNumber;
  htmlString = @"<div style=\"font-family:Helvetica,

             Arial, sans-serif; font-size:48pt;\"
             align=\"center\">";
  htmlString = [htmlString stringByAppendingString:
             appDelegate.savedNumber];
  htmlString = [htmlString stringByAppendingString:
             @"</span>"];

  [webView loadHTMLString:htmlString baseURL:nil];
```

```objc
    if (![appDelegate.savedNumber isEqualToString:@"650 555
            1212"]) {
      textField.enabled=NO;
//  label.enabled=YES;
//  label.userInteractionEnabled = YES;
      }
    [super viewDidLoad];
}


- (void)viewWillAppear:(BOOL)animated {

    [[NSNotificationCenter defaultCenter] addObserver:self
            selector:@selector(keyboardWillShow:)  name:UI
            KeyboardWillShowNotification object:self.view.
            window];

    [super viewWillAppear:animated];
}

- (void)viewWillDisappear:(BOOL)animated {

    [[NSNotificationCenter defaultCenter]
            removeObserver:self name:UIKeyboardWillShowNoti
            fication object:nil];

    [super viewWillDisappear:animated];
}

#pragma mark - ReturnMeTo methods

- (void)keyboardWillShow:(NSNotification *)notif {

    NSDictionary* info = [notif userInfo];

    NSValue* aValue = [info objectForKey:UIKeyboardBoundsUse
            rInfoKey];
    CGSize keyboardSize = [aValue CGRectValue].size;
    float bottomPoint = (textField.frame.origin.y+
            textField.frame.size.height+10);
    scrollAmount = keyboardSize.height - (self.view.frame.
            size.height-  bottomPoint) ;

    if (scrollAmount >0)  {
      moveViewUp =YES;
      [self scrollTheView:YES];
    }
    else
```

(continued)

Listing 11-15 *(continued)*

```
      moveViewUp =NO;
      webView.userInteractionEnabled=NO;
}

- (void)scrollTheView:(BOOL)movedUp {

  [UIView beginAnimations:nil context:NULL];
  [UIView setAnimationDuration:0.3];
  CGRect rect = self.view.frame;
  if (movedUp){
    rect.origin.y -= scrollAmount;
    }
  else {
    rect.origin.y += scrollAmount;
    }
  self.view.frame = rect;

  [UIView commitAnimations];
}

#pragma mark - UIResponder methods

- (void)touchesBegan:(NSSet *)touches withEvent:(UIEvent
          *)event {

// if (!textField.enabled) {
//    UITouch *touch = [touches anyObject];
//    if (CGRectContainsPoint([label frame], [touch
//        locationInView:self.view])) {
//      textField.enabled = YES;
//      label.text = @"You found it, touch below";
//      textField.placeholder = @"You may now enter the
//        number";
//    }
// }
// else {

  if( textField.editing) {
  [textField resignFirstResponder];
  [self updateCallNumber];
    if (moveViewUp) [self scrollTheView:NO];
    webView.userInteractionEnabled=YES;
  }
// }

  [super touchesBegan:touches withEvent:event];
}
```

```
#pragma mark - NSObject methods

- (void)didReceiveMemoryWarning {
    [super didReceiveMemoryWarning];
}

- (void)dealloc {

        [textField release];
        // [label release];
        [webView release];
        [callNumber release];
        [htmlString release];

    [super dealloc];
}

#pragma mark - UITextField delegate methods

- (BOOL)textFieldShouldBeginEditing:(UITextField *)
        currentTextField {

  if(currentTextField == self.textField )
        moveViewUp = YES;
  else
        moveViewUp == NO;
  return YES;
}

-(BOOL)textFieldShouldReturn:(UITextField *)theTextField {

  [textField resignFirstResponder];
  webView.userInteractionEnabled=YES;
  if (moveViewUp) [self scrollTheView:NO];
  [self updateCallNumber];
  webView.userInteractionEnabled=YES;

  return YES;
}

#pragma mark - Target Action methods

-(IBAction)buttonPressed:(id)sender{

  textField.enabled = YES;

  // label.text = @"You found it, touch below";
```

(continued)

Listing 11-15 *(continued)*

```
    htmlString =  @"<div style=\"font-family:Helvetica,
           Arial, sans-serif; font-size:48pt;\"
           align=\"center\">";

 htmlString =  [ htmlString stringByAppendingString: @"You
           found it, touch below"];
   htmlString =  [ htmlString stringByAppendingString: @"</
           span>"];
   [webView loadHTMLString:htmlString baseURL:nil];


   textField.placeholder = @"You may now enter the number";
}

#pragma mark - "Model" methods

- (void)updateCallNumber {

   self.callNumber = textField.text;
//  label.text = self.callNumber;
       htmlString =  @"<div style=\"font-family:Helvetica,
           Arial, sans-serif; font-size:48pt;\"
           align=\"center\">";
   htmlString =  [ htmlString stringByAppendingString:
           callNumber];
   htmlString =  [ htmlString stringByAppendingString: @"</
           span>"];

   [webView loadHTMLString:htmlString baseURL:nil];

   ReturnMeToAppDelegate *appDelegate = [[UIApplication
           sharedApplication] delegate];
   appDelegate.savedNumber = self.callNumber;
}

@end
```

Chapter 12

Checking Your Code Using Xcode's Instruments Application

*B*efore you attempt to get your application into the App Store, or even run it on anyone's iPhone, you need to make sure it's behaving properly. By that I mean not only delivering the promised functionality, but also avoiding the unintentional misuse of iPhone resources. Keep in mind that the iPhone, as cool as it may very well be, is nevertheless somewhat resource-constrained when it comes to memory usage and battery life. Such restraints can have a direct effect on what you can (and can't) do in your application. Xcode's Instruments application lets you know how your application uses iPhone resources such as the CPU, memory, network, and so on.

The Instruments application allows you to observe the performance of your application while running it on the IPhone, and to a lesser extent, while running it on the Simulator. Here *instrument* means a specialized feature of the Instruments application that zeroes in on a particular aspect of your app's performance (such as memory usage, system load, disk usage, and the like) and measures it. What's really neat, however, is the fact that you can look at these different aspects simultaneously along a timeline — and then store data from multiple runs, so you get a picture of how your application's performance changes when you tune it.

The Instruments application is a very powerful piece of software, with so many features that an in-depth discussion would be beyond the scope of this book. I am going to focus on how the Instruments application can help you deal with object-allocation issues and with memory leaks — two of the most common performance deficits that plague app developers around the world. After you get object-allocation issues and memory leaks under your belt, you can explore other capabilities of the Instruments application at your leisure.

The Instruments Application

To use Instruments, you start with your compiled application — meaning you've already done the Build stuff. Launch your application by choosing Run⇨Start With Performance Tool⇨Leaks from the main menu. (If you're curious, this menu shows the various tools you can use in the Simulator — Activity Monitor, CPU Sampler, Leaks, Object Allocations, and the like.)

When you start your application using Instruments — the "performance tool" mentioned in the Run menu — your app starts either in the Simulator or the device (if you're running it on an iPhone). Where it starts depends on the kind of SDK you've selected in Xcode. Check out Figure 12-1, paying special attention to the drop-down menu in the upper-right corner of the Project window; the figure shows Simulator - 2.2.1 Release selected. That's fine for now. But when the time comes to test your app on a real device, you'll have to let the Instruments application know that by choosing the device from this drop-down menu. (I explain the differences between running the Instruments application on the Simulator and on a real device later in this chapter.)

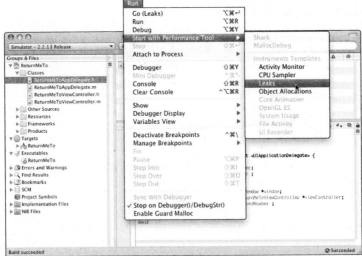

Figure 12-1:
Starting the Instruments application.

Starting your application via the Instruments application *will* launch your application, as you can see in Figure 12-2. This stands to reason; your app has to be *running* in order for there to be data for Instruments to display. Wait for your app to load fully, and then keep your eye out for the Instruments window, which should look something like Figure 12-3.

The top pane of the Instruments window shows what instruments you're currently running. Figure 12-3 shows that, besides Leaks (which I chose from the menu), the ObjectAlloc instrument is also running. Next to each instrument listed you see a graphical summary of the data that that the running instruments generate; each instrument has its own "track." (I guess that's why they call that part of the top pane the Track pane.) You can use the Time Scale slider — located right under the instrument listing in the top pane — to expand the tracks, letting you see the finer details of how each instrument is running. Similar to Interface Builder, the Library button allows you to drag more instruments into the Instruments pane.

In the current SDK, you may come up against a situation where the Instruments application doesn't recognize a device for some reason. If that happens, launch Xcode and choose Window➪Organizer from the main menu. When the Organizer window appears on-screen, right-click the listed device and then choose Remove From Organizer from the contextual menu that appears. Disconnect the device from your computer and then reconnect it. Shortly, you'll see Xcode's New Device dialog. Select Continue Using For Development and you should be able to proceed.

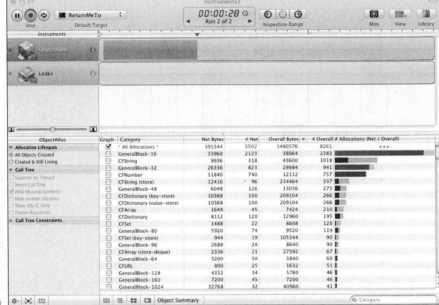

Figure 12-3:
The
Instruments
window
starts out
looking
pretty
boring.

The ObjectAlloc instrument

The ObjectAlloc instrument — one of the many tools at Instrument's disposal — shows you how your application is using memory. The Track pane in Figure 12-3 graphs the net amount of memory that your app is currently using.

Using the Inspector — accessed using the info button for the instrument in the Instruments pane you are interested in, as shown in Figure 12-4 — you can change this view to show memory allocation details in other ways — in particular, these:

- ✔ **Allocation Density:** This shows you where the memory allocations occur (generally new objects created during runtime). You would expect new objects to be created when the application is launched, and whenever you invoke a new application function. If they seem to be happening at random, you may have a problem — or then again maybe not. The way your application creates new objects is idiosyncratic to your particular application, and you need to be aware of when that should be occurring.

- ✔ **Current Bytes:** This shows you how much memory your application has currently allocated. Again, depending on your application's character-istics, this may increase and then decrease as you run your application through its functionality.

- ✔ **Stack Depth:** using this is beyond the scope of our discussion here.

In Figure 12-4, I selected Allocation Density — and as you would expect, Figure 12-5 shows that all memory allocations happened early in the program. This makes sense — I really haven't taxed any of my app's resources yet — I've just started it and let it run. No taps, touches, or slides means it can just lay back and go along for the ride.

The Detail Pane provides you with a ton of information you can use to understand object allocation of your application. Here are a couple of handy examples:

- **The Allocations (Net/Overall) column:** This column shows a histogram of the currently active objects and the total number that were ever created. Blue is the normal color, but as the ratio of net allocations to overall allocations shrinks, meaning that you're having to deal with a lot of temporary allocations, the color of the histogram shifts towards the red spectrum. This may not necessarily mean you have a problem. It may be normal for the application, or where in the application lifecycle you are, or for the object type.

- **The Graph column:** This column contains checkboxes for selecting which objects you want to graph. If you want to look at a particular kind of memory allocation, unchecking the All Allocations checkbox (which is enabled by default) and checking the checkbox for another object type determines what you will see in the Track pane. If you check more than one box, the ObjectAlloc instrument either stacks the graphs or overlays them on top of each other using different colors.

    You control the kind of display you want to see, either Stacked, or Overlay, by using the Type drop-down menu in the Inspector (the info button for the instrument in the Instruments pane). I'll leave it to you to decide which you prefer.

For any of these instruments to be really useful to you, you need to watch the displays *over time* and not rely on a single snapshot of the application.

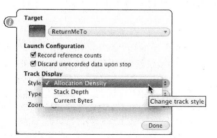

Figure 12-4:
The
Inspector.

In Figure 12-6, I run the ObjectAlloc instrument again, but this time I actually *do* something with the application. As it's running, I select the iPhone image button to enter a new phone number. (Notice that I've changed the Track Display to Current Bytes.)

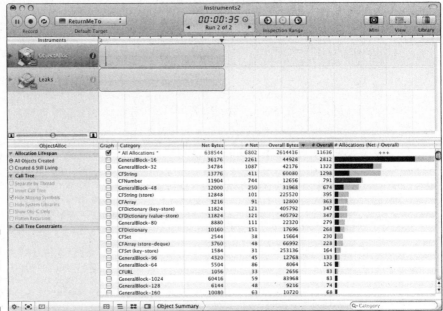

Figure 12-5:
Monitoring
allocation
density.

Miracle of miracles, I have changed the Track Display to Allocation Density and that
has also changed as a result of my action, a change documented in Figure 12-7.

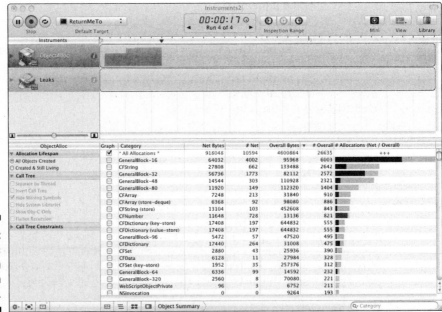

Figure 12-6:
ObjectAlloc
showing an
increase in
allocations.

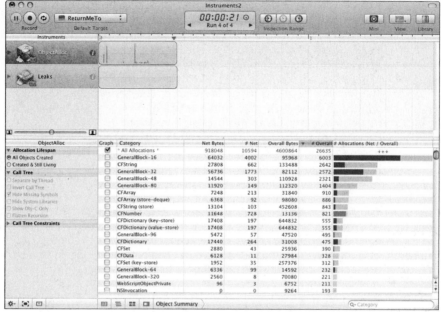

Figure 12-7: Here's what allocation density looks like when you use the application.

That's about all you need to demonstrate the basics of this instrument. While it is somewhat interesting to watch what is going on in an application like ReturnMeTo (at least one level above watching paint dry), it can be very useful in more complex applications. In these applications, you can exercise your app and see if memory is being allocated in the way you expect. You can also find out at what points you are at maximum memory usage, and tune your app if necessary. Here again you should start with an idea of how your application works and the ObjectAlloc traces can confirm or call into question your understanding. You may have been mistaken, or your application may not be behaving in the way you intended (ah yes, our old nemesis logic error rears it ugly head). In either case, you now have the information you need to do something about it.

Using the Leaks instrument

When a block of allocated memory is no longer being referenced from any of the objects in your application you have a *memory leak*. The Leaks instrument shows you where to go to fix the leak. It works by recording all allocation events in your application and then scanning the application's writable memory, registers, and stack to see whether it can still find references to those particular blocks. If there's no way to either use or free those blocks in your application, the instrument reports them as memory leaks.

The problem is, memory leaks are just sitting there, taking up space until your application terminates. If your application needs to run for a long time, or requires a lot of memory, leaks can seriously reduce its performance. That's especially important on the iPhone, which, as I explained in Chapter 6, isn't able to expand memory use beyond physical memory.

Memory is a precious iPhone resource. Too many leaks, and eventually your application may be reduced to a crawl, and even crash because it cannot get the memory it needs to perform an operation.

Now, expert developer that I am, you'll notice that my ReturnMeTo application has no leaks in my application. So let me create one. Figure 12-8 shows my intentional memory leak.

In Figure 12-9, the leak appears in the Instruments' Track Pane as a noticeable blip.

In Figure 12-10, I've selected the Leaks instrument in the Instruments Pane, which calls up a detailed view of the Leaks instrument. In this detailed view, the leaked object is revealed to be a UIView object.

When I click the entry showing the culprit in Figure 12-11, a Follow link appears in the Address column. Clicking the Follow Link button takes you to an allocation history (a listing of the allocations and deallocations) for memory blocks at that address.

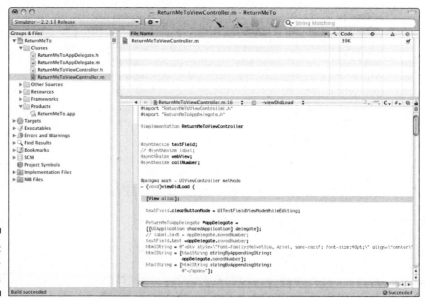

Figure 12-8:
An intentional leak.

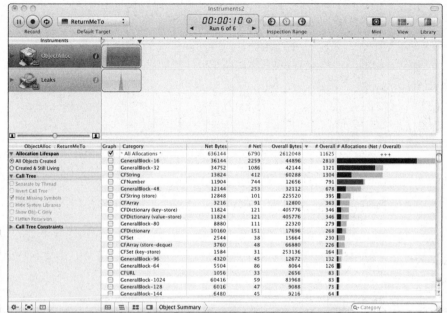

Figure 12-9:
Gotcha, intentional leak.

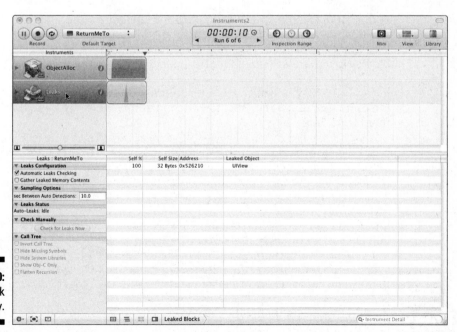

Figure 12-10:
The Leak entry.

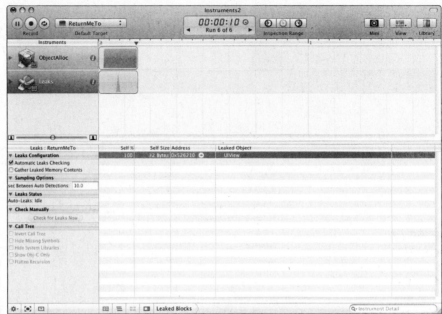

Figure 12-11:
Follow Link.

In this view, I am looking for an allocation (Malloc) without a matching deallocation (Free) for that block. To refresh your memory, you create a memory leak when you allocate (Malloc) memory and don't deallocate (Free) that block when there are no longer any objects referencing it.

In Figure 12-12, you can see that for the first three Malloc's of 32 bytes there is a corresponding Free. But after the fourth Malloc — by ReturnMeTo — there is no Free.

Next I want to look at this in an Extended Detail View. To show the Extended Detail View, click the icon my mouse pointer is pointing to, as shown in Figure 12-12. (I could also get to this view by choosing View ⇨Extended Detail or by pressing ⌘+E, or even by selecting the View Button on the right side of top toolbar.)

When I am in the Extended Detail View, I can see a stack trace (a trace of the objects and methods that got you to where you are now) in the Extended Detail pane on the right, as shown in Figure 12-13. When I select an allocation event in the Detail Pane, the Extended Detail Pane displays the stack trace for that event. This stack is organized starting with the oldest call at the top.

If you right-click in that pane you can see a number of options, including inverting the stack.

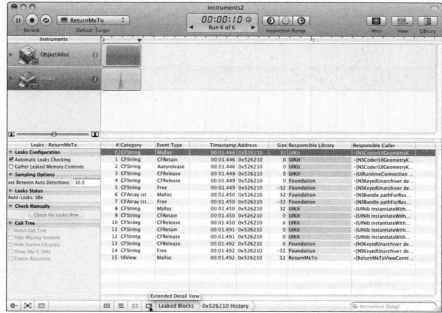

Figure 12-12:
You can
see the
allocations.

Figure 12-13:
Adding an
Expanded
Detail Pane.

In Figure 12-14, I've selected the allocation event in the Detail Pane that allocated the 32 bytes that were leaked — displaying the stack at that point. The last entry in the stack that was one of my own application methods — `ReturnMeToViewController: viewDidLoad` — was where the memory allocation that caused the leak was done. Up to that point, you can see paired Malloc's and Free's, but there was no Free after the last Malloc that occurred in my application.

When I double-click the `ReturnMeToViewController viewDidLoad` stack entry, as you can see in Figure 12-15, I am shown the problem line of code.

Very cool.

Figure 12-14: The last call from my application.

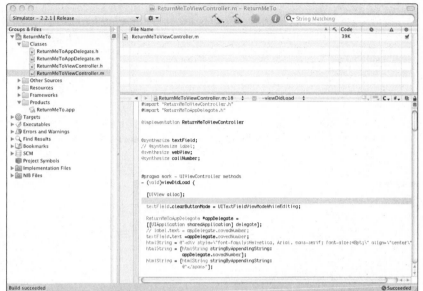

Figure 12-15:
There's the
problem.

Running Instruments on the iPhone

I've said it before and I'll say it again: Running an app on the Simulator is not like running it on the device. So I want to show you what happens when I test the same application when it's running on an iPhone. In Figure 12-16, you can see that I changed the target SDK to the device (in the upper-left corner) and then chose Run⇨Start With Performance Tool⇨Leaks. (You'll notice that when the Instruments application runs your application on the device, there are more tools available to you than when it runs in the Simulator; compare Figure 12-1.)

If you compare the ObjectAlloc track in Figure 12-17 to the one in Figure 12-3 — where I was running the application in the Simulator — you can see it has changed.

More importantly, notice now that there are *two* leaks in the Detail pane!

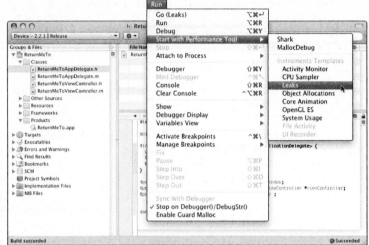

Figure 12-16:
Changing
the target.

Figure 12-17:
Yikes —
two leaks.

I know about the UIView entry — that's the one I just looked at in the previous section. Let's examine the first entry, though: If I click the Follow Link button to display the allocations, and switch to the Extended Detail View, the last call on the stack from my application (as you can see in Figure 12-18) was applicationDidFinishLaunching.

If I double-click the stack entry, you can see in Figure 12-19 that the problem occurs at the end of that method.

Going back to the Extended Detail View in Figure 12-20, you can see the culprit (a.k.a. the Responsible Library) was System Configuration. Examining the stack, you can see that from the sequence of calls there was a UIWebView initialization involved and a ReachabilityRequest.

Because the hardware (and the frameworks) on the Mac and the device are different, the code may execute differently, and not just from a performance standpoint. While it is possible there is a memory leak here, another explanation is *autorelease pool timing*. Objects can be "tagged" as *autorelease*, which means they're sent a periodic release message automatically, usually at the end of the current event loop. If a sample was taken after the object was no longer being used but *before* it was purged, then the object shows up as a memory leak.

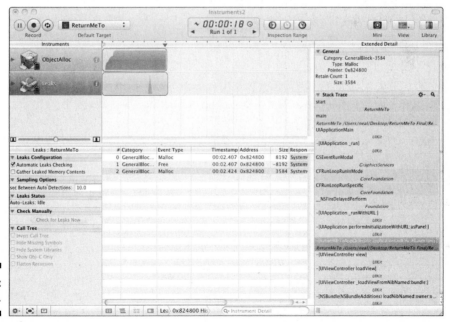

Figure 12-18:
The stack.

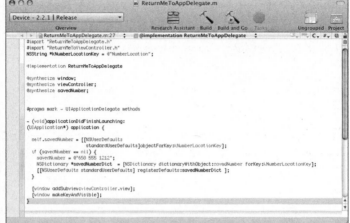

Figure 12-19:
Looks like
addSubview
is implicated
in a memory
leak.

This illustration shows one way that running on the Simulator differs from running the app on an actual device. The simulator is a great place to see how your code is working as you are developing your application, and some design decisions. It does not, however, emulate processor speed or memory allocation — and even network access may be different. There also are some slight but real differences in the frameworks themselves.

Yes, I Am Finally Done

After I take out my intentional memory leak, I am ready to submit ReturnMeTo to the App Store. But before you get carried way with thoughts of fame and fortune, you need to take that not-so-small step of running, testing, and monitoring *your* application's performance on a real iPhone. I'll show you how to do that, as well as guide you through the process of submitting an application to the App Store in Chapter 13.

If you haven't joined the developer program yet, you can skip to Chapter 14, where I start the discussion of the design process for the MobileTravel411 application.

In the ReturnMeTo application, I could have done one more thing to follow my own rules — implement `didReceiveMemoryWarning`. Well, not really. In this application, there would be nothing that I could do if I ran out of memory. I only have a single view, and there is nothing for me to free up. In a more complicated application, however, taking care of this detail would be something I'd have to pay attention to. I talk about that in Chapter 17.

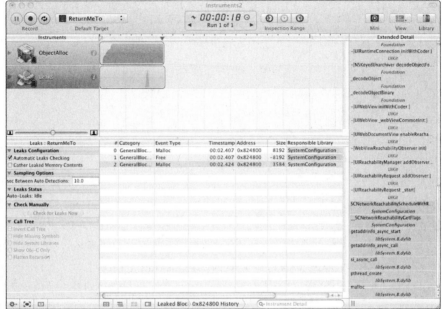

Chapter 13

Death, Taxes, and the iPhone Provisioning

In This Chapter

▶ Running your application on the iPhone

▶ Getting the app ready for distribution

▶ Taking the app to market — that is, the App Store

*B*enjamin Franklin once said, "in this world nothing can be said to be certain, except death and taxes." I've discovered one other certainty in this earthly vale of tears: Everybody has the same hoops to jump through to get an application onto an iPhone and then into the App Store — and nobody much likes them, but there they are.

So you're working on your application, running it in the Simulator, as happy as a virtual clam, and all of a sudden you get this urge to see what your creation will look like on the iPhone itself. Assuming that you have joined the requisite developer program (see Chapter 3), what do you have to do to get it to run on the iPhone?

For most developers, getting their application to run on the iPhone during development can be one of the most frustrating things about developing software for the iPhone. The sticking point has to do with a rather technical concept called *code signing,* a rather complicated process designed to ensure the integrity of the code and positively identify the code's originator. Apple requires all iPhone applications to be digitally signed with a signing certificate — one issued by Apple to a registered iPhone developer — before the application can be run on a development system and before they are submitted to Apple for distribution. As I mention earlier, this signature authenticates the identity of the developer of the application and ensures that there have been no changes to the application after it was signed. As to why this is a big deal, here's the short and sweet (and, to my ears, convincing) answer: Code signing is your way of guaranteeing that no bad guys have done anything to your code that can harm the innocent user.

Now, as I said, nobody really likes the process, but it is doable. In this chapter, I'm going to start by giving you an overview of how it all works by jumping right to that point where you're getting your application ready to be uploaded to the App Store and then distributed to end users. I realize I am starting at the end of the process, which for all practical purposes begins with getting your application to run on a device during development. I am doing the overview in this order because the hoops you have to jump through to get an application to run on a single iPhone during development are a direct consequence of code signing, and of how Apple manages it through the App Store and on the device.

After the overview, which will give you some context for the whole process, I'll revert back to the natural order of things and start with getting your application to run on your iPhone during development.

How the Process Works

Before you can build a version of your application that will actually run on your users' iPhones, Apple insists that you have the following:

✔ **A Distribution Certificate:** An electronic document that associates a *digital identity* (which it creates) with other information that identifies you, including a name, e-mail address, or business that you have provided. The Distribution Certificate is placed on your *keychain* — that place on your Mac that securely stores passwords, keys, certificates, and notes for users.

✔ **A Distribution Provisioning Profile:** These profiles are code elements that Xcode builds into your application, creating a kind of "code fingerprint" that acts as a unique *digital signature*.

After you've built your application for distribution, you then send it to Apple for approval and distribution, Apple verifies the signature to be sure that the code came from a registered developer (you) and has not been corrupted. Apple then adds its own digital signature to your signed application. The iPhone OS will only run applications that have that digital signature. Doing it this way ensures iPhone owners that the applications they download from iTunes have been written by registered developers and have not been altered since they were created.

To install your distribution-ready application on a device, you can also create an *Ad Hoc Provisioning Profile*, which allows you to actually have your application used on up to 100 devices.

The system works pretty well, but leaving aside the fact that Apple essentially has veto rights on every application that comes its way, there are some significant consequences for developers:

✔ You need to be able to test your application on the device it's going to run on — and (as Chapter 12 shows) the Simulator only gets you so far.

✔ You can't run your app on an actual device until it's been code-signed by Apple *but* Apple is hardly going to code-sign something that may not be working correctly.

✔ Even if Apple did sign an app that hadn't yet run on an iPhone, that would mean an additional hassle: Every time you recompiled, you'd have to upload the app to the App Store again — *and* have it code-signed again because you had changed it, *and* then download it to your device.

Bit of a Catch-22 here.

To deal with this problem, Apple has developed a process in which you can create a *Development Certificate* (as opposed to a Distribution Certificate) and a *Development Provisioning Profile* (as opposed to a Distribution Provisioning Profile). With these items in hand, you can run your application on a *specific* device.

The Development Provisioning Profile is a collection of your App ID, Apple device UDID (a unique identifier for each iPhone), and iPhone Development Certificate. This Profile must be installed on each device on which you want to run your application code (you'll see how that is done later). Devices specified within the Development Provisioning Profile can be used for testing only by developers whose iPhone Development Certificates are included in the Provisioning Profile. A single device can also contain multiple provisioning profiles.

Even with your provisioning profile(s) in place when you compile your program, Xcode will only build and sign (create the required signature for) your application if it finds one of those Development Certificates in your Keychain. Then, when you install a signed application on your provisioned device, the iPhone OS verifies the signature to make sure that (a) the application was signed and (b) the application has not been altered since it was signed. If the signature is not valid or if you didn't sign the code, the iPhone OS will not let the application run.

The process you're about to go through is akin to filling out taxes: You have to follow the rules or there can be some dire consequences. But if you do follow the rules, everything works out and you don't have to worry about it again. (Until it's time to upload the next app, of course.)

While this is definitely not my favorite part of iPhone software development, I've made peace with it, and so should you. Now I'll go back to the natural order of things and start by explaining the process of getting your device ready for development. I'm happy to give you an overview of the process, but it will be up to you to go through it step by step on your own. Although Apple documents the steps very well, do keep in mind that you really have to carry them out in exactly the way Apple tells you. There are no shortcuts. But if you do it the way they prescribe, you'll be up and running on a real device very quickly.

With your app up and running, it's time for the next step: getting your creation ready for distribution. (I find that process to be somewhat easier.) Finally, you'll definitely want to find out how to get your application into the App Store. I aim to please, so I spell out those steps as well. After that, all you have to do is sit back and wait for fame and fortune to come your way.

This is the way things looked when I was writing this book. What you see when you go through this process yourself may be slightly different from what you see here. Don't panic. It's because Apple changes things from time to time.

Provisioning Your Device for Development

Until just recently, getting your application to run on the iPhone during development was a really painful process. In fact, I had written a 30-page chapter on it, detailing step after painful step. Then, lo and behold, right when I had put the finishing touches on my *magnum opus*, Apple changed the process and actually made it much easier. In fact, the process is now so easy that there's no real need for me to linger over the details. (Okay, I have some mixed feelings about that — but they're mostly *relief*.)

Here's the drill:

1. **Go to the iPhone Dev Center Web site at**

   `http://developer.apple.com/iphone/`

   The Program Portal Button in the iPhone Developer Program section on the right side of the Web page (shown in Figure 13-1) appears. (Well, it does if you're a registered developer. You did take care of that, right? If not, look back at Chapter 3 for more on how to register.)

2. **Click the Program Portal Button.**

   The Program Portal screen appears, as shown in Figure 13-2.

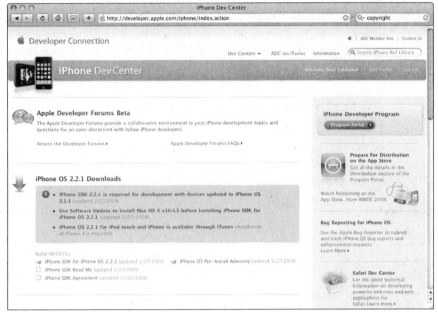

Figure 13-1:
The gateway to the Program Portal

3. **Assuming you're a Team Admin or Team Agent or are enrolled in the Developer Program as an individual, use the Development Provisioning Assistant to create and install a Provisioning Profile and iPhone Development Certificate as shown in the next section.**

   You need these to build and install applications on the iPhone. But you knew that.

You have already identified yourself to Apple as one of two types of developers:

✔ If you are enrolled in the Developer Program as an individual, you are considered a Team Agent with all the rights and responsibilities.

✔ If you're part of a company, you have set up a team already. If not, click the Setting up a Team link on the right side of the iPhone Developer Program Portal page — right there under the Portal Resources heading — to get more info about setting up a team and who needs to do what when.

Development Provisioning Profile and iPhone Development Certificate

When you've settled the matter of which kind of developer you are (for Apple's purposes), click the Launch Assistant button and you should see what I see in Figure 13-3.

Figure 13-2:
Behold
the iPhone
Developer
Program
Portal.

As I mention earlier in the chapter, to run an application you're developing for iPhone, you must have a Provisioning Profile installed on the device on which you're running your app, as well as a Development Certificate on your Mac. The whole point of the Development Provisioning Assistant is to guide you through the steps to create and install your Development Provisioning Profile and iPhone Development Certificate.

Development and Distribution stay off each other's turf. The Development Provisioning Assistant creates a *Development* Provisioning Profile, not *Distribution* Provisioning Profile. You have to use the Provisioning section of the Program Portal to create a Distribution Provisioning Profile required for distribution to customers on the App Store. I'll get to that later in the chapter.

Here's what the Development Provisioning Assistant has you do:

1. **Choose an App ID.**

   An App ID is a unique identifier that is one part of your Development Provisioning Profile.

2. **Choose an Apple Device.**

   Development provisioning is also about the device, so you have to specify which particular device you are going to use. You do that by providing the Assistant with the device's Unique Device Identifier (UDID), which the Assistant shows you how to locate using Xcode.

Figure 13-3:
The Devel-
opment
Provisioning
Assistant.

3. Provide your Development Certificate.

Since all applications must be signed by a valid certificate before they can run an Apple device, you will have to create one at this point. The Development Provisioning Assistant will guide you through that process.

For an Individual developer, the assistant will guide you through the process, step-by-step. For a Company (that is, a team), each developer will first have to create a Certificate Signing Request, which will then have to be approved by your Program Admin or Team Agent. The Development Provisioning Assistant will take you through that as well.

4. Name your Provisioning Profile.

A Provisioning Profile pulls together your App ID (Step 1), Apple device UDID (Step 2), and iPhone Development Certificate (Step 3). The assistant will step you though downloading it and handing it over to Xcode, which will install it on your device.

At that point, you'll be able to choose Device - iPhone OS 2.2.1 (see Figure 13-4) as the active SDK in the project window. You can then build your application and have it installed on the provisioned device. You'll notice that in Figure 13-4 I also have Distribution as one of my active configurations. Not to worry, you'll be there soon.

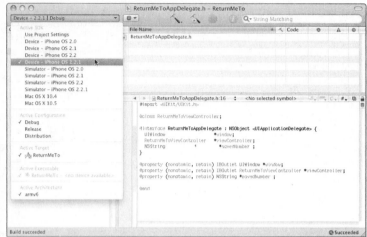

Figure 13-4:
Ready to run
your app on
the iPhone.

Provisioning Your Application for the App Store

Although there's no dedicated Assistant to help you provision your application for the App Store, that process is actually a little easier — which may be why they didn't bother coming up with an Assistant for it. You start at the Developer Portal (refer to Figure 13-2), but this time you select Distribution from the menu on the left side of the page. Doing so takes you to the screen shown in Figure 13-5 — an overview of the process, as well as links that take you where you need to go when you click them.

You actually jump through some of the very same hoops you did when you provisioned your device for development — except this time you're going after a distribution certificate.

Here's the step-by-step account:

1. **Obtain your iPhone Distribution Certificate.**

   In order to distribute your iPhone OS application, a Team Agent has to create an iPhone Distribution Certificate. This works much like the Development Certificate, except only the Team Agent (or whoever is enrolled as an Individual developer) can get one. Clicking the Obtaining Your iPhone Distribution Certificate link (shown in Figure 13-5) leads you through the process.

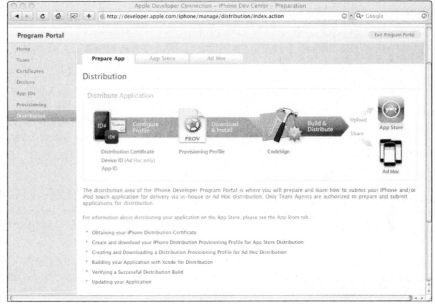

Figure 13-5:
Getting your
app ready
for distribu-
tion: You
are here.

2. Create your iPhone Distribution Provisioning Profile for App Store Distribution.

To build your application successfully with Xcode for distribution via the App Store, first you have to create and download an App Store Distribution Provisioning Profile — which is (lest we forget) *different* from the Development Provisioning Profiles I talk about in the previous section.

Apple will only accept an application when it's built with an App Store Distribution Provisioning Profile.

3. Click the Create and Download Your iPhone Distribution Provisioning Profile for App Store Distribution link.

The link (refer to Figure 13-5) leads you through this process.

4. When you're done creating the Distribution Provisioning Profile, download it and drag it into Xcode in the dock.

That loads your Distribution Profile into Xcode and you're ready to build an app you can distribute for use on actual iPhones.

5. (Optional) You can also create and download a Distribution Provisioning Profile for Ad Hoc Distribution.

Going the Ad Hoc Distribution route enables you to distribute your application to up to 100 users without going through the App Store.

Clicking the Creating and Downloading a Distribution Provisioning Profile for Ad Hoc Distribution link (refer to Figure 13-5 again) leads you through the process. (Ad Hoc Distribution is beyond the scope of this book, but the iPhone Developer Program Portal has more info about this option.)

6. **Build your application with Xcode for distribution.**

   After you download the distribution profile, you can build your application for distribution — rather than just building it for testing purposes, which is what you've been doing so far. It is a well-documented process that you start by clicking the Building Your Application with Xcode for Distribution link (shown in Figure 13-5).

7. **Verify that it worked.**

   Click the Verifying a Successful Distribution Build link (refer to Figure 13-5) to get the verification process started. In this case, I find there are some things missing in the heretofore well explained step-by-step documentation, so I'll help you along.

   If you check the handy documentation that is part of the Verifying a Successful Distribution Build link, it tells you to open the Build Log detail view and confirm the presence of the `embedded.mobileprovision` file. It doesn't tell you how to do that, so I will — choose Build⇨Build Results.

   If you have never opened the Build Log before for this project, you may be surprised to see a blank screen, looking something like Figure 13-6. Don't panic; select the Show/Hide button for the transcript, as I did in Figure 13-6. Clicking that button gets you the entire Build Log.

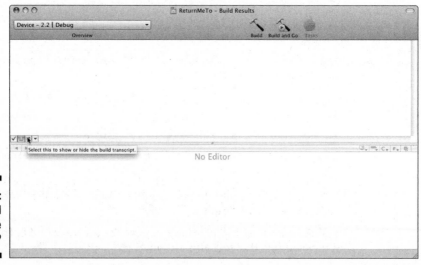

Figure 13-6:
And
where's the
transcript?

As you might imagine, an entire Build Log can mean a lot of material to slough through. To find exactly what you need (`embedded.mobileprovision`, in this case) press ⌘+F or choose Edit⟹Find⟹Single File Find to open the Single File Find dialog, as shown in Figure 13-7. Enter the file you want to search on in the Find field and click Next; you should see something like Figure 13-8.

Figure 13-7:
Finding embedded. mobile provision.

This process takes you to the line in the build log that shows you the provisioning profile was successfully included.

8. At this point, do a couple of prudent checks . . . .

Figure 13-8:
There's that pesky embedded. mobile provision.

- Verify that the `embedded.mobileprovision` is located in the "Distribution" build directory and is *not* located in a "Debug" or "Release" build directory.

- Make sure that the destination path (at the very end of the build message) is the app you are building.

When you've done this elaborate (but necessary) song and dance, you can go to iTunes Connect — your entry way to the App store. This is where the *real* fun starts.

iTunes Connect

iTunes Connect is a group of Web-based tools that enable developers to submit and manage their applications for sale via the App Store. It's actually the very same set of tools that the other content providers — the music and video types — use to get their content into iTunes. In iTunes Connect, you can check on your contracts, manage users, and submit your application with all its supporting documentation — the *metadata*, as Apple calls it — to the App Store. This is also where you get financial reports and daily/weekly sales trend data (yea!).

Your first stopping point is the App Store, Logo Licensing, and Affiliate Program page (shown in Figure 13-9). Here's how you get there:

✔ Select the App Store tab in the Distribution section of the Developer Portal.

(Select Learn More right under the App Store heading if you don't see what I have in Figure 13-9.)

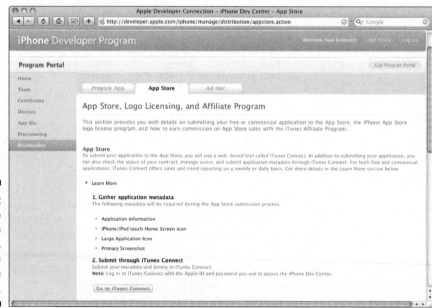

Figure 13-9:
The App Store, Logo Licensing, and Affiliate Program page.

At this point, get your bearings and proceed:

✔ A Team Agent or Individual developer will see the Go to iTunes Connect button. Click this button to call up the login page of iTunes Connect.

✔ You need to use the same AppleID and password you use to log in to the iPhone Developer Program Portal.

✔ Before you can do anything, you're asked to review and accept the iTunes Distribution Terms & Conditions. After taking care of that chore, you land on the iTunes Connect page shown in Figure 13-10.

At some point, you should also select To Become an Authorized Licensee, which is a little further down the App Store, Logo Licensing, and Affiliate Program page you see back in Figure 13-9. This will allow you to use the iPhone App Store artwork and iPhone images in your advertising, Web sites, and other marketing materials.

When you want to add an application to the App Store, or manage what you already have there, the iTunes Connect main page is your control panel for getting that done.

What you'll need to get your application into the App Store

Actually, the Uploading Your Application to the App Store part is pretty easy. The hard part is collecting all the little bits of information you'll need to enter into all the text fields in the upload page. Here's an overview of the kind of information you'll need:

✔ **Metadata:** The ever-present data about data. Here's what Apple wants from you:

- *Application Name*: It must conform to guidelines for using Apple trademarks and copyrights. They take this very seriously, as evidenced by Apple sending a cease-and-desist order to my ISP when I tried (innocently) to use iPhoneDev411 as my domain name. (A word to the wise: Don't mess with Apple.)

- *Application Description*: When you go through the process of uploading your data, the field you have to paste this into will say you're limited to 700 characters. In fact, the documentation says that 4000 is permitted, but they suggest no more that 700.

  This is what users will see when they click on your app in the App Store, so it's important that this description be well written and point out all your app's key features.

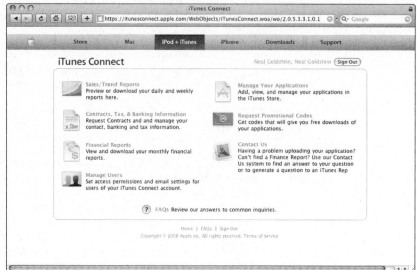

Figure 13-10:
The iTunes
Connect
main page.

Don't include HTML tags; they will be stripped out when the data is uploaded. Only line breaks are respected.

- *Device*: Basically, we're talking iPhone and/or iPod touch.

- *Primary Category*: There will be a drop-down menu from which to choose the primary category for your app. There are about 20 choices, ranging from Business to Games to Social Networking to Travel to Utility.

- *Secondary Category*: (Optional) Same categories as above.

If you've selected Games as the primary or secondary category for your application, you'll be asked to provide additional information describing the content. You'll see things like Cartoon or Fantasy Violence, Simulated Gambling, Mature/Suggestive Themes and so on. For each type of content, you'll need to describe the level of frequency for that content — None, Infrequent/Mild, Frequent/Intense. Apple has strict rules stating that content and games (or any other app) must not contain any obscene, pornographic, or offensive content. Oh and by the way, it is entirely up to them what is to be considered offensive or inappropriate.

- *Copyright*: I use this line:

© Copyright Neal Goldstein 2009. All rights reserved.

You can get the copyright symbol, in Word at least, by choosing Insert⇨Symbol. If you have any questions about copyright registration, talk to your lawyer or check out www.copyright.gov.

- *Version Number*: People usually start with 1.0. Then, as you get more and more suggestions and "constructive criticism" you can move on to 1.1, and some day even version 2.0.

- *SKU Number*: A Stock Keeping Unit (SKU), any alphanumeric sequence of letters and numbers that is used to uniquely identify your application in the system. (If you don't really care, put in A1 or something fairly obvious like that.)

- *Support URL for the Company*: You need a support URL, which basically means you need a Web site. That's not that hard. If you don't have a Web site yet and don't know how to build one, just go to your friendly ISP, find a domain name, get a package designed for folks who don't know HTML, and build yourself a Web site. Later on, you can get a hold of David Crowder's *Building a Web Site For Dummies*, 3rd Edition, which can help you build a "more professional" site. There will be a link to your support URL on the application product page at the App store and this is the link users will click on if they need technical support from you or have a question about your app.

- *Support E-mail Address*: (for use by Apple only). Likely this address will be the one you used when you registered for the developer program.

- *End User License Agreement*: (Optional). If you don't know what this is, don't worry. It is the legal document that spells out to the end users what they're agreeing to do in order to use your app. Fortunately, the iTunes Store has a standard one. By this time, I think they probably know what they're doing — but you should read it anyway before you use it.

- *Territories application to be distributed in*: You can choose these when you get to the upload.

- *Application Availability Date:* When it will be available for purchase.

- *Application Price*: Free is easier, but later on I show you what you have to do if you want to get *paid* (what a concept) for all the work you did getting your application to the public.

- *Localization desired*: Additional languages (besides English) for your metadata. You can have your text and images in Italian in all Italian speaking stores, for example.

✔ **Artwork:** A picture is worth a thousand words, so the App store gives you the opportunity to dazzle your app's potential users with some nice imagery:

- *iPhone/iPod touch Home Screen Icon*: Your built application must have a 57×57 pixels icon included for it, following the procedure I showed you back in Chapter 7. This icon is what will be displayed on the iPod touch or iPhone home screen.

- *Large Application Icon:* This icon will be used to display your application on the App Storefront. It needs to meet the following requirements:

    512×512 pixels (flattened, square image)

    72 DPI

    .jpg, .jpeg, or .tiff format

- *Primary Screenshot:* This shot will be used on your *application product page* in the App Store.

    Apple doesn't want you to include the iPhone status bar in your screenshot. The shot itself needs to meet these requirements:

    320×460 portrait (without status bar) minimum

    480×300 landscape (without status bar) minimum

    320×480 portrait (full screen)

    Up to four additional optional screenshots can be on the application product page. These may be resized to fit the space provided. Follow the same requirements as above.

- **Additional Artwork: (not required):** If you are really lucky — I mean *really* lucky (or that good) — you might get to be featured on the App Store. They will want "high-quality layered artwork with a title treatment for your application," which will then be used in small posters to feature your application on the App Store.

We're not done yet

If you're going to charge for your application, you have to provide even more information. Most of it is pretty straightforward, except for some of the banking information, which you do need to have available, *and which you can't change afterward* (although you can create a new contract, it seems). Here's what I'm talking about:

- ✔ **Bank name**
- ✔ **Bank address**
- ✔ **Account number**
- ✔ **Branch/Branch ID**

- ✔ **ABA/Routing Transit Number:** Generally, this is the first nine digits of that that long number at the bottom of your checks that also contains the account number. If you aren't sure what the routing number is, contact your bank.
- ✔ **Your Bank Swift Code:** You will have to get that from your bank.

Take it from me, it's far easier if you have all bits and pieces together *before you start the actual upload process*, rather than having to scramble at 3:00 in the morning to find some obscure piece of information they want. (The Bank Swift Code was the one that got me.)

Uploading your information

At this point, you can start the application-upload process by clicking the Manage Your Applications link on the iTunes Connect main page. (Refer to Figure 13-9.) But hold it. Better to look before leaping: Check out the requisite Contracts, Tax & Banking Information.

Here's why: If you plan on selling your application, you'll need to have your paid commercial agreement in place and signed before your application can be posted to the App Store.

If your application is free, you've already entered into the freeware distribution agreement by being accepted into the iPhone Developer Program. I am not going to charge for the ReturnMeTo application, but just like with anything else at Apple, contract approval can take a while, so you should probably fill out the contract information just to get it out of the way. That's my style, and if it's not yours, feel free to skip to the next section.

Start by clicking the Contracts, Tax & Banking Information link on the iTunes Connect main page. The Manage your Contracts page appears, as shown in Figure 13-11. You use this page to create a contract for your paid application.

You can also see that you already have, by default, a contract in effect for free applications. To create a new contract, select the box under Request Contract in the Request New Contracts section, and you're taken though a series of pages that ask you to provide the information Apple needs, including the bank information I called your attention to earlier.

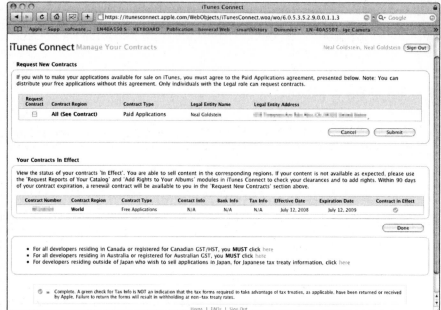

Figure 13-11:
Create a
contract
for a paid
application.

Upload your application and its data

After you've set the wheels in motion, you can then go back to the iTunes
Connect main page and upload your data. Click the Manage Your Applications
link (refer to Figure 3-10) to call up the Manage Your Applications page shown in
Figure 13-12. In that page, click the Add New Application button and go to town.
Fill in all the blanks, using all that info I ask you to collect in the "What you'll
need to get your application into the App Store" section, earlier in the chapter.
Along the way, you'll upload your metadata and the application itself to Apple.

Figure 13-12:
Add your
application.

When it comes time to enter your Application Description, you can safely paste in more than the 700 character limit. In fact, you can enter up to 4000 characters.

Now What?

You get to find out when I do. I did everything I just described in this chapter for the ReturnMeTo application — and I now wait with bated breath for Apple's response.

It can take days, weeks, or even months, and Apple may reject it or require more information, or ask me to make changes. You hear lots of stories (good and bad) from developers out there.

Update 1: About a week later

> Dear Neal,
>
> Thank you for submitting Return Me To to the App Store. We've reviewed Return Me To and determined that we cannot post this version of your iPhone application to the App Store because of an Apple trademark image. The application features the Apple iPhone in the icon. We want to remind you of the importance of following Apple's posted Guidelines for Using Apple's Trademarks and Copyrights: <http://www.apple.com/legal/trademark/guidelinesfor3rdparties.html.

So I changed the icon, but I left the iPhone image in the app — you know, the button to enable the text. It was a picture of *my* iPhone after all. Well, it might not surprise you to see what happened next.

Update 2: About a week later

> Dear Neal,
>
> Thank you for submitting Return Me To to the App Store. We've reviewed Return Me To and determined that we cannot post this version of your iPhone application to the App Store because of an Apple trademark image of the iPhone. We want to remind you of the importance of following Apple's posted Guidelines for Using Apple's Trademarks and Copyrights: <http://www.apple.com/legal/trademark/guidelinesfor3rdparties.html.

I've resubmitted it with a new image, so stay tuned. I'll keep you updated on my Web site, www.nealgoldstein.com.

Part IV

An Industrial-Strength Application

The 5th Wave   By Rich Tennant

"He seemed nice, but I could never connect with someone who had a ring tone like his."

In this part . . .

After the realization dawns that you have to sell a lot of 99-cent applications to afford a meal in London, you can start thinking about raising the bar. Maybe what you need to do is develop an industrial-strength application that you can charge real money for — something so good that people will actually pay the big bucks for it. In this part, I explain the design of an application that has big muscles: a context-driven user interface, lots of functionality, Web access, and an application architecture that you can use to build your own version of The Next Great Thing.

Chapter 14

Designing Your Application

ReturnMeTo, the star of Part III, is a useful little application and a great way to learn about iPhone software development. Apple considers it a utility application — like the Weather application, but with a single view.

Utility applications can provide real value to the user and are also fun and easy to write — not a bad combination. The good news is that by now, if you have been following along with me in the book, you understand enough about the framework, its architecture, components, and control flow to figure out how to build a nice little utility application on your own.

Not that you're all set right now to do everything you'd like — far from it. The way the Weather application flips the view, for example, may seem a total mystery. But Apple goes out of its way to provide samples for many of the neater tricks and features out there, all in hopes of demystifying how they work. In Chapter 18, I'll give you an annotated tour of the samples. With the ReturnMeTo application under your belt, it'll be a lot easier to understand and use all the resources Apple provides to help you develop iPhone applications.

What Apple doesn't show you (and where there's a real opportunity to develop a killer app) is how to design and develop more complex applications. Now, "more complex" doesn't necessarily — and shouldn't — mean "more complex *to the user*." The real challenge and opportunity is in creating complex applications that are as easy to use as simple ones.

In this chapter, I take you through an overview of the design cycle of a more complex application (MobileTravel411) and the resulting user interface and program architecture. While there are at least a half a dozen models for the process (I'm a recovering software development methodologist myself) the one I'll go through here is pretty simple and is well suited for the iPhone to boot. Here goes:

1. Defining the problems

2. Designing the user experience

    a. Defining the constraints

    b. Categorizing the problems and defining the solutions

3. Creating the program architecture

    a. A main view

    b. Content views

    c. View controllers

    d. Models

4. Writing the code

5. Doing it until you get it right

After taking you through all that, I show you how to develop a subset (iPhoneTravel411) of the application.

Of course, the actual analysis, design, and programming (not to mention testing) process has a bit more to it than this — and the specification and design definitely involves more than what you see in these few pages. But from a process perspective, it's pretty close to the real thing. It does give you an idea of the questions you need to ask — and have answered — to develop an iPhone application.

A word of caution, though. Even though iPhone apps are smaller and much easier to get your head around than, say, a full-blown enterprise service oriented architecture, they come equipped with a unique set of challenges. Between the iPhone platform limitations I talk about in Chapter 1 and the high expectation of iPhone users, you will have your hands full.

Defining the Problems

Innovation is usually born of frustration, and the MobileTravel411 project was no exception. It just turns out that my frustration was linked to a trip to beautiful Venice rather than, say, the vacuum cleaner doing a terrible job of picking up cat hair.

My wife and I were going to arrive late at night, and rather than trying to get into Venice at that hour, we decided we'd stay at a hotel near the airport and then go into Venice the next day. We were going to meet some friends who were leaving the day after that. That meant we wanted to get a relatively early start so we could spend the day with them.

I was a little concerned about the logistics. I thought we would have to go back to the airport terminal and then get on a water bus or water taxi. Both the water taxi stand and the water bus stop are a distance from the terminal, and that meant more time and more trudging about. The water taxi was the fastest way, but very pricey (around $140 USD at the time). The water bus was much cheaper but more confusing — and only ran once an hour. It seemed like a major excursion.

My friends said, "Why not take a taxi or a bus?"

I said, "A bus to Venice — it's an island, for crying out loud."

Okay, it *is* an island, but there's a causeway running from the mainland to Piazzale Roma, where you can then get a water bus or water taxi — or meet your friends.

Although it is more romantic to arrive by sea, it's a lot easier by land. Having been to Venice a couple times before, and considering our time constraints, we opted for the land route.

Now, I'm sure that information was in a guidebook someplace, but it would have taken a lot of work to dig it out; most guidebooks focus on attractions. Also, guidebooks go out of date quickly; the one I had for Venice was already two years old. Of course, I could have used the Internet before I left home to find the information, but that can also be a real chore.

What I wanted was something that made it easier to travel — reducing all those hassles — getting to and from a strange airport, getting around the city, getting the best exchange rate, knowing how much should I tip in a restaurant — that sort of thing. (Not too much to ask, right?)

Don't get me wrong — I actually do a lot of research before I go someplace, and often I have that information handy already. But I end up with lots of paper because I usually don't take a laptop with me on vacation; even when I do, it's terribly inconvenient to have to take it out on a bus or in an airline terminal to find some information. And then there's the challenge of finding a Wi-Fi connection when you really need it.

The iPhone is the perfect device to solve all those problems, so I decided to develop an iPhone application. It became MobileTravel411.

Designing the User Experience

To meet my Venetian (and other travel) needs, I didn't need a lot of information at any one time. In fact, what I wanted was as little as possible — just the facts ma'am — but I wanted it to be as current as possible. It doesn't help to have last year's train schedule.

To get the design ball of my application rolling, I started with a list of constraints. Okay, some people may consider these as requirements — that's up to them. But what I like to do is take the device's limitations — along with a small, non-negotiable set of requirements — as the frame within which I operate. The rest of the requirements may be traded off, but the non-negotiable set I come up with here is inviolate.

Defining the constraints

For those of you out there who love lists, here's one I came up with for my MobileTravle411 application:

- ✔ **Limited screen real estate:** Although scrolling is built into an iPhone and is relatively easy to do, I still believe that you should require as little scrolling as possible. Okay, there may be times when scrolling is unavoidable, but keep those times to a minimum. One thing I was certain of: I didn't want to have to scroll the *main view* of the application, the one you see the first time you use it.

- ✔ **Keeping things quick:** As a corollary to the first constraint, I wanted to be able to get to the information I needed quickly, without having to drill down, around, and through a hierarchy.

- ✔ **Keeping things accurate:** I wanted all the information to be right, and by that I meant *up to date*. Although some of the information rarely changes — the Brits are still partial to their pound sterling as the world's oldest currency — most of it can change at any time. This meant I had to have real-time access to the latest info.

- ✔ **Keeping things cheap:** For a user with a U.S. cell-phone account (like me), international roaming charges can be expensive; at the time of this writing, they still are. So I wanted to allow the user to minimize real-time access to data on the Internet — which conflicts with my Keeping Things Accurate goal, doesn't it? Welcome to the real world.

- ✔ **Keeping things localized:** With the world growing even flatter (from a communications perspective, anyway) and the iPhone available in more than 80 counties, the potential market for the app was considerably larger than just the folks who happen to speak English. So the application had to be *localized* — meaning it needed to have all of it information, content and even the text used in dialogs in the user's language of choice. I want anybody to be able to use it to go almost anyplace — especially visitors to the U.S. who might not speak English. If you plan to release applications through the iPhone App Store, your market is greatly expanded when your application can be localized.

Some of these goals overlap, of course, and that's where the real challenges are.

Categorizing the problems and defining the solutions

Because the app's requirements — and common sense — precluded scrolling through lots of information to get to what I needed, I had to create a *hierarchy* — a way of ordering the information or functionality into groups that make sense to the user. On desktop or laptop machines, features are often categorized by function, but given the way the iPhone is used (as I describe in Chapter 1), categorizing by *context* makes more sense. (If you're interested in the function vs. context discussion, check out my Web site at www.nealgoldstein.com for more information.). So once I settled on the information and functionality I needed when I was traveling, I grouped things into the following contexts.

✔ **Getting and using money:** What is the country's currency (including denominations and coins) and what's the best way to exchange my currency for it? I want to understand the costs of using credit cards versus an ATM card, or exchanging at a *bureau de change*. I also wanted to be able to understand how the dreaded VAT (*v*alue-*a*dded *t*ax) really worked.

✔ **Getting to and from the airport:** What choices do I really have when it comes to things terminal? What are the costs, advantages, and disadvantages — and logistics — of each? Do I have to buy a ticket in advance? How do I find said ticket? What is the schedule?

✔ **Getting around the city.** Same kind of pickle as getting to and from the airport — what's available *and* best for a traveler's purposes? I once spent several days in Barcelona before I realized there was a subway system.

✔ **Seeing what's happening right now in the city:** Guidebooks are fine for visiting the sights, and I had no need to recreate one on the iPhone. But I *would* like to know if there is anything special happening when I am in some particular place at some particular time. Bastille Day in Paris can be fun if you know about the Bastille Day parade, and less of a hassle if you know you can't cross the Champs-Élysées for a few hours.

✔ **Knowing the practical day-to-day stuff:** How do you make calls into, out of, and within a given city? How much and when should I tip? What is acceptable and unacceptable behavior? For example, that it might be impolite to eat or drink something while walking down the street in Japan might not occur to someone from New York City.

✔ **Staying safe:** Being immediately informed of breaking news that could make things unsafe — large demonstrations or terrorist attacks for example — would be high on my wish list. But even the more mundane things like the "dangerous" neighborhoods are important. What should you do in an emergency? A friend of ours had her passport stolen in Prague — at times like that, it would be nice to have the locations and phone numbers of embassies or consulates. This is stuff you hardly ever need, but when you need it, you need it right away.

✔ **What to do before I go:** In the past, I have forgotten to call my cell-phone company before I leave home to get a roaming package and notify my credit-card company that I'll be out of the country or far from home, so please, *please* don't decline my hotel charge in Vladivostok. I also want to be able to download all the information before I leave so I can look at it on the plane, or as part of my strategy for avoiding roaming changes or handling an unexpected lack of connections.

I also wanted to make the app easy to use for someone who was not intimately involved with the design — and perhaps did not immediately share my take on the best way to organize the information. So, for each choice in the main window, I wanted to be able to add a few words of explanation about what each category contained.

The final user interface I came up with looks like the left side of Figure 14-1. On the right side of Figure 14-1 is the iPhoneTravell411 version — a subset of the MobileTravel411 application. Although it's a subset, there is enough there for me to introduce you to almost all the technology I used to create the real application.

The rest of the views follow the same general format — some general information with specific information about each category.

Part of making the app easy to use involves giving users a way to set their preferences for how the app should work. On the left side of Figure 14-6 you can see the MobileTravel411 Settings view, on the right the iPhoneTravel411 subset. The most important of these settings involves being able to work in a *stored data mode* — using previously stored data, rather than the current real-time version that would require Internet access. The idea is to download the information I need before I leave — and then only update it occasionally while I'm gone, so I can avoid data roaming charges and afford food other than ramen noodles on my trip.

In Figures 14-2 through 14-5, you can see some of the application's content.

Figure 14-3:
Currency
selector.

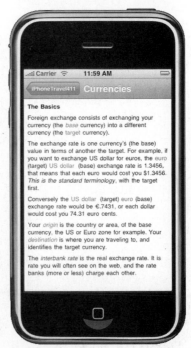

Figure 14-4:
Displaying
value in
dollars and
exchange-
rate
information.

Figure 14-5:
Weather
views.

Figure 14-6:
Use offline
data.

Creating the Program Architecture

Given the user interface I just described, how did I get from there to here?

Keeping things at a basic level — a level that will be familiar to those of you who worked through the ReturnMeTo application — the MobelTravel411 is made up of the following:

- **Models:** Model objects encapsulate the logic and (data) content of the application. There was no model object in ReturnMeTo per se (although I opine on model functionally in Chapter 8). For iPhoneTravel411, I show you how to design, implement, and use model objects.

- **Views:** Views present the user experience; you have to decide what information to display and how to display it. In the ReturnMeTo application there was a single content view with controls as subviews. Now, with the iPhoneTravel411 app, there will be a main view and several content views.

- **Controllers:** Controllers manage the user experience. They connect the views that present the user experience with the models that provide the necessary content. In addition (as you'll see), controllers also manage the way the user navigates the application.

No big surprises here — especially because the MVC model (Model-View-Controller) is pretty much the basis for all iPhone application development projects. The trick here is coming up with just the right views, controllers, and model objects to get your project off the ground. Within the requirements I spelled out in the "Designing the User Experience" section earlier in the chapter, I came up with the elements highlighted in the next few sections.

I'm going to start with the views, since they determine the functionality and information available in a given context — being at an airport and needing to get into the city for example.

A main view

This one was a no-brainer. The main view for MobileTravel411 (and for iPhoneTravel411) is a `UITableView`, no question about it. Table views are used a lot in iPhone applications to do two things:

- **Display hierarchal data:** Think of the iPod application, which gives you a list of albums, and if you select one, a list of songs.

- **Act as a table of contents (or for my purposes, contexts).** Now think of the Settings application, which gives you a list of applications that you can set preferences for. When you select one of those applications from the list, it takes you to a view that lists what preferences you are able to set, and a way to set them.

Content views

Content views are views that display the information the user wants — stuff like how many Zimbabwean dollars I can get for $2.75 or the weather in Aruba next week.

The views you create are based on the information and functionality that a user needs in that context. At the risk of oversimplification, there are two types of views I had to think about:

- **The How Many Zimbabwean Dollars Can I Get For $2.75 (US) View.** These kinds of views are characterized by the fact that user input is required to be able to deliver the goods. The user would have to enter $2.75 US and then request to see the equivalent amount in Zimbabwean Dollars. (According to MobileTravel411, the answer by the way, at the end of February 2009, is a little over 103 million).

  Examples of this kind of view in the MobileTravel411 application are shown in Figure 14-3, Figure 14-4 (left), and Figure 14-5 (right). These are all `UIView`'s with controls, constructed the same way as you constructed the view in the ReturnMeTo app. You won't be creating any of them in the next few chapters, but once you create the application structure, they are easy to add on your own.

- **The Weather In Aruba Next Week View.** This view, and others like it, simply displays information that it gets for the view controller. These are views like Figure 14-2, 14-4 (right) and 14-5 (left).

These second types of view (and all the views in the iPhoneTravel411 application) are *Web views* for some good practical reasons. First and foremost, some of the views must be updated regularly. If I want the current price and schedule of the Heathrow Express, for example, data from last year (or even last week) may not help me. I also want the most current information about what's happening in the city I plan to visit.

Web views, in that context, are the perfect solution; they make it easy to access data from a central repository on the Internet. (Client-server is alive and well!)

As for other benefits of Web views, keep in mind that real-time access is not always necessary — sometimes it's perfectly fine to store some data on the iPhone. It turns out that Web views can easily display formatted data that's locally stored — very handy. (We took advantage of that fact when building the ReturnMeTo application.)

Finally, I use Web views because they can access Web sites. If users want more information on the Heathrow Express, they can get to the Heathrow Express Web site by simply touching a link.

View controllers

View controllers are responsible for not only providing the data for a view to display, but also responding to user input and navigation as well.

For each How Many Zimbabwean Dollars Can I Get For $2.75 (US) View, like the ones in Figure 14-3, on the left of 14-4, and on the right in Figure 14-5, I created a custom subclass of UIViewController to connect a control selected in the view (a button tapped, for example) with the model that has the logic and data to respond to the tap.

But for the views like those Figure 14-2, the one on the right in Figure 14-4 and even the one on the left in Figure 14-5, I actually designed a single subclass of UIViewController that connects the view to a model and can navigate from view to view for any context. That allowed me to use the same view controller to send to its Web view different content, from Getting To And From The Airport Data to Getting Around The City Data to Practical Day-To-Day Stuff Data. I did this by designing a view controller that can be initialized with the context information it needs when it is created (its model, the number of tabs, other things). While (fortunately for you) I won't be getting into the details of this, I will explain its architecture in enough detail in Chapter 17 to give you a good start on implementing it on your own.

Models

While you could write a book on model design (in fact, I've written a couple, not to mention an Apple video — but that's another story), I want to concentrate on a couple things now to keep you focused. I'll elaborate more in Chapter 17.

When you begin to think about the models that you need for the application, you may think you've opened up a very large can of worms.

If you want to cover 160 cities or so — not unreasonable if you want your app to appeal to a broad, international audience — are you going to need a separate model object to deal with every city, airport, airport transportation option (trains, busses taxis etc) city transportation option (busses cars, subways, trains), how to tip in every country, the way to make a phone call into out of and within every city, and so on? If so, you would end up with thousands of classes (models, nib files and so on). Definitely an unmanageable (not to mention resource-intensive) situation, and because there would also be a lot of redundancy in the code, maintenance would be a nightmare.

Fortunately, with some careful thought, you will come to the same conclusion I did: No, not today, not tomorrow, not on your life.

No use re-inventing the wheel

To show you the proper (and far less work-intensive) way to think about it, I want to review what the model objects need to do.

- ✔ **The models own the data and the application logic.** In the MobileTravel411 application, for example, one model converts U.S. dollars to pounds (or any other currency) and vice versa.

- ✔ **The design of model objects is closely tied to the functionality of the view it is connected to.** The How Many Zimbabwean Dollars Can I Get For $2.75 (US) View requires a model that can compute exchange rates, and here is where the real world objects associated with object oriented programming come into play. In the MobileTrave411 app, I have a Currency (model) object that knows how to compute exchange rates, and a VAT (Value Added Tax) object that does something similar. So for each view like those two, I created a separate model.

When it comes to the Weather In Aruba Next Week View, though, the same approach doesn't hold. You don't need a weather object here. The model object doesn't have to really care about the weather; all it really needs to do is have the logic to go out and get the data from a file, database, or server. For my purposes, a model object that gets weather information and a model object that gets information on the Heathrow schedule are pretty much the same (although there are some differences that need to be incorporated in the object functionality). The logic for this object revolves around how to access the data, how to deal with the data itself and how this data may be connected to other data — the logic isn't about the *content* of the data. This means that, like the single view controller I mention above, I only need a single model object to support views like those Figure 14-2, the one on the right in Figure 14-4 and even the one on the left in Figure 14-5.

So my path is clear: I'll design this model object in the same way I designed the view controller it is paired with — essentially creating a structure that can be filled with new content whenever necessary. (Programmers call such model objects parameterized models.) All you need to do is initialize the model with the context information it needs when the model is created.

Putting property lists to good use

All the model objects are of a subclass NSObject, because NSObject provides the basic interface to the runtime system. It already has methods for allocation, initialization, memory management, introspection (what class am I?), encoding and decoding (which makes it quite easy to save objects as objects), message dispatch, and a host of other equally obscure methods that I won't get into but are required for objects to be able to behave like they're expected to in an iPhone OS/Objective-C world.

To implement parameterized models and view controllers, you need something to provide the parameters. I used *property lists* — XML files, in other words — to take care of that because they're well suited for the job task and (more importantly) support for them is built into the iPhone frameworks.

Setting up property lists is a bit beyond the scope of this book, but in Chapter 17 I show you how to structure your application so you can implement property lists on your own.

Just as with the single view controller class, I won't be getting into the details of the single model class, but I will explain its architecture in enough detail in Chapter 17 to give you a good start on implementing it on your own.

In the iPhoneTravel411 application, I'll actually create three models and three view controllers to illustrate what you need to know about the model, view and controller relationship, how to access and display data stored locally or on a server, as well as how to simply display a Web site. That will be enough to keep you busy for a while.

Stored data mode, saving state, and localization

Using the application design I've described, adding these particular features is easy; I explain them as I work through the implementation in Chapters 15 and 16. Although I don't dig too deeply into localization in this book, I show you how to build your application to make that handy feature as easy as possible to include in your app.

The Iterative Nature of the Process

If there's one thing I can guarantee about development, it's that *nobody gets it right the first time*. Although object-oriented design and development is in itself a fun intellectual exercise (at least for some of us), it also is very valuable. It makes it possible to modify and extend the program with relative ease, not just during initial development, but also over time from version to version. (Actually, "initial development" and "version updating" are both the same; they differ only by their periods of rest and vacation.)

The design of my MobileTravel411 application evolved over time, as I learned the capabilities and intricacies of the platform and the impact of my design decisions. What I've tried to do in this chapter, and the ones following, is to help you avoid (at least most of) the blind alleys I stumbled down while developing my first application. So get ready for a stumble-free experience. On to Chapters 15, 16, and 17.

Chapter 15

Setting the Table

*V*iews are the user's window into your application; they present the user experience on a silver platter, as it were. Their associated view controllers manage the user experience by providing the data displayed in the view, as well as by enabling user interaction.

In this chapter, you get a closer look at the iPhoneTravel411 *main view* — the view you see when you launch the application — as well as the view controller that enables it. As part of your tour of the main view, I show you how to use one of the most powerful features of the framework — table views. In the chapters that follow, I show you how to implement the views that you set up to deliver the content of your application — how to get from Point A to Point B, convert yen to yaun, or check on the weather in Anaheim, Azusa, or Cucamonga.

My running example here will be the iPhoneTravel411 application described in Chapter 14. Space prohibits dotting every *i* and crossing every *t* in implementing the application, but I can show you how to use the technology you need to do the detailed work on your own. And while I also won't have the complete listing in this book, I'll make a copy available on my Web site.

Working with Table Views

Table views are front and center in several applications that come with the iPhone out of the box; they play a major role in many of the more complex applications you can download from the App Store. (Obvious examples: Almost all the views in the Mail, iPod, and Contacts applications are table views). Table views not only display data, but also serve as a way to navigate a hierarchy.

If you take a look at an application such as Mail or iPod, you'll find that table views present a scrollable list of *items* (or *rows* or *entries* — I use all three terms interchangeably) that may be divided into *sections*. A row can display text or images. So, when you select a row, you may be presented with another table — or with some other view that may display a Web page or even some controls such as buttons and text fields. You can see an illustration of this diversity in Figure 15-1: selecting Heathrow on the left leads to a content view devoted to Heathrow information.

Figure 15-1:
A table and
Web view.

But while a table view is an instance of the class `UITableView`, each visible row of the table uses an `UITableViewCell` to draw its contents. Think of a *table view* as the object that creates and manages the table structure, and the *table view cell* as being responsible for displaying the content of a single row of the table.

Creating the table view

Although powerful, table views are surprisingly easy to work with. To create a table, you need only to do four — count 'em, four — things, in the following order:

1. **Create and format the view itself.**

   This includes specifying the table style and a few other parameters — most of which is done in Interface Builder.

2. **Specify the table view configuration.**

   Not too complicated, actually: You let `UITableView` know how many sections you want, how many rows you want in each section, and what you want to call your section headers. You do that what the help of the `numberOfSectionsInTableView:` method, the `tableView:number OfRowsInSection:` method, and the `tableView:titleForHeader InSection:` method, respectively.

3. **Supply the text (or graphic) for each row**.

   You return that from the implementation of the `tableView:cellFor RowAtIndexPath:` method. This message is sent for each visible row in the table view and you return a table view cell to display the text or graphic.

4. **Respond to a user selection of the row.**

   You use the `tableView:didSelectRowAtIndexPath:` method to take care of this task. In this method, you create a view controller and a new view. For example, when the user selects Heathrow in Figure 15-1, this method is called, and then an Airport controller and an Airport view are created and displayed.

A `UITableView` object must have a *data source* and a *delegate*. The data source supplies the content for the table view and the delegate manages the appearance and behavior of the table view. The data source adopts the `UITableViewDataSource` protocol and the delegate adopts the `UITableViewDelegate` protocol — no surprises there. Of the above methods, only the `tableView:didSelectRowAtIndexPath:` is included in the `UITableViewDelegate` protocol. All the others I listed earlier are included in the `UITableViewDelegate` protocol.

The data source and the delegate are often (but not necessarily) implemented in the same object — which is often a subclass of `UITableViewController`. I plan to use the `RootViewController` for my iPhone411Travel app.

Implementing these five (count 'em, five) methods — and taking Interface Builder for a spin or two, along with the same kind of initialization methods and the standard memory-management methods you used in the ReturnMeTo application, creates the table view that can respond to a selection made in the table.

Not bad.

Creating and formatting a grouped table view

Table views come in two basic styles. The default style is called *plain* and looks really unadorned — plain vanilla. It's a listing: just one darn thing after another. You can index it, though, just as the table view in the Contacts application is indexed, so it can be a pretty powerful tool.

The other style is the *grouped* table view; unsurprisingly, it allows you to clump entries into various categories. In Figure 15-2, you can see a grouped table view on the right; the one on the left is a plain table view.

Grouped tables cannot have an index.

When you configure a grouped table view, you can also have header, footer, and section titles. I show you how to do the latter shortly.

To see how table views work, you of course need a project you can use to show them off. With that in mind, fire up Xcode and officially launch the iPhoneTravel411 project. (If you need a refresher on how to set up a project in Xcode, take another look at Chapter 4.) As you can see in Figure 15-3, I'm recommending that you go with a Navigation-Based Application template.

Figure 15-2:
Plain and grouped tables.

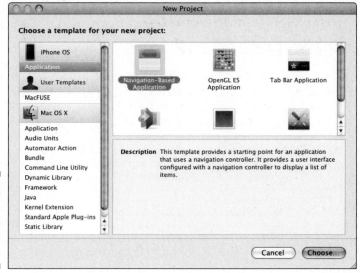

Figure 15-3:
Navigation-
Based
Application
template.

I then save the project as **iPhoneTravel411** in a folder on my desktop, as you can see in Figure 15-4.

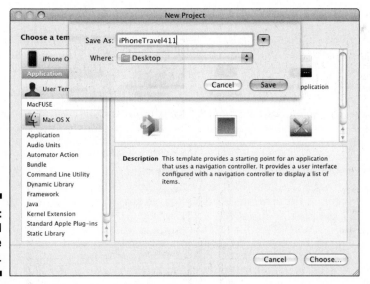

Figure 15-4:
Naming and
saving the
project.

Your new project gets added to the Groups & Files listing on the left side of the Xcode project window. Next, take look at what happens when you drill down in your project folder in the Groups & Files listing until you end up selecting `RootViewController` (as shown in Figure 15-5): The main pane of the Xcode project window reveals that `RootViewController` is derived from a `UITableViewController`.

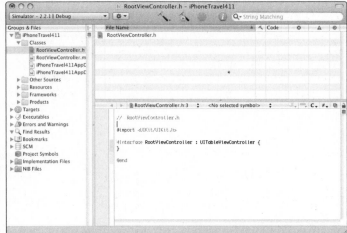

Figure 15-5:
The
RootView
Controller.

Inquisitive type that you are, you look up `UITableViewController` in the API reference by right-clicking its entry and choosing Find Selected Text in API Reference from the pop-up menu that appears. The API reference tells you that `UITableViewController` conforms to the `UITableViewDelegate` and `UITableViewDataSource` protocols — the two protocols I said were necessary to implement table views. What luck. (Kidding. It's all intentional.)

Always on the lookout for more information, you continue down the Groups & Files listing to open your project's Resources folder, where you double-click the `RootViewController.xib` file to launch Interface Builder. You are reassured to see a table view set up in front of you — admittedly, a plain table view rather than the grouped table view we want, but a table view none-theless. To get the final duck in a row, choose Grouped from the Style drop-down menu in the Attributes Inspector, as shown in Figure 15-6, to make the switch from plain to grouped.

At this point, you can build and run this project; go for it. What you see in the Simulator is a table view — and if you try to scroll it you get a "bounce scroll," where the view just bounces back up when you scroll it, but not much else. In fact, you won't even see it as a grouped view. What you do have is the basic framework, however, and now you can format it the way you'd like.

Figure 15-6:
RootView
Controller
nib file.

Making UITableViewController work for you

The data source and the delegate for table views are often (but not necessarily) the same object — and that object is frequently a custom subclass of UITable ViewController. For the iPhoneTravel411 project, the RootViewController created by the Navigation-Based Application template is a subclass of UITable ViewController — and the UITableViewController has adopted the UITableViewDelegate and UITableViewDataSource protocols. So you're free to implement those handy methods I mention in the "Creating the table view" section, earlier in the chapter. (Just remember that you need to implement them in RootViewController to make your table usable.) Start with the methods that format the table the way you'd like.

Adding sections

In a grouped table view, each group is referred to as a *section*.

In an indexed table, each indexed grouping of data is also called a section. For example, in the iPod application all the albums beginning with "A" would be one section, those beginning with "B" another section, and so on. While having the same name, this is not the same thing as sections in a grouped table (which doesn't have an index).

The two methods you need to start things off are as follows:

```
numberOfSectionsInTableView:(UITableView *)tableView
tableView:(UITableView *)tableView numberOfRowsInSection:(
        NSInteger)section
```

Each of these methods returns an integer and that tells the table view something — the number of sections and the number of rows in a given section, respectively.

In Listing 15-1, you can see the code that results in two sections with three rows in each section. These methods are already implemented for you by the Navigation-Based Application template in the `RootViewController.m` file. You'll just need to remove the existing code and replace it with what you see in Listing 15-1.

Listing 15-1:   Modify numberOfSectionsInTableView and numberOfRowsInSection

```
- (NSInteger)numberOfSectionsInTableView:(UITableView *)
         tableView {

   return 2;
}

- (NSInteger)tableView:(UITableView *)tableView numberOf
         RowsInSection:(NSInteger)section {

   NSInteger rows;
   switch (section) {
     case 0:
       rows = 3;
       break;
     case 1:
       rows = 3;
       break;
     default:
       break;
   }

   return rows;
}
```

You can implement `numberOfRowsInSection:` using a simple `switch` statement:

```
switch (section) {
```

Keep in mind that the first section is zero, as is the first row.

Although that's as easy as it gets, it's not really the best way to do it. Read on.

In the interests of showing you how to implement a robust application, I am going to use constants to represent the number of sections *and* the number of rows in each section. I'll put those constants in a file, `Constants.h`, which will eventually contain other constants. I do this for purely defensive reasons: Both of these values will be used often in this application (I know that because hindsight is 20-20) and declaring them as constants makes changing the number of rows and sections easy and it also helps avoid hard-to-detect typing mistakes.

I'll show you some techniques here that make life much, much easier later. It means paying attention to some of the less glamorous application nuts and bolts functionality — can you say, "memory management"? — that may be annoying to implement along the way, but are *really* hard to retrofit later. I want to head you away from the boulder-strewn paths that so many developers have gone down (me included), much to their later sorrow.

To implement the `Constants.h` file, you should do the following:

1. **Choose File⇨New File from the Xcode main menu.**

   I recommend having the `Classes` folder selected in the Groups & Files listing so the file will be placed in there.

2. **In the New File dialog that appears, choose Other from the listing on the left (under the Mac OS X heading) and then choose Empty File in the main pane, as shown in Figure 15-7.**

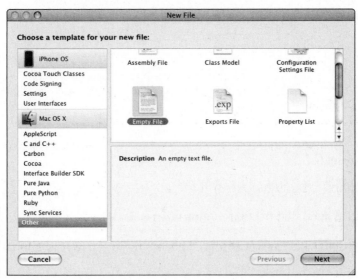

Figure 15-7: Creating an empty file.

3. **In the new dialog that appears, name the file** `Constants.h` **(as shown in Figure 15-8), and then click Finish.**

The new empty file is saved in the Classes folder, as shown in Figure 15-9.

With a new home for your constants all set up and waiting, all you have to do is add the constants you need so far. (Listing 15-2 shows you the constants you need to add to the `Constants.h` file.)

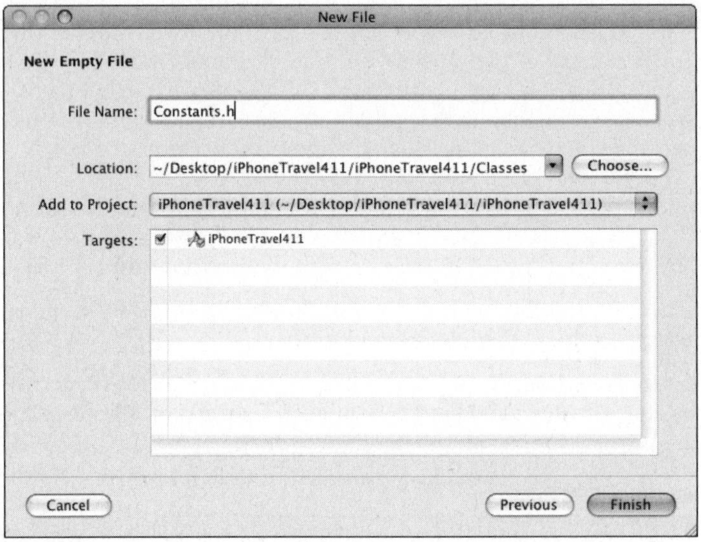

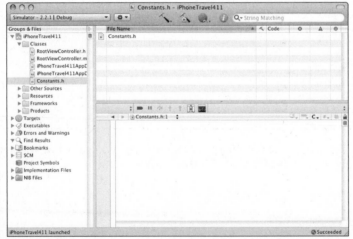

Figure 15-8:
Naming the new file.

Figure 15-9:
The Constants.h file.

Listing 15-2:   Adding to the Constants.h file

```
#define kSections      2
#define kSection1Rows  3
#define kSection2Rows  3
```

Having a `Constants.h` file in hand is great, but you have to let `RootView Controller.m` know that you plan to use it. To include `Constants.h` in `RootViewController.m`, open `RootViewController.m` in Xcode and add the following statement:

```
#import "Constants.h"
```

You can then use these constants in all the various methods used to create your table view, as shown in Listing 15-3.

Listing 15-3:   Sections and rows done the right way

```
- (NSInteger)numberOfSectionsInTableView:(UITableView *)
          tableView {

  return kSections;
}

- (NSInteger)tableView:(UITableView *)tableView numberOf
          RowsInSection:(NSInteger)section {

  NSInteger rows;
  switch (section) {
    case 0:
      rows = kSection1Rows;
      break;
    case 1:
      rows = kSection2Rows;
      break;

    default:
      break;
  }
  return rows;
}
```

When you build and run this (provisional) app, you get what you see in Figure 15-10 — two sections with three rows each.

Figure 15-10:
Now I have
sections.

Adding titles for the sections

With sections in place, you now need to title them so users know what the sections are for. Luckily for you, the `UITableViewdataSource` protocol has a handy method — titled, appropriately enough, the `titleForHeaderIn-Section:` method — that enables you to add a title for each section. Listing 15-4 shows how to implement the method.

Listing 15-4:   Add Section titles

```
- (NSString *)tableView:(UITableView *)tableView titleFor
            HeaderInSection:(NSInteger)section {

  NSString *title = nil;
  switch (section) {
    case 0:
      title = @"Welcome to London";
      break;
    case 1:
      title =  @"Getting there";
      break;
    default:
      break;
  }
  return title;
}
```

This (again) is a simple `switch` statement. For `case 0`, or the first section, you'll want the title to be `"Welcome to London"`, and for `case 1`, or the second section, you'll want the title to be `"Getting there"`.

Okay, this, too, was really easy — so you probably won't be surprised to learn that it's *not* the best way to tackle the whole titling business. Another path not to take — in fact a really *important* one not to take. Really Serious Application Developers insist on catering to the needs of an increasingly global audience, which means — paradoxically — that they have to *localize* their applications. In other words, an app must be created in such a way that it presents a different view to different, local audiences. The next section explains how this is done.

Localization

Localizing an application isn't hard, just tedious. To localize your application, you create a folder in your application bundle (I'll get to that) for each language you want to support. Each folder has the application's translated resources.

In the Settings application for the iPhoneTravel411 app, we're going to set things up so the user can set the language — Spanish or Italian, for example — and the region format.

For example, if the user's language is Spanish, available regions range from Spain to Argentina to the United States and lots of places in between. When a localized application needs to load a resource (such as an image, property list, or nib), the application checks the user's language and region and looks for a localization folder that corresponds to the selected language and region. If it finds one, it loads the localized version of the resource instead of the *base* version — the one you're working in.

Showing you all the ins and outs of localizing your application is a bit too Byzantine for this book. But I *will* show you what you must do to make your app localizable when you're ready to tackle the chore on your own.

What you have to get right — right from the start — are the strings you use in your application that get presented to the user. (If the user has chosen Spanish as his or her language of choice, what's expected in the main view is now *Moneda*, not *Currency*.) You ensure that the users see what they're expecting by storing the strings you use in your application in a `strings` text file; this file contains a list of string pairs, each identified by a comment. You would create one of these files for each language you support.

Here is an example of what a `strings` file might look like for this application:

```
/*Airport choices */
"Getting there"  = "Getting there";
```

The values between the /* and the */ characters are just comments for the (human) translator you task with creating the right translation for the phrase — assuming, of course, that you're not fluent in the ten-or-so languages you'll probably want to include in your app, and therefore will need some translating help. You write such comments to provide some context — how that string is being used in the application.

Okay, this example has two strings — the one to the left of the equals sign is used as a key; the one to the right of the equals sign is the one displayed. In the example, both strings are the same — but in the string file used for a Spanish speaker, here's what you'd see:

```
/*Airport choices */
"Getting there"  = "Cómo llegar";
```

Looking up such values in the table is handled by the NSLocalizedString macro in your code.

To show you how to use the macro, I take one of the section headings as an example. Instead of

```
title = Getting there;
```

I code it as follows:

```
title = NSLocalizedString(@"Getting there",
                              @"Airport choices");
```

As you can see, the macro has two inputs. The first is the string in your language, the second the general comment for the translator. At run time, NSLocalizedString looks for a strings file named localizable. strings in the language that has been set: Spanish, for example. (A user would have done that by going to Settings, selecting General⇨International⇨ Language⇨Español). If NSLocalizedString finds the strings file, it searches the file for a line that matches the first parameter. In this case it would return "Cómo llegar", and that is what would be displayed as the section header. If the macro doesn't find the file or a specified string, it returns its first parameter — and the string will appear in the base language.

To create the localizable.strings file, you run a command-line program named genstrings, which searches your code files for the macro and places them all in a localizable.strings file (which it creates), ready for the (human) translator. genstrings is beyond the scope of this book, but it is well documented. When you are ready, I leave you to explore it on your own.

Okay, sure, it's really annoying to have to do this sort of thing as you write your code (yes, I know, *really really* annoying). But that's not nearly as annoying as having to go back and *find and replace all the strings you want to localize* after the application is almost done. Take my word for it!

Listing 15-5 shows how to use the NSLocalizedString macros to create localizable section titles.

Listing 15-5:   Add localizable section titles

```
- (NSString *)tableView:(UITableView *)tableView titleForH
        eaderInSection:(NSInteger)section {

  NSString *title = nil;
  switch (section) {
    case 0:
      title = NSLocalizedString(@"Welcome to London",
                                        @"City name");
      break;
    case 1:
      title = NSLocalizedString(@"Getting there",
                                     @"Airport choices");
      break;
    default:
      break;
  }
  return title;
}
```

Creating the model

As all good iPhone app developers know, the model-view-controller design pattern is the basis for the design of the framework you use to develop your applications. In this design pattern, each element (model, view, or controller) concentrates on the task at hand; it doesn't much care what the other elements are doing. For table views, that means the method that draws the content doesn't know what the content is — and the method that decides what to do when a selection is made in a particular row is equally ignorant of what the selection is. The important thing is to have a model object — one for each row — to hold and provide that information.

You usually want to deal with the model-object business by creating an array of models for each row. In our case, the model object will be a dictionary that holds the following three items:

✔ **The selection text:** Heathrow, for example.

✔ **The description text:** International airport, for example.

✔ **The view controller to be created when the user selects that row:** AirportController, for example.

You can see all three items illustrated in Figure 15-11.

In more complex applications, you could provide a dictionary *within* the dictionary, and use it to provide the same kind of information for the next level in the hierarchy. The iPod application is an example: It presents you with a list of albums, and then, when you select an album, shows you a list of songs on that the album.

Below is the code that shows you how to create a single dictionary for a row. Later I'll show you how to create all of the dictionaries and where all this code needs to go.

```
self.menuList = [[NSMutableArray alloc] init];

[menuList addObject:[NSMutableDictionary
                            dictionaryWithObjectsAndKeys:
     NSLocalizedString(@"Heathrow",
          @"Heathrow Section"), kSelectKey,
     NSLocalizedString(@"International airport",
          @"Heathrow Explain"), kDescriptKey,
     nil,kControllerKey,
     nil]];
```

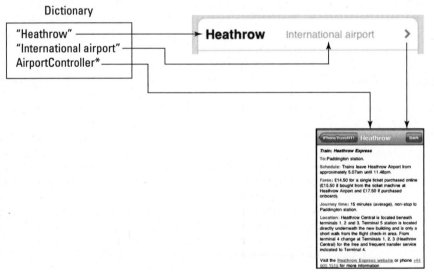

Figure 15-11:
The model
for a row.

Here's the blow-by-blow account:

1. **Create an array to hold the model for each row.**

    An NSMutableArray is a good choice here, because it allows you to easily insert and delete objects.

In such an array, the position of the dictionary corresponds to the row it implements, that is, relative to row zero in the table and not taking into account the section.

2. **Create an** NSMutableDictionary **with three entries and the following keys:**

   - kSelectKey: The entry that corresponds to the main entry in the table view. ("Heathrow," for example.)

   - kDescriptKey: The entry that corresponds to the description in the table view. ("International Airport," for example.)

   - kControllerKey: This entry contains a pointer to a view controller that will display the Heathrow information. I'll create an entry for the controller, but not just yet; I just use nil for now. The first time the user selects a row, I'll create the view controller and save that value in here. That way, if the user selects that row again, the controller will simply be reused.

3. **Add the keys to the** Constants.h **file.**

```
#define kSelectKey        @"selection"
#define kDescriptKey      @"description"
#define kControllerKey    @"viewController"
```

The @ before each of the strings above tells the compiler that this is an NSString.

You'd use the same mechanism to get rid of these controllers if you ever get a low-memory warning. You'd simply go through each dictionary in the array and release every controller except the one that's currently active.

You'll want to create this array and all of the dictionaries in an initialization method awakeFromNib, which you'll need to add to the RootView Controller.m file, and can see in Listing 15-6. When the RootView Controller's nib file is loaded, the awakeFromNib message is sent to the RootViewController after all the objects in the nib file have been loaded and the RootViewController's outlet instance variables have been set. Typically, the object that owns the nib file (File's Owner, in this case the RootViewController) implements awakeFromNib to do initialization that requires that outlet and target-action connections be set.

You really should create a model class that creates this data-model array, reading the data from a file or property list. I do it this way in my Mobile Travel411 application — but for simplicity's sake, do it in the awakeFromNib method for the iPhoneTravel411 app. Think of this as a model method that lives in a view controller object.

Listing 15-6: awakeFromNib

```
- (void)awakeFromNib {

    self.title = [[[NSBundle mainBundle] infoDictionary]
            objectForKey:@"CFBundleName"];

    self.menuList = [[NSMutableArray alloc] init];

    [menuList addObject:[NSMutableDictionary
                                dictionaryWithObjectsAndKeys:
      NSLocalizedString(@"London", @"City Section"),
                                                    kSelectKey,
      NSLocalizedString(@"US dollars to pounds",
                        @"City Explain"), kDescriptKey,
      nil,kControllerKey, nil]];
    [menuList addObject:[NSMutableDictionary
                                dictionaryWithObjectsAndKeys:
      NSLocalizedString(@"Currency", @"Currency Section"),
                                                    kSelectKey,
      NSLocalizedString(@"Cost in dollars",
                        @"Currency Explain"), kDescriptKey,
      nil,kControllerKey, nil]];
    [menuList addObject:[NSMutableDictionary
                                dictionaryWithObjectsAndKeys:
      NSLocalizedString(@"Weather", @"Weather Section"),
                                                    kSelectKey,
      NSLocalizedString(@"Current conditions",
                        @"Weather Explain"), kDescriptKey,
      nil,kControllerKey, nil]];
    [menuList addObject:[NSMutableDictionary
                                dictionaryWithObjectsAndKeys:
      NSLocalizedString(@"Heathrow", @"Heathrow Section"),
                                                    kSelectKey,
      NSLocalizedString(@"International airport",
                        @"Heathrow Explain"), kDescriptKey,
      nil,kControllerKey, nil]];
    [menuList addObject:[NSMutableDictionary
                                dictionaryWithObjectsAndKeys:
      NSLocalizedString(@"Gatwick", @"Gatwick Section"),
                                                    kSelectKey,
      NSLocalizedString(@"European flights",
                        @"Gatwick Explain"), kDescriptKey,
      nil,kControllerKey, nil]];
    [menuList addObject:[NSMutableDictionary
                                dictionaryWithObjectsAndKeys:
      NSLocalizedString(@"Stansted", @"Stansted Section"),
                                                    kSelectKey,
      NSLocalizedString(@"UK flights",
                        @"Stansted Explain"), kDescriptKey,
      nil,kControllerKey, nil]];
}
```

Going through the code, you can see that the first thing you do is get the application name from the bundle so you can use it as the main view title.

```
self.title = [[[NSBundle mainBundle] infoDictionary]
        objectForKey:@"CFBundleName"];
```

"What bundle?" you say? Well, when you build your iPhone application, Xcode packages it as a bundle — containing

- ✔ The application's executable code.

- ✔ Any resources that the app has to use (for instance, the application icon, other images, and localized content).

- ✔ The info.plist, also known as the information property list, which defines key values for the application, such as bundle ID, version number, and display name.

infoDictionary: returns a dictionary that's constructed from the bundle's info.plist. CFBundleName is the key to the entry that contains the (local-izable) application name on the home page. The title is what will be displayed in the Navigation bar at the top of the screen.

Going through the rest of the code, you can see that for each entry in the main view, you have to create a dictionary and put it in the menuList array. You'll put the dictionary menuList array so you can use it later when you need to provide the row's content or create a view controller when the user selects the row.

Seeing how cells work

We've been going steadily from macro to micro, so it makes sense that after setting up a model for each row, we get to talk about cells, the individual constituents of each row.

Cell objects are what draw the contents of a row in a table view. The method tableView:cellForRowAtIndexPath: is called for each visible row in the table view. It's expected that the method will configure and return a UITableViewCell object for each row. The UITableView object uses this cell to draw the row.

When providing cells for the table view, you have three general approaches you can take:

- ✔ Use vanilla (not subclassed) UITableViewCell cell objects.

- ✔ Add subviews to a UITableViewCell cell object's content view.

- ✔ Use cell objects created from a custom subclass of UITableViewCell.

The next few sections take a look at these options, one by one.

Using vanilla cell objects

Using the UITableViewCell class directly, you can create cell objects with text and an optional image. (If a cell has no image, the text starts near the left edge of the cell.) You also have an area on the right of the cell for accessory views, such as disclosure indicators (the one shaped like a regular chevron), detail disclosure controls (the one that looks like a white chevron in a blue button), and even control objects such as sliders, switches, or custom views. (The layout of a cell is shown in Figure 15-12.) If you like, you can format the font, alignment, and color of the text (as well as have a different format when the row is selected).

Display Mode

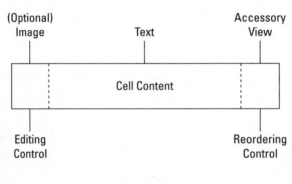

Figure 15-12: The cell architecture.

Editing Mode

Adding subviews to a cell's content view

Although you can specify the font, color, size, alignment, and other characteristics of the text in a cell using the UITableViewCell class directly, the formatting is applied to all of the text in the cell. To get the variation that I suspect you want between the selection and description text (and, it turns out, the alignment as well), you have to create subviews within the cell.

A cell that a table view uses for displaying a row is, in reality, a view in its own right. UITableViewCell inherits from UIView, and it has a content view. With content views, you can add one subview (containing, say, the selection text "Weather") formatted the way I want — and a second subview (holding, say, the description text, "current conditions") formatted an entirely different way. You may remember that you already experienced adding subviews (the button, text field, and labels) in creating the ReturnMeTo applications main view, although you may not have known you were doing that at the time. Well, now it can be told.

Creating a custom subclass UITableViewCell

Finally, you can create a custom cell subclass when your content requires it — usually when you need to change the default behavior of the cell.

Creating the cell

As I mentioned in the previous section, you're going to use the UITableView Cell class to create the cells for your table views and then add the subviews you need in order to do the formatting you want. The place to create the cell is cellForRowAtIndexPath:. This method is called for each visible row in the table view, as shown in Listing 15-7. You'll find that a code stub is already included in the RootViewController.m file, courtesy of the template.

Listing 15-7:   Drawing the text

```
- (UITableViewCell *)tableView:(UITableView * )tableView
          cellForRowAtIndexPath:(NSIndexPath *)indexPath {
 #define CellIdentifier  @"Cell"

 UITableViewCell *cell = [tableView dequeueReusableCell
          WithIdentifier:CellIdentifier];

 if (cell == nil) {
   cell = [[[UITableViewCell alloc]
          initWithFrame:CGRectZero
          reuseIdentifier:CellIdentifier] autorelease];

   cell.accessoryType =
          UITableViewCellAccessoryDisclosureIndicator;

   CGRect subViewFrame = cell.contentView.frame;
   subViewFrame.origin.x += kInset;
   subViewFrame.size.width = kInset+kSelectLabelWidth;

   UILabel *selectLabel = [[UILabel alloc]
                           initWithFrame:subViewFrame];
   selectLabel.textColor = [UIColor blackColor];
   selectLabel.highlightedTextColor = [UIColor
          whiteColor];
   selectLabel.font = [UIFont boldSystemFontOfSize:18];
```

(continued)

Listing 15-7 *(continued)*

```
        selectLabel.backgroundColor = [UIColor clearColor];
        [cell.contentView addSubview:selectLabel];

        subViewFrame.origin.x += kInset+kSelectLabelWidth;
        subViewFrame.size.width = kDescriptLabelWidth;

        UILabel *descriptLabel = [[UILabel alloc]
              initWithFrame:subViewFrame];
        descriptLabel.textColor = [UIColor grayColor];
        descriptLabel.highlightedTextColor = [UIColor
              whiteColor];
        descriptLabel.font = [UIFont systemFontOfSize:14];
        descriptLabel.backgroundColor = [UIColor clearColor];
        [cell.contentView addSubview:descriptLabel];

        int menuOffset = (indexPath.section*kSection1Rows)+
                                            indexPath.row;
        NSDictionary *cellText= [menuList
                            objectAtIndex:menuOffset];

        selectLabel.text = [cellText objectForKey:kSelectKey];
        descriptLabel.text = [cellText
                            objectForKey:kDescriptKey];
        [selectLabel release];
        [descriptLabel release];
    }
  return cell;
}
```

Here's the logic behind all that code:

1. **Determine if there are any cells lying around that you can use.**

   Although a table view can only display a few rows at a time on iPhone's small screen, the table itself can conceivably hold a lot more. A large table would chew up a lot of memory if you created cells for every row. Fortunately, table views are designed to *reuse* cells. As a table view's cells scroll off the screen, they're placed in a queue of cells available to be reused.

2. **Create a *cell identifier* that indicates what cell type you're using.**

   ```
   #define CellIdentifier  @"Cell"
   ```

   Table views support multiple cell types, which makes the identifier necessary. In this case, you only need one cell type, but sometimes you may want more than one.

If the system runs low on memory, the table view gets rid of the cells in the queue, but as long as it's got some available memory for them, it will hold on to them in case you want to use them again.

You can ask the table view for a specific reusable cell object by sending it a `dequeueReusableCellWithIdentifier:` message:

```
UITableViewCell *cell = [tableView         dequeueReusabl
     eCellWithIdentifier:CellIdentifier];
```

This asks whether any cells of the type you want are available.

3. **If there aren't any cells lying around, you'll have to create a cell, using the cell identifier you just created.**

```
if (cell == nil) {
   cell = [[[UITableViewCell alloc]
      initWithFrame:CGRectZero
      reuseIdentifier:CellIdentifier] autorelease];
```

You now have a table view cell that you can return to the table view.

4. **Define the accessory type for the cell.**

```
cell.accessoryType =
      UITableViewCellAccessoryDisclosureIndicator;
```

As I mentioned earlier in our brief tour of a cell, its layout includes a place for an accessory — usually something like a disclosure indicator.

In this case, use `UITableViewCellAccessoryDisclosureIndicator` (the one shaped like a regular chevron). It lets the user know that tapping this entry will result in something (hopefully wonderful) happening — the display of the current weather conditions, for example.

If you're using a table view, and you want to display more detailed information about the entry itself, you might use a Detail Disclosure button. This allows you to then use a tap on the row for something else. In the Favorites view in the Phone application, for example, selecting the Detail Disclosure button gives you a view of the contact information; if you just tap the row, it places the call for you.

You're not limited to these kinds of indicators; you also have the option of creating your own view — you can put in any kind of control. (That's what you see in the Settings application, for example.)

5. **Create the subviews.**

Here I show you just one example (the other is the same except for the font size and text color): I get the `contentView` frame, and base the subview on it. The inset from the left (`kInset`) and the width of the subview, (`kLabelWidth`) are defined in the `Constants.h` file. It looks like this:

```
#define kInset              10
#define kSelectLabelWidth    100
#define kDescriptLabelWidth  160
```

To hold the text, the subview I am creating is a `UILabelView`, which meets my needs exactly:

```
CGRect subViewFrame = cell.contentView.frame;
subViewFrame.origin.x += kInset;
subViewFrame.size.width = kInset+kSelectLabelWidth;
UILabel *selectLabel = [[UILabel alloc]
                initWithFrame:subViewFrame];
```

You then set the label properties that you are interested in, just as when you created the labels in the ReturnMeTo application. This time however, you'll do it by manually writing code rather than using Interface Builder. Just set the font color and size — the highlighted font color when an item selected, and the background color of the label (as indicated in the code that follows). Setting the background color to transparent allows me to see the bottom line of the last cell in the group.

```
selectLabel.textColor = [UIColor blackColor];
selectLabel.highlightedTextColor = [UIColor
        whiteColor];
selectLabel.font = [UIFont boldSystemFontOfSize:18];
selectLabel.backgroundColor = [UIColor clearColor];
[cell.contentView addSubview:selectLabel];
```

I could have inset the view one pixel up from the bottom, made the label opaque, and given it a white (not clear) background — which would be more efficient to draw. But with such a small number of rows, making that effort really has no appreciable performance impact — and the way I've set it up here requires less code for you to go through. Feel free to do it the "right way" on your own.

After you have your label, you just set its text to one of the values you get from the dictionary created in `awakeFromNib` representing this row.

The trouble is, you won't get the absolute row passed to you. You get only the row within a particular section — and you need the absolute row to get the right dictionary from the array. Fortunately, one of the arguments used when this method is called is the `indexPath`, which contains the section and row information in a single object. To get the row or the section out of an `NSIndexPath`, you just have to call either its section method (`indexPath.section`) or its row method (`index Path.row`), each of which returns an `int`. This neat trick enables you to compute the offset for the row in the array you created in `awake FromNib`. This is also why it is so handy to have the number of rows in a section as a constant.

So the first thing you do in the code below is compute that. And then you can use that dictionary to assign the text to the label.

```
int menuOffset = (indexPath.section*kSection1Rows)+
                                        indexPath.row;
NSDictionary *cellText = [menuList
                            objectAtIndex:menuOffset];
selectLabel.text = [cellText objectForKey:kSelectKey];
descriptLabel.text = [cellText
                            objectForKey:kDescriptKey];
```

Finally, since I no longer need the labels I created I release them:

```
[selectLabel release];
[descriptLabel release];
```

and return the cell formatted and with the text it needs to display in that row.

```
return cell;
```

Responding to a selection

When the user taps on a table-view entry, what happens next depends on what you want your table view to do for you.

If this application were using the table view to display data (as the Albums view in the iPod application does, for example), you'd show the next level in the hierarchy — such as the list of songs, to stick with the iPod application — or a detail view of an item, such as information about a song.

In our case, we're using the table view as a table of contents, so tapping a table-view entry transfers the user to the view that presents the desired information — the Heathrow Express, for example.

For the iPhoneTravel411 application, I'm going to show you the table-of-contents approach; in Chapter 18, I direct you to some Apple-supplied sample code that deals with data hierarchies.

To move from one content view to a new (content) view, first you need to create a new view controller for that view; then you launch it so it creates and installs the view on the screen. But you also have to give the a user a way to get back to the main view!

Brass-tacks time: What kind of code-writing gymnastics do you have to do to get all this stuff to happen?

Actually, not much. Table views are usually paired with *navigation bars*, whose job it is to implement the back stuff. And to get a navigation bar all you have to do is include a *navigation controller* in your application. What's more, if you wisely chose the Navigation-Based Application template at the outset of your iPhoneTravel411 project, a navigation controller was already put in place for you in the appDelegate created by the template. Here's the code that the template quite generously provided you with (the navigation controller is bolded so you can find it easier):

```
@interface iPhoneTravel411AppDelegate : NSObject
          <UIApplicationDelegate> {

    UIWindow *window;
    UINavigationController *navigationController;
}

@property (nonatomic, retain) IBOutlet UIWindow *window;
@property (nonatomic, retain) IBOutlet
          UINavigationController *navigationController;
@end
```

This navigation controller is created for you in the MainWindow.xib file (see Figure 15-13) which you can access by double-clicking the MainWindow.xib file in the Groups & Files pane in your project. If you take a closer look at Figure 5-13, you can see that, when the navigation controller is selected, it points to the RootViewController.nib in the View window — which is to say, it's pointing to the RootViewController and its table view. This links together the navigation controller, the root view controller, and the view.

But not only did the Navigation-Based Application template deliver the goods in the iPhoneTravel411AppDelegate.h file and nib file, it also created the code I need in the iPhoneTravel411AppDelegate.m file.

To get the navigation controller view to load in the window, you don't have to do anything. When you chose Navigation-Based Application template, the code below was automatically generated for you.

```
- (void)applicationDidFinishLaunching:(UIApplication *)
          application {
    [window addSubview:[navigationController view]];
    [window makeKeyAndVisible];
}
```

When all is said and done, you have a table view with a navigation bar ready to go to work.

Figure 15-13:
The
navigation
controller.

Navigating the navigation controller

As the previous section made clear, to give users the option of returning to a view higher up in the hierarchy (in our case, the main view), table views are paired with navigation bars that enable a user to navigate the hierarchy. Here's what you need to know to make that work:

- ✔ The view below the navigation bar presents the current level of data.

- ✔ A navigation bar includes a title for the current view.

- ✔ If the current view is lower in the hierarchy than the top level, a Back button appears on the left side of the bar; the user can tap it to return to the previous level, as shown in Figure 15-14. The text in the back button tells the user what the previous level was. In this case, it's the application's main view, so you will see the application's name — iPhoneTravel411.

- ✔ A navigation bar may also have an Edit button (on the right side) — used to enter editing mode for the current view — or even custom buttons.

In the case of our iPhoneTravel411 application, you'll create a custom button — an additional back button. I explain why that is needed shortly.

The navigation bar for each level is managed by a navigation controller — again, as mentioned in the previous section. The navigation controller maintains a stack of view controllers, one for each of the views displayed, starting with the root view controller (hence the name `RootViewController` given to the table view controller by the template). The root view controller is the very first view controller that the navigation controller pushes onto its stack when a user launches the application; it remains active until the user selects the next view to look at.

Time for a concrete example: When the user taps a row of the table view to get the Heathrow Express information, the root view controller pushes the next view controller onto the stack. The new controller's view (the Heathrow Express information) slides into place, and the navigation bar items are updated appropriately. When the user taps the Back button in the navigation bar, the current view controller pops off the stack, the Heathrow Views slides off the screen, and the user lands (so to speak) back in the main (table) view.

A *stack* is a commonly used data structure that works on the principle of last in, first out. Imagine an "ideal" boarding scenario for an airplane: You would start with the last seat in the last row, and board the plane in back-to-front order until you got to the first seat in the first row — that would be the seat for the last person to board. When you got to your destination you'd deplane (is that really a word?) in the reverse order. That last person on — the person in row one seat one — would be the first person off.

A computer stack is pretty much the same. Adding an object is called a *push* — in this case, when you select Heathrow, the view controller for the Heathrow view is pushed on to the stack. Removing an object is called a *pop* — touching the back button pops the view controller for the Heathrow view. When you pop an object off the stack, it's always the last one you pushed onto it. The controller that was there before the push is still there, and now becomes the active one — in this case, it's the root view controller.

I mentioned earlier that I wanted two Back buttons in place. Now you get to find out why. In my design, I wanted to be able to tap a link in the content views to access a Web site. (You can see such a link on the left in Figure 15-14.) When I do that, the iPhoneTravel411 application *replaces* the content of the view, rather than *creating* a new view controller. Tapping the link doesn't change the controller in any way, so the left button won't change; you won't be able to use it to get back to a previous view — you'll only go back to the main view, as the control text tells you. To solve this quandary, I created another button and labeled it "Back," so the user knows he or she can use it to get back to the previous view. I show you how to create such a Back button in Chapter 17.

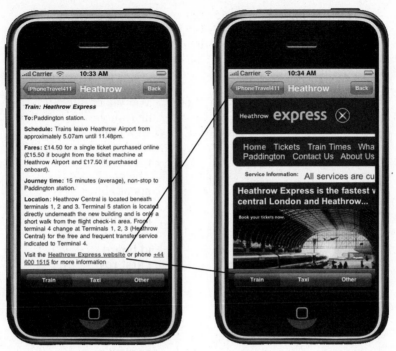

Figure 15-14:
Getting
back.

Implementing the selection

At some point you have to make sure that something actually happens when a user makes a selection. To do that, all you really need to do is implement the `didSelectRowAtIndexPath:` method to set up a response to a user tap in the main view. This method, too, is already in the `RootViewController.m` file, courtesy of the template. Listing 15-8 shows you not only how to implement the tap, but also how to use the array and dictionary I created back in Listing 15-6 when you added the code to `awakeFromNib` to manage the view controllers.

Listing 15-8:   didSelectRowAtIndexPath:

```
- (void)tableView:(UITableView *)tableView
      didSelectRowAtIndexPath:(NSIndexPath *)indexPath {

  [tableView deselectRowAtIndexPath:indexPath
        animated:YES];
```

(continued)

Listing 15-8 *(continued)*

```
int menuOffset = (indexPath.section*kSection1Rows)+
        indexPath.row;


UIViewController *targetController =
        [[menuList objectAtIndex: menuOffset]
        objectForKey:kControllerKey];

if (targetController == nil) {

  switch (menuOffset) {
    case 0:
      targetController = [[LondonController alloc]
        initWithCity:NSLocalizedString(@"London",
        @"London") cityID: 1];
      break;
    case 1:
      targetController = [[CurrencyController alloc]
        initWithCurrency:NSLocalizedString(@"Pound",
        @"Pound Currency") currencyID: @"GBP"];
      break;
    case 2:
      targetController = [[WeatherController alloc]
        initWithCity:NSLocalizedString(@"London",
        @"London") cityID: 1];
      break;
    case 3:
      targetController = [[AirportController alloc]
        initWithAirport:NSLocalizedString(@"Heathrow",
        @"Heathrow") cityID: 1];
      break;
    case 4:
      targetController = [[AirportController alloc]
        initWithAirport:NSLocalizedString(@"Gatwick",
        @"Gatwick") cityID: 1];
      break;
    case 5:
      targetController = [[AirportController alloc]
        initWithAirport:NSLocalizedString(@"Stansted",
        @"Stansted") cityID: 3];
      break;
  }
  [[menuList  objectAtIndex: (indexPath.row +
      (indexPath.section*kSection1Rows))]
        setObject:targetController
        forKey:kControllerKey];
}
[[self navigationController]
        pushViewController:targetController
        animated:YES];
}
```

Again, here's the blow-by-blow:

1. **Deselect the row the user selected.**

```
[tableView deselectRowAtIndexPath:indexPath
        animated:YES];
```

It stands to reason that if you want your app to move on to a new view, you have to deselect the row where you currently are.

2. **Compute the offset (based on section and row) into the menu array.**

```
int menuOffset = (indexPath.section*kSection1Rows)+
                                    indexPath.row;
```

You need to figure out where you want your app to land, right?

3. **Check to see whether the controller for that particular view has already been created.**

```
UIViewController *targetController = [[menuList
                objectAtIndex: menuOffset]
                objectForKey:kControllerKey];

if (targetController == nil) {
```

4. **If no controller exists, create and initialize a new controller.**

I explain the mechanics of this in Chapter 17. As you can see, you're going to use another switch statement to get to the right controller:

```
switch (menuOffset) {
  case 0:
    targetController = [[someController alloc]
                initWithNibName:@" someController"
                bundle:nil];
    break;
```

5. **Save a reference to the newly created controller in the dictionary for that row.**

```
[[menuList  objectAtIndex: (indexPath.row +
                (indexPath.section*kSection1Rows))]
        setObject:targetController
        forKey:kControllerKey];
```

6. **Push the controller onto the stack, and let the navigation controller do the rest.**

```
[[self navigationController] pushViewController:
                targetController animated:YES];
```

I want to remind you of something. In Chapter 12, I said I would not implement the `didReceiveMemoryWarning:` in the ReturnMeTo application, but that I would explain a strategy of how to use it in more complex applications. Well, here you are. If I get a `didReceiveMemoryWarning:` message. I can go through the array and release the controllers (and their views and models) that are not currently active.

And now . . .

We're off to a good start — and we only had to use five methods to create the table and handle user selections. We still have to create the content views and models, but before we do that, I want to show you how to improve the user experience by saving state and allowing the user to set preferences.

Chapter 16

Enhancing the User Experience

. . . .

In This Chapter

▶ Getting back to where you once belonged

▶ Avoiding bankruptcy because of exorbitant roaming charges

. . . .

"*K*eep the customer satisfied" is my mantra. If that means constantly refining an application design, so be it. In thinking about my iPhone Travel411 design, two things struck me as essential if I really wanted to make this an application that really focuses on the user. The first is part of the Human Interface Guidelines, so it's not really something I can claim credit for; the second is something that flowed straight out of the nature of my design.

In this chapter, I show how I incorporated elements into my design that directly addressed issues relating to an enhanced user experience.

Saving and Restoring State

When the user taps the Home button, the iPhone OS terminates your application and returns to the Home screen. The `applicationWillTerminate:` method is called and your application is terminated — no ifs, ands, or buts. That means you have to save any unsaved data — as well as the current state of your application — if you want to restore the application to its previous state the next time the user launches it. Now, in situations like this one, you have to use common sense to decide what *state* really means. Generally you wouldn't need to restore the application to where the user last stopped in a scrollable list for example. For purposes of explanation I chose to save the last category view that the user selected in the main table view, which corresponds to a row in a section in the table view. You, the reader, might also consider saving that last view that was selected in that category.

Saving state information

Here's the sequence of events that go into saving the state:

1. **Add new instance variable** lastView **and declare the** @property **in the** iPhoneTravel411AppDelegate.h **file.**

   I explain properties in Chapter 8.

   This is shown in Listing 16-1. (Again, the new stuff is bold.)

   As you can see, lastView is a mutable array. You'll save the section as the first element in the array and the row as the second element. As I mentioned in Chapter 15, since it is mutable, it will be easier to update when the users selects a new row in a section.

2. **Add the** @synthesize **statement to the** iPhoneTravel411App Delegate.m **file, to tell the compiler to create the accessors for you.**

   This is shown in Listing 16-2. (You guessed it — new is bold.)

3. **Define the filename you'll use when saving the state information in the** Constants.h **file.**

   ```
   #define kState  @"LastState"
   ```

4. **Save the section and row that the user last tapped, in the** iPhone Travel411AppDelegate**'s** lastView **instance variable, by adding the following code to the beginning of the** didSelectRowAtIndexPath: **method in the** RootViewController.m**, as shown in Listing 16-3.**

   The didSelectRowAtIndexPath: method is called when the user taps a row in a section. As you recall from Chapter 15, the section and row information is in the indexPath argument of the didSelectRowAt IndexPath: method. All you have to do to save that information is to save the indexPath.section as the first array entry, and the index-Path.row as the second. (The reason I do it this way will become obvious when I show you how to write this out to a file.)

5. **When the user goes back to the main view, save that main view location in the** viewWillAppear: **method. You will need to add this method to the RootViewController.m file as shown in Listing 16-4. (It's already there; all you have to do is uncomment it out.)**

   The last step is to deal with the case when the user moves back to the main view, and then quits the application. To indicate that the user is at the main view, I use –1 to represent the section and –1 to represent the row. I use minus ones in this case because, as you recall, the first section and row in a table are both 0, which requires me to represent the table (main) view itself in this (clever) way.

6. **Save the section and row in the `ApplicationWillTerminate:` method. The method stub is already in the** `iPhoneTravel411App Delegate`**.m file, you just have to add the code in Listing 16-5.**

In `applicationWillTerminate:` I am saving the `lastView` instance variable (which contains the last section and row the user tapped) to a file `kState`, which is the constant which I defined in Step 3 to represent the filename `LastState`.

As you can see, reading or writing to the file system on the iPhone is pretty simple: You tell the system which directory to put the file in, specify the file's name — and then pass that information to the `writeTo File` method. Let me take you through what I just did in Step 6

- *Got the path to the* `Documents` *directory.*

```
NSArray *paths = NSSearchPathForDirectoriesInDomains(
        NSDocumentDirectory, NSUserDomainMask, YES);
NSString *documentsDirectory =[paths objectAtIndex:0];
```

On the iPhone, you really don't have much choice about where the file goes. Although there is a `/tmp` directory, I'm going to place this file in the `Documents` directory — because (as I explain in Chapter 2) this is part of my application's sandbox, so it's the natural home for all the app's files.

`NSSearchPathForDirectoriesInDomains`: returns an array of directories; because I'm only interested in the `Documents` directory, I use the constant `NSDocumentDirectory` — and because I'm restricted to my home directory/sandbox, the constant `NSUserDomainMask` limits the search to that *domain*. There will be only one directory in the domain, so the one I want will be the first one returned.

- *Created the complete path by appending the path filename to the directory.*

```
NSString *filePath = [documentsDirectory stringBy
        AppendingPathComponent:fileName];
```

`stringByAppendingPathComponent`: precedes the filename with a path separator (/) if necessary.

Unfortunately this does not work if you are trying to create a string representation of a URL.

- *Write the data to the file.*

```
[lastView writeToFile:filePath atomically:YES];
```

`writeToFile`: is an `NSData` method and does what it implies. I am actually telling the array here to write itself to a file, which

TIP

is why I decided to save the location in this way in the first place. There are a number of other classes that implement that method, including NSData, NSDate, NSNumber, NSString, and NSDictionary. You can also add this behavior to your own objects, and they could save themselves — but I won't get into that here. The atomically parameter first writes the data to an auxiliary file and once that is successful, it is renamed to the path you have specified. This guarantees that the file won't be corrupted even if the system crashed during the write operation.

Listing 16-1:   Add the instance variable to the interface

```
#import <UIKit/UIKit.h>

@interface iPhoneTravel411AppDelegate : NSObject
        <UIApplicationDelegate> {

UIWindow               *window;
UINavigationController *navigationController;
NSMutableArray         *lastView;

}

@property (nonatomic, retain) IBOutlet UIWindow *window;
@property (nonatomic, retain) IBOutlet
        UINavigationController *navigationController;
@property (nonatomic, retain) NSMutableArray *lastView;

@end
```

Listing 16-2:   Add the synthesize to the implementation

```
#import "iPhoneTravel411AppDelegate.h"
#import "RootViewController.h"
#import "Constants.h"

@implementation iPhoneTravel411AppDelegate

@synthesize window;
@synthesize navigationController;
@synthesize lastView;
```

Listing 16-3:   Saving indexPath

```
iPhoneTravel411AppDelegate *appDelegate =
        (iPhoneTravel411AppDelegate *)[[UIApplication
        sharedApplication] delegate];
```

```
[appDelegate.lastView replaceObjectAtIndex:0
          withObject:[NSNumber
          numberWithInteger:indexPath.section]];
[appDelegate.lastView replaceObjectAtIndex:1
          withObject:[NSNumber
          numberWithInteger:indexPath.row]];
```

Listing 16-4: Adding `viewWillAppear`:

```
- (void)viewWillAppear:(BOOL)animated {

  iPhoneTravel411AppDelegate *appDelegate =
          (iPhoneTravel411AppDelegate *)
          [[UIApplication sharedApplication] delegate];

  [appDelegate.lastView replaceObjectAtIndex:0
          withObject:[NSNumber numberWithInteger:-1]];
  [appDelegate.lastView replaceObjectAtIndex:1
          withObject:[NSNumber numberWithInteger:-1]];
}
```

Listing 16-5: Adding `applicationWillTerminate`:

```
- (void)applicationWillTerminate:(UIApplication *)
          application {

  NSArray *paths = NSSearchPathForDirectoriesInDomains
          (NSDocumentDirectory, NSUserDomainMask, YES);
  NSString *documentsDirectory = [paths objectAtIndex:0];
  NSString *filePath = [documentsDirectory stringBy
          AppendingPathComponent:kState];
  [lastView writeToFile:filePath atomically:YES];
}
```

Restoring the state

Now that I've saved the state, I need to restore it when the application is launched. I use our old friend `applicationDidFinishLaunching:` to carry out that task (as shown in Listing 16-6). `applicationDidFinish Launching` is a method you will find in the `iPhoneTravel411App Delegate.m` file. The code you need to add is in bold.

Listing 16-6: Add to `applicationDidFinishLaunching` :

```
- (void)applicationDidFinishLaunching:(UIApplication *)
                                      application {
```

(continued)

Listing 16-6 *(continued)*

```
    NSArray *paths = NSSearchPathForDirectoriesInDomains
            (NSDocumentDirectory, NSUserDomainMask, YES);
    NSString *documentsDirectory = [paths objectAtIndex:0];
    NSString *filePath = [documentsDirectory stringByAppendi
            ngPathComponent:kState];
    lastView =[[NSMutableArray alloc]  initWithContentsOfFil
            e:filePath];
    if (lastView == nil) {
      lastView = [[NSMutableArray arrayWithObjects:
                [NSNumber numberWithInteger:-1],
                [NSNumber numberWithInteger:-1],
                 nil] retain];
    }
    [window addSubview:[navigationController view]];
    [window makeKeyAndVisible];
}
```

Reading is the mirror image of writing. I create the complete path, including the file name, just as I did when I saved the file. This time I call `initWith ContentsOfFile:`, instead of `writeToFile:`, which allocates the `last View` array and initializes it with the file. If the result is `nil`, there is no file, meaning that this is the first time the application is being used. In that case, I create the array with the value of section and row set to –1 and –1. (As I said earlier, in Step 5 above, I use –1 –1 to indicate the main view because 0 0 is actually the first row in the first section.)

`initWithContentsOfFile:` is an `NSData` method similar to `writeTo File:`. The classes that implement `writeToFile` and those that implement `initWithContentsOfFile:` are the same.

Fortunately, restoring the current state is actually straightforward, given the program architecture. The `RootViewController`'s `viewDidLoad` method is called at application launch — after the first view is in place but not yet visible. At that point, you are getting ready to display the (table) view. But instead of just doing that, you see if the saved view was something other than the table view, and if it was, you take advantage of the same mechanisms that are used when the user taps a row in the table view. You call the `didSelect RowAtIndexPath:` method which already knows how to display a particular view represented by the `indexPath`, i.e. section and row. This is shown in Listing 16-7.

`viewDidLoad` is already in the `RootViewController.m` file. All you have to do is uncomment it out.

Listing 16-7:   Specify the view to be displayed at launch

```
- (void)viewDidLoad {

iPhoneTravel411AppDelegate *appDelegate =
        (iPhoneTravel411AppDelegate *)[[UIApplication
        sharedApplication] delegate];

if ([(( NSNumber*) [appDelegate.lastView
        objectAtIndex:0]) intValue] != -1) {
    NSIndexPath* indexPath = [NSIndexPath
        indexPathForRow:[[appDelegate.
        lastView objectAtIndex:1]intValue]
        inSection:[[appDelegate.lastView
        objectAtIndex:0] intValue]];

    [self tableView: ((UITableView*) self.tableView )did
        SelectRowAtIndexPath:indexPath ];
    }
}
```

Here's what you're up to in Listing 16-7:

1. Check to see if the last view was the table view.

```
if ([(( NSNumber*) [appDelegate.lastView
        objectAtIndex:0]) intValue] != -1) {
```

2. If the last view wasn't the table view, create the index path using the last section and row information that was loaded into the lastView **instance variable by** applicationDidFinishLaunching:.

```
NSIndexPath* indexPath = [NSIndexPath
        indexPathForRow:[[appDelegate.
        lastView objectAtIndex:1]intValue]
        inSection:[[appDelegate.lastView
        objectAtIndex:0] intValue]];
```

3. Call the didSelectRowAtIndexPath **method to display the right view.**

```
[self tableView: ((UITableView*) self.tableView ) did
        SelectRowAtIndexPath:indexPath ];
```

The reason I created an index path was to be able to take advantage of the didSelectRowAtIndexPath: method. This is our old friend from Chapter 15; we handle it by replaying the last user tap in the main view.

Respecting User Preferences

Figure 16-1 shows you the Settings screen for my MobileTravel411 application. There you can see that I've provisioned my app with three preferences. In this chapter, I show you how to implement the most critical of these preferences — the Use Stored Data option.

Use Stored Data tells the application to use the last version of the data that it accessed, rather than going out on the Internet for the latest information. While this does violate my I Want The Most Up To Date Information, it can save the user from excessive roaming charges, depending on their cell provider's data plan.

Figure 16-1:
The
required
preferences.

No doubt it's way cool to put user preferences in Settings. Some programmers abuse this trick, though; they make you go into Settings, when it's just as easy to give the user a preference-setting capability within the program itself. You should only put something in Settings if the user changes it infrequently. In this case, stored data doesn't change often; Use Stored Data mode definitely belongs in Settings.

In this part of the chapter, I'm going to show you how to put a toggle switch in Settings that lets you specify whether to use only stored data — and then show you how to retrieve the setting. In the next chapter, I show you how to actually use the toggle switch setting in your code.

The Settings application uses a property list, called `Root.plist`, found in the Settings bundle inside your application. The Settings application takes what you put in the property list and builds a Settings section for your application in its list of application settings as well as the views that display and enable the user to change those settings. The next sections spell out how to put that Settings section to work for you.

Adding a Settings bundle to your project

For openers, you'll have to add a Settings bundle to your application. Here are the moves:

1. **In the Groups & Files listing (at left in the Xcode project window), select the iPhoneTravel411 folder and then chose File⇨New File from the main menu, or press ⇨cmd+n.**

   The New File dialog appears.

2. **Choose Settings under the iPhone OS heading in the left pane, and then select the Settings Bundle icon, as shown in Figure 16-2.**

3. **Click the Next button.**

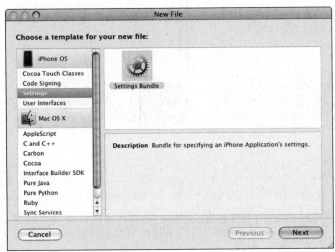

Figure 16-2: Creating the application bundle.

4. **Choose the default name of** `Settings.bundle`, **then press Return (Enter) or click Finish.**

   You should now see a new item called `Settings.bundle` in the iPhone Travel411 folder, in the Groups & Files listing.

5. **Click the triangle to expand the** `Settings.bundle` **subfolder.**

   You'll see the `Root.plist` file as well as an `en.lproj` folder — the latter is used for dealing with localization issues, as discussed in Chapter 15.

Setting up the property list

Property lists are widely used in iPhone applications because they provide an easy way to create structured data using named values for a number of object types.

In the MobileTravel411 application, I use property lists extensively as a way to "parameterize" view controllers and models. (I de-buzz this word and provide details in the next chapter.)

Property lists all have a single root node — a Dictionary, which means it stores items using a key-value pair, just as an `NSDictionary` does: All dictionary entries must have both a key and a value. In this dictionary there are three keys:

- ✔ Title
- ✔ StringsTable
- ✔ PreferenceSpecifiers

The values for each of the first two entries are strings. The first is the name of your application, whereas the second is the name of a strings table used for localization, which I won't get into here. The third entry is an array of dictionaries — one dictionary for each preference. You'll probably need some time to wrap you head around that one. It will become clearer as I take you through it.

`PreferenceSpecifiers` is where you put a toggle switch so the user can choose to use (or not use, since it's a toggle) only stored data — I'll refer to that choice later as *stored-data mode*. Here's how it's done:

1. **In the Groups & Files pane of the project window, select the triangle next to the** `Settings.bundle` **file to reveal the** `Root.plist` **file, as shown in Figure 16-3.**

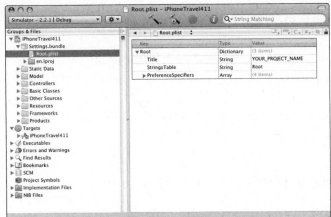

2. **Double-click the** Root.plist **file to open it in a separate window.**

   Okay, you don't *really* have to do this, but I find it easier to work with this file when it's sitting in its own window.

3. **In the** Root.plist **window you just opened, expand the triangles next to all the nodes by clicking all those triangles, as shown in Figure 16-4.**

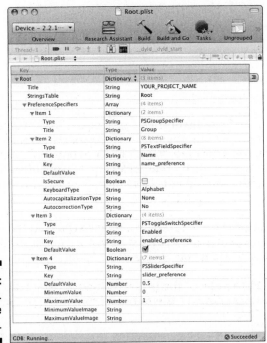

4. **Still in the** Root.plist **window, double-click the current value next to Title — the first item under the Root node — and change it from YOUR_PROJECT_NAME to iPhoneTravel411.**

5. **Under the next heading in the** Root.plist **window —** Preference Specifiers **— move to Item 1.**

   PreferenceSpecifiers is an array designed to hold a set of diction- ary nodes, each of which represents a single preference. For each item listed in the array, the first row under it has a key of Type; every prop- erty list node in the PreferenceSpecifiers array must have an entry with this key, which identifies what kind of entry this is. The Type value for the current Item 1 — PSGroupSpecifier — is used to indicate that a new group should be started. The value for this key actually acts like a section heading for a table view (like you created in Chapter 15). Double- click into the value next to Title (refer to Figure 16-4) and replace the default Group with IPhoneTravel411 Preferences (or be creative if you would like).

6. **Seeing that Item 3 is already defined as a toggle switch, you can just modify it by changing the** Title **value from** Enabled **to** Use stored data **and the key from** enabled_preference **to** useStoredData Preference. **This is the key you will use in your application to access the preference.**

7. **Continue your modifications by unchecking the Boolean checkbox next to** DefaultValue.

   I want the Use Stored Data preference initially to be set to Off because I expect most people will still want to go out on the Internet for the latest information, despite the high roaming charges involved.

   When you're done, the Root.plist window should look like Figure 16-5.

8. **Collapse the little triangles next to items 2 and 4 (as shown in Figure 16-6), and then select those items one by one and delete them.**

   The item numbers do change as you delete them, so be careful. That's why you need to leave the preference item you care about open, so you can see not to delete it. Fortunately, Undo is supported here; if you make a mistake, press ⌘+z to undo the delete.

9. **Save the property file by pressing ⌘+S.**

Time to see if everything is set up and working as it should. Start out by selecting Build and Run from the Build menu. Then, if you click the Home button and then the icon for the Settings application, you should find an entry for our application. Clicking on that and you should see the right hand view in Figure 16-1. (You'll have to download iPhone Travel411 from my Web site to get this to compile correctly.)

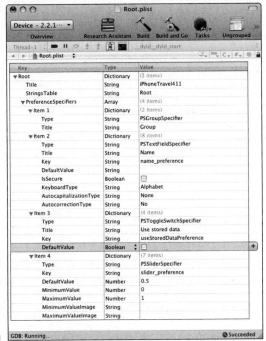

Figure 16-5:
Preferences
for IPhone
Travel411.

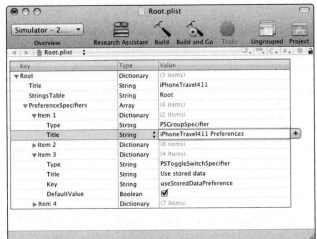

Figure 16-6:
Delete these
items.

Reading Settings in the Application

After you've set it up so your users can let their preferences be known in Settings, you'll need to read those preferences back into the application. You do that in the iPhoneTravel411AppDelegate's applicationDidFinish Launching: method. But first, a little housekeeping.

1. **Add the new instance variable** useStoredData **and declare the @property in the** iPhoneTravel411AppDelegate.h **file.**

   This is shown in Listing 16-8. (Again, the new stuff is bold.)

   Notice that the @property declaration is a little different than what you have been using so far. Up to now, all your properties have been declared (nonatomic, retain), — as was explained back in Chapter 7. What's this readwrite stuff? Since useStoredData: is not an object (it is a Boolean value) retain is not applicable. Instead you'll enable it be read and assigned to.

2. **Add the** @synthesize **statement to the** iPhoneTravel411AppDelegate.m **file, to tell the compiler to create the accessors for you.**

   This is shown in Listing 16-9. (You guessed it — new is bold.)

Listing 16-8:   Add the instance variable to the interface

```
#import <UIKit/UIKit.h>

@interface iPhoneTravel411AppDelegate : NSObject
                              <UIApplicationDelegate> {

  UIWindow                   *window;
  UINavigationController     *navigationController;
  NSMutableArray             *lastView;
  BOOL                       useStoredData;
}


@property (nonatomic, retain) IBOutlet UIWindow *window;
@property (nonatomic, retain) IBOutlet
          UINavigationController *navigationController;
@property (nonatomic, retain) NSMutableArray *lastView;
@property (nonatomic, readwrite) BOOL useStoredData;

@end
```

Listing 16-9: Add the synthesize to the implementation

```
#import "iPhoneTravel411AppDelegate.h"
#import "RootViewController.h"
#import "Constants.h"

@implementation iPhoneTravel411AppDelegate

@synthesize window;
@synthesize navigationController;
@synthesize lastView;
@synthesize useStoredData;
```

With your housekeeping done, it's time to add the necessary code to the `applicationDidFinishLaunching:` method. Listing 16-10 shows the code you need:

Listing 16-10: Add to applicationDidFinishLaunching

```
- (void)applicationDidFinishLaunching:(UIApplication *)
                                        application {
 if (![[NSUserDefaults standardUserDefaults] objectForKey:
        kUseStoredDataPreference] ){
    [[NSUserDefaults standardUserDefaults]setBool:NO
                      forKey:kUseStoredDataPreference];
    useStoredData = NO;
    }
  else
    useStoredData = [[NSUserDefaults standardUserDefaults]
                    boolForKey:kUseStoredDataPreference];

  NSArray *paths = NSSearchPathForDirectoriesInDomains
          (NSDocumentDirectory, NSUserDomainMask, YES);
  NSString *documentsDirectory = [paths objectAtIndex:0];
  NSString *filePath = [documentsDirectory stringBy
          AppendingPathComponent:kState];
  lastView =[[NSMutableArray alloc]  initWithContentsOf
          File:filePath];
  if (lastView == nil) {
    lastView = [[NSMutableArray arrayWithObjects:
              [NSNumber numberWithInteger:-1],
              [NSNumber numberWithInteger:-1],
              nil] retain];
  }
  [window addSubview:[navigationController view]];
          [window makeKeyAndVisible];
}
```

Here's what you want all that code to do for you:

1. **Check to see whether the settings have been moved into** NSUser Defaults.

```
if (![[NSUserDefaults standardUserDefaults] objectFor
      Key:kUseStoredDataPreference] ){
```

   I explain NSUserDefaults back in Chapter 9. The Settings application moves the user's preferences from Settings into NSUserDefaults only *after* the user opens them up for the first time; Settings will, however, update them in NSUserDefaults if the user makes any changes.

2. **If the settings have not been moved into** NSUserDefaults **yet, then use the default of** NO **(which corresponds to the default I used for the initial preference value).**

```
[[NSUserDefaults standardUserDefaults]setBool:NO
                 forKey:kUseStoredDataPreference];
    useStoredData = NO;
```

3. **If the settings** *have* **been moved into** NSUserDefaults, **read them in, and then set the** useStoredData **instance variable to whatever the user's preference is.**

```
else
   useStoredData =
           [[NSUserDefaults   standardUserDefaults]
           boolForKey:kUseStoredDataPreference];
```

   I show you how to use useStoredData in your code in Chapter 17.

This App Is Almost Done

In the next chapter, I show you how to implement the content view controllers, views, and models. Then you'll be ready to march off and create your own applications.

Chapter 17

Creating Controllers and Their Models

In This Chapter
▶ Taking another look at model objects
▶ Taking advantage of reusable view controllers and models
▶ Accessing data on the Internet
▶ Saving and reading files

Getting the infrastructure in place for a new iPhone application is certainly a crucial part of the development process, but in the grand scheme of things it's only the spadework that prepares the way for the really cool stuff. After all is said and done, you still need to add the content that the users will see or interact with. Content is, after all, the reason they bought this application.

Chapter 15 was all about infrastructure — and a very interesting chapter it was — but this chapter moves on from there to content views and how to implement them.

This is actually less difficult than it sounds. The real key to creating an extensible application — one where you can easily add new views — is the program architecture. Once you have a table view in place, you have the structure necessary for navigation in your application. With that navigation architecture — along with the MVC pattern I've been touting all along — creating the views, view controllers, and models turns out to be somewhat pedestrian. You do more or less the same thing over again for each new content view. (Oh well, boring is sometimes good; computers love consistency.)

If you've been dutifully following along in this book chapter by chapter, you probably already know the basics of creating a view and its view controller. If so, no big surprise that what I do here is almost identical to creating the view controller for my other sample application (the ReturnMeTo app) in Chapters 5, 7, 8, 9 and 11 — although this time I get to do it in a single chapter!

To kick off the process, you'll first need to decide what you want to see in each view whenever the user selects a particular row in the main view. You'll also need to decide where that information is going to be located. You have a number of options here. It can be a program resource (kind of like a local file, which I'll get to later), a Web page, or data located on a server on the Internet. To ease your mind, I'll show you how to work with all three. And, oh yes, you'll also have to decide what you want to do if the user is offline, which is not as ominous as it may seem.

My running examples in this chapter are going to involve implementing the Currency, Weather, and Heathrow selections for the iPhoneTravel411 application. To see the full listings of each of those, you'll have to go to my Web site — www.nealgoldstein.com. At this stage of the game, the listings have gotten so big that it would be a bear for you to flip back and forth between them in printed-text form. Having them in electronic form also means that, if you download them, you can create an Xcode project and both work along and experiment with changing parameters or even logic just to see what happens — both are very helpful in learning what's going on.

Let's go to work.

Specifying the Content

If the user selects **Currency** from the main view in the iPhoneTravel411 application, he or she will see some very basic information about exchange rates, as illustrated in Figure 17-1. Since this information changes rarely (if ever), I'm going to include this information in the application. The way to do this is to include it as a *resource*, which I will explain in a later section. The view the user sees will be the same regardless if the user is online or in stored data mode.

If the user selects **Weather** from the main view, what the user sees *does* depend on whether the device is online or in stored data mode. If the device is online, the user sees a Web page from a Web site with the weather information, as illustrated in Figure 17-2 (left) When in stored data mode, the user gets a message stating that weather data is unavailable when offline, as you can see in Figure 17-2 (right).

If the user selects **Heathrow** from the main view, he or she sees what's illustrated in Figure 17-3: A view of one particular means of transportation (Heathrow Express, for example), with tabs that will enable her or him to look at the others. When the user is online, I'll get this data off of a server on the Internet where I keep the (up to date) information. The only difference between being online and being in stored data mode (offline) is the freshness of the data. In stored data mode, what the user sees is a copy of the information that I saved the last time the user was online.

Figure 17-1:
Currency
view.

Figure 17-2:
Weather
views.

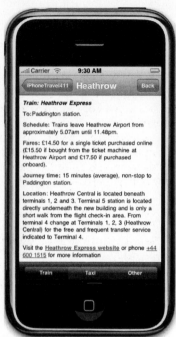

Figure 17-3:
Heathrow
view.

In this chapter, I show you how to code the views, view controllers, and models for each of the examples listed above. The views will all be UIWeb Views (see Chapter 14 for more on those) and I'll have you creating a unique view controller (WeatherController, for example) and model (Weather, for example) for each.

If you've had a chance to make your way through Chapter 14, you'll remember that I told you that you could use the same *generic* view controller and model to display any of the views you are about to create. Well, you can, but I'm not going to recommend doing that in this example for two reasons. It will be a lot easier to follow the logic in each of these view controllers and models if I keep them separate, because then I can use more context-specific data names and logic. But more importantly, while not rocket science, what you'd have to do to generalize the behavior of a model and view controller involves some pretty nifty work with property lists or databases, and that's not in the cards for this book.

What I *will* do though, is explain afterwards the approach you'd have to take to turn your work into a general solution. I'll even put more advanced information on my Web site for you to use as well.

Fair enough?

Creating the View Controller, Nib, and Model Files

Standard operating procedure for iPhone applications is to have a user tap an entry in a main view to get to a subsequent view. For this to work, you need to create a new controller and push in on to the stack. (For more on controllers and stacks as they apply to the iPhoneTravel411 application, see Chapter 15.) From there, you need to get your view controller interface and implementation files, your nib files, and then your model interface and implementation files all lined up. (Yes, we're talking a lot of files here — deal with it.)

Going from abstract to concrete, read on as I spell out what you need to have in place before your users can jump from one view to another in iPhone Travel411 — say, when a user selects the "Heathrow" row in the main view of the app and fully expects to find a new view full of information about (yep) Heathrow airport. This will be the general pattern you can follow for the rest of the rows in this application, or in any application that uses a table view. (For more on table views, check out Chapter 15.)

Adding the controller and nib file

So many files, so little time. Actually, after you get a rhythm going, cranking out the various view controller, nib, and model files necessary to fill your application architecture with content isn't *that* much work. I want to start with what happens when the user taps Heathrow because it allows me to also explain a bit about navigating between views in your program.

OK, check out how easy it is to come up with the view controller and nib files:

1. **In the iPhoneTravel411 project window, select the Classes folder, and then select File⇨New from the main menu (or press ⌘+n) to get the New File dialog you see in Figure 17-4.**

2. **In the left column of the dialog, select Cocoa Touch Classes under the iPhone OS heading, select the UIViewController subclass template in the top right pane, and then click Next.**

   You'll see a new dialog asking for some more information.

3. **Enter AirportController.m in the File Name field, as I did in Figure 17-5, and then select Finish.**

   I'm using Airport here instead of Heathrow to get you started thinking more in terms of generic controllers — an airport is an airport after all. What would you have to do to re-use this controller for the other two airports in the main view?

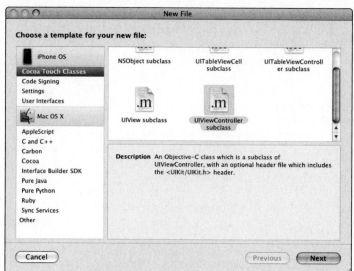

Figure 17-4:
Select
UIView
Controller
subclass.

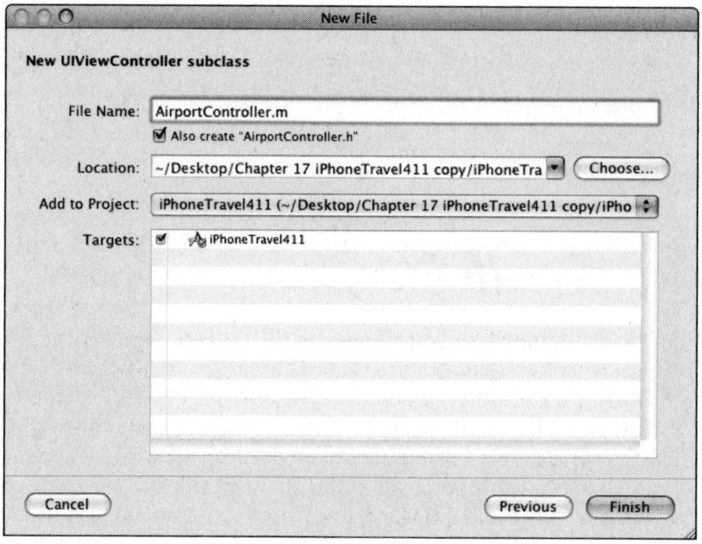

Figure 17-5:
Save as
Airport
Controller.m.

4. **In the iPhoneTravel411 project window, select the Resources folder, and then select File⇨New or press ⌘+n to get the template chooser you see in Figure 17-6.**

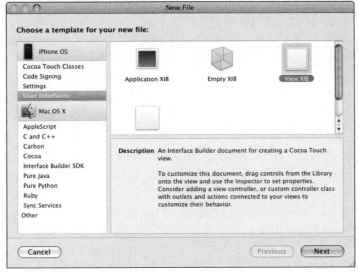

Figure 17-6:
Create a
new xib
view in
Xcode.

5. **In the left column, choose user Interfaces under iPhone OS, choose the View XIB template in the top-right window, and then select Next.**

   You'll see a dialog similar to that in Figure 17-5.

6. **Type** AirportController.xib **in the File Name field and then select Finish.**

Set up the nib file

For the iPhoneTravel411 application, you'll want to use a UIWebView to display the airport information you think your users will need. (For the reasoning behind that choice, check out Chapter 14.) You'll set the UIWebView up using Interface Builder, but you'll also need a reference to it from the AirportController so it can pass the content from the model to the view. To do *that*, you need to create an *outlet* (a special kind of instance that can refer to objects in the nib) in the view controller, just as you did back in Chapter 7 when you were working on the ReturnMeTo application. The outlet reference will be "filled in" automatically when your application is initialized.

Here's how you should deal with this outlet business:

1. **Within Xcode, add an** airportView (UIWebView) **outlet to the** Airport Controller.h **interface file.**

You declare an outlet by using the keyword IBOutlet in the Airport Controller interface file.

2. **While you're at it, make the AirportController a UIWebView delegate as well (you'll need that later).**

Here's what it should look like when you are done, changes are in bold.

```
@interface AirportController : UIViewController
                              <UIWebViewDelegate> {
    IBOutlet UIWebView *airportView;
```

3. **Do the File⇨Save thing to save the file.**

After it's saved — and only then — Interface Builder can find the new outlet.

4. **Use the Groups & Files listing on the left in the project window to drill down to the** AirportController.xib **file, then double-click the file to launch it in Interface Builder.**

Interface Builder should display the windows you see in Figure 17-7. If the Attributes Inspector window is open, you'll see four icons across the top — corresponding to the Attributes, Connections, Size Inspector and Identity Inspectors, respectively. Make sure the Identity Inspector is chosen.

If the Attributes Inspector window is not open, choose Tools⇨Inspector or press shift+ ⌘+1. If the View window is not visible, double-click the View icon in the AirportController.xib window.

If you can't find the AirportController.xib window (you may have minimized it — accidentally, on purpose, whatever) you can get it back by choosing Window⇨AirportController.xib or whichever nib file you're working on.

5. **Select File's Owner in the** AirportController.xib **window.**

6. **Select** AirportController **from the Class drop-down menu in the Identity Inspector, as shown in Figure 17-7.**

Doing so (surprise, surprise) tells Interface Builder that the File's Owner is AirportController.

7. **Click in the View window and then choose** UIWebView **from the Class drop-down menu in the Identity Inspector, as shown in Figure 17-8.**

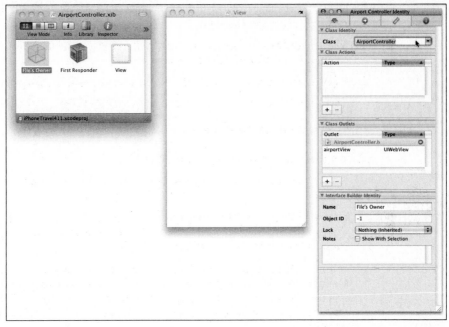

Figure 17-7:
Make the
File's owner
an Airport
controller.

8. **Back in the** AirportController.xib **window, right-click File's Owner to call up a contextual menu with a list of connections**.

You can get the same list using the Connections tab in the Attributes Inspector.

9. **Drag from the little circle next to the** airportView **outlet in the list onto the View window, as shown in Figure 17-9.**

Doing so connects the AirportController's airportView outlet to the Web view.

10. **Right-click File's Owner again to call up the very same list of connections, but this time drag from the little circle next to the view outlet to the View window, as shown in Figure 17-10.**

Doing so connects the AirportController's view outlet to the Web view.

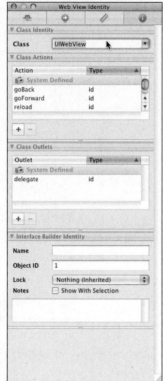

Figure 17-8:
Make the
view a
UIWebView.

If you think about it though, why do you need the `airportView`? There is already a pointer to the `view` object safely nestled in the view controller. There are two reasons.

✔ **I'm lazy.** If a create a second outlet of type `UIWebView`, then every time I access it I don't have to cast the vanilla Web view into a `UIWebView`, as you can see below.

```
(UIWebView*) [self view] or (UIWebView*) self.view
```

✔ **I'm doing it for you.** It makes the code easier to follow.

At this point, you have the view controller class set up and you've arranged for the nib loader to create a `UIWebView` object and set all the outlets for you when the user selects Heathrow for the main view.

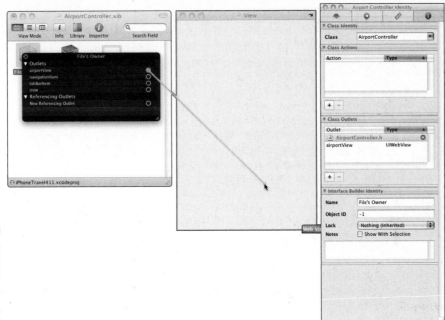

Figure 17-9:
Connecting the airportView outlet.

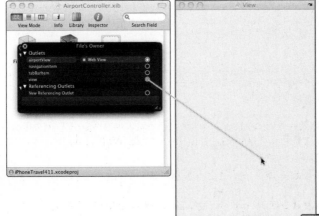

Figure 17-10:
Connect the view outlet.

Adding the model class

At some point you'll definitely want to add a model class — and you'll do it following the same procedure you used when you added the `Airport Controller`.

It would be a good idea to add a new folder in the Groups & Files pane to hold all your new model classes. To do so, select the iPhoneTravel411 project icon and then choose Project⇨New Group. You'll get a brand spanking new folder, named New Group, already selected and waiting for you to type in the name you want. To change what folder a file is in, select and then drag the file to the folder you want it to occupy. The same goes for folders as well (after all, they can go into other folders).

1. **Select File⇨New from the main menu (or press ⌘+n) to get the New File dialog.**

2. **In the left-most column of the dialog, first select Cocoa Touch Classes under the iPhone OS heading, select the NSObject subclass template in the topmost pane as I have in Figure 17-11 and then click Next.**

   You'll see a new dialog asking for some more information.

3. **Enter** Airport.m **in the File Name field and then click Finish.**

At this point, you have the classes defined for the `Airport` model object. All that's left for you to do is enter the code to make it do something — well, maybe not just *something*. How about *exactly* what you want it do?

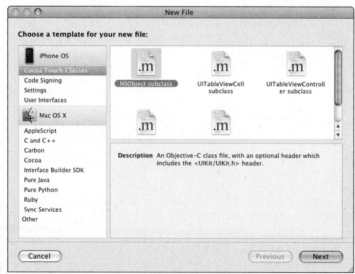

Figure 17-11: Adding a model class.

Implementing the View, View Controller, and the Model

You now have all the classes/objects you need to actually implement a view similar to what you see in Figure 17-3.

Check out all the little things you need to do next.

The initialization chain

Initialization is one of those nuts and bolts things that is a good idea to pay attention to. It is the way you connect your controller and models, as well as one of the key places to pass the information you'll need when you create a generic view controller and model. It's best to think of this process as an *initialization chain*, rather than as separate steps, and it is illustrated in Figure 17-12. To see how it works, follow along as I walk you through it using the Airport controller and model as an example.

It all starts in `RootViewController.m`.

1. **In the** RootViewController's didSelectRowAtIndexPath: **method — create and initialize the view controller that implements the row selected by the user.**

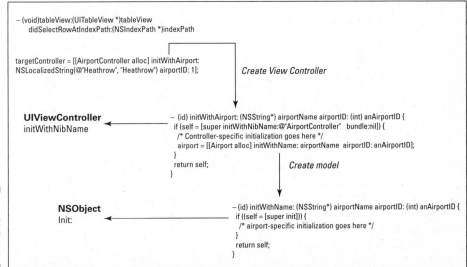

Figure 17-12: The great chain of initialization.

The code below allocates an Airport Controller (a view controller) and then calls the `AirportController`'s `initWithAirport:cityID:` method. (You did this at the very end of Chapter 15; you might want to review that if it has been a while since you looked at it.) The parameters here are for illustrative purposes only. I've included a `cityID` — which I don't use — to show you how you would create an `init` method with more than one parameter.

```
targetController = [[AirportController
      alloc] initWithAirport:
      NSLocalizedString(@"Heathrow", "Heathrow")
      cityID: 1];
```

Now on to `AirportController.m`.

2. **Add the** initWithAirport: **method, shown in Listing 17-1, to** `Airport Controller.m`.

First call the superclass's `initWithNibName: bundle:` method

```
- (id) initWithAirport: (NSString*) airportName
                         cityID: (int) aCityID {
   if (self = [super initWithNibName:
         @"AirportController" bundle:nil])
```

This method is the next link in the chain. I pass it the nib file name (the one I just created in a previous section) and `nil` as the bundle, telling it to look in the main bundle.

Note that the message to `super` precedes the initialization code added in the method. This sequencing ensures that initialization proceeds in the order of inheritance. Calling the superclass's `initWithNibName: bundle:` method initializes the controller, loads and initializes the objects in the nib file (views and controls for example), and then sets all its outlet instance variables and Target-Action connections for good measure.

The `init...:` methods all return back a pointer to the object created. While not the case here, the reason you assign whatever comes back from an `init...:` method to `self` is that some classes actually return back a different class than what you created. The assignment to `self` becomes important if your class is derived from one of those kinds of classes. Keep in mind as well that an `init...:` method can also return `nil:` if there's a problem initializing an object. If you're creating an object where that is a possibility, you have to take that into account. (Both of those situations are beyond the scope of this book.)

Next, create the `Airport` model, as shown in Listing 17-2.

After the return from this call, the `Airport` controller is ready to do its own initialization, including setting the title and creating and initializing the Airport model(s).

Time for `Airport.m`.

3. **Add the** initWithName: **method, shown in Listing 17-3, to** `Airport.m`.

   This is the standard way to initialize an object. I didn't have to do this in the `AirportController` because it's taken care of in the super-class hierarchy. But when you create your own objects derived from `NSObject`, as I did here, you are where the rubber meets the road, so to speak. After the return from this method, you would do any other initial-ization needed.

   In both cases, some of that initialization, of course, could involve initial-izing generic airport and airport controller objects for a specific airport. More on this later.

Listing 17-1: Adding the `initWithAirport:` method

```
- (id) initWithAirport: (NSString*) airportName cityID:
                                          (int) aCityID  {

  if (self = [super initWithNibName:@"AirportController"
                                          bundle:nil]) {
    self.title = airportName;
    airport = [[Airport alloc] initWithName: airportName];
    }
  return self;
}
```

Listing 17-2: Creating the `Airport` model

```
    self.title = airportName;
    airport = [[Airport alloc] initWithName: airportName
          ];
    }
```

Listing 17-3: Adding the `initWithName:` method,

```
- (id) initWithName: (NSString*) airportName {

  if ((self = [super init])) {
    /* airport-specific initialization goes here */
  }
    return self;
  }
```

If your eyes are beginning to glaze over after this section, don't worry about it. It does get easier after this. I know it's a lot to absorb, if you regularly come back and reread this section as you gain more experience, you won't be alone. I have included it because it's my responsibility to start you down the right path. At some point, you may wonder, "Why did I think that was so hard?" or have an "Aha!" moment — "Here's a *better* way to do what Neal wants me to do." Both are good signs.

Setting up the view

Your AirportController is going to be getting the content for any view you've set up from the Airport object — content which it then passes on to the view itself. But before you get a crack at doing that, you need to know how set up the view. If you take a look back at Figure 17-3, what you see is UIWebView, with a segmented control at the bottom (Train— Taxi — Other, in this example). You use the ViewDidLoad method to get your view nice and prepped for its big day. This method was created for you in AirportController.m by the UIViewController subclass template you chose in the "Adding the Controller and Nib File" section, earlier in the chapter. You can see the code that was automatically added below:

```
/*
// Implement viewDidLoad to do additional setup after
          loading the view, typically from a nib.
- (void)viewDidLoad {
    [super viewDidLoad];
}
*/
```

Simply uncomment out this method and follow these steps to add the needed code after [super viewDidLoad]:

1. **Create and add the Back button.**

```
UIBarButtonItem *backButton = [[[UIBarButtonItem
        alloc]
            initWithTitle: @"Back"
            style:UIBarButtonItemStylePlain
            target:self
            action:@selector(goBack:)] autorelease];
self.navigationItem.rightBarButtonItem = backButton;
```

In this method, you allocate the button and then assign it to an instance variable that the UINavigationController will later use to set up the Navigation Bar. The action:@selector(goBack:) argument is the standard way to specify Target-Action — and is exactly what you did when you created the button that enabled text entry in Chapter 12. It says when the button is tapped, send the goBack: message to the target: self, which is the AirportController. I'll show you how to implement this shortly.

2. **Create the choice bar to be used for the segmented control at the bottom of the screen.**

```
choiceBar = [UIToolbar new];
choiceBar.barStyle = UIBarStyleBlackOpaque;
CGRect viewBounds = self.view.frame;
viewBounds.origin.y =  viewBounds.size.height -
    self.navigationController.navigationBar.frame.
    size.height-kToolbarHeight -
    [UIApplication sharedApplication].
                        statusBarFrame.size.height;
viewBounds.size.height =  kToolbarHeight;
[choiceBar setFrame:viewBounds];
```

Here, you're computing a subview's frame using viewBounds and taking into account the height of the Navigation and Status bars. (You're also setting the style to BlackOpaque, my personal favorite — I hope you don't mind.)

3. Create the segmented control.

```
choiceBarSegmentedControl = [[UISegmentedControl
    alloc] initWithItems: [NSArray
    arrayWithObjects: @"Train", @"Taxi", @"Other",
    nil]];
[choiceBarSegmentedControl addTarget:self action:@
    selector(selectTrans:) forControlEvents:UICont
    rolEventValueChanged];
choiceBarSegmentedControl.segmentedControlStyle =
                        UISegmentedControlStyleBar;
choiceBarSegmentedControl.tintColor = [UIColor
                            darkGrayColor];
CGRect segmentedControlFrame =  choiceBar.frame;
segmentedControlFrame.size.width =
                choiceBar.frame.size.width -
                kLeftMargin;
segmentedControlFrame.size.height =
                            kSegControlHeight;
choiceBarSegmentedControl.frame =
                        segmentedControlFrame;
choiceBarSegmentedControl.selectedSegmentIndex = 0;
```

In the first line of code, you're creating a segmented control and an array that specifies the text for each segment. You then set the Target-Action parameters saying that if a segment is tapped by the user (UIControlEventValueChanged), then the selectTrans: message (I've shortened that from selectTransportation because I am getting tired of typing those long names) is sent to self, that's to say the AirportController. You then compute the size of the segmented control as you would for any other subview. The last line specifies the initial segment (0) selected when the view is created; before the view is displayed, the `selectTrans:` message is sent to display the content associated with segment 0. (You can see the code for `selectTrans:` in all its glory in Listing 17-4.)

4. **Add the segmented control to the control bar.**

```
UIBarButtonItem *choiceItem = [[UIBarButtonItem alloc]
        initWithCustomView:choiceBarSegmentedControl]

    choiceBar.items = [NSArray
    arrayWithObject:choiceItem];
[choiceItem release];
```

You get the `choiceBar` (`UIToolbar`) to display controls by creating an array of instances of `UIBarButtonItems` and assigning the array to the `items` property of the `UIToolbar` object (our `choiceBar`). In this case, you create a `UIBarButtonItem` and initialize it with the segmented control you just created. You then create the array and assign it to `items`.

I then can release `choiceItem` since the `NSArray` has a reference it.

5. **Add the choice bar to the view.**

```
[self.view addSubview:choiceBar];
```

At this point, you now have the view set up, waiting for data, and the segmented control across the bottom that will allow the user to select @"Train", @"Taxi", @"Other".

Responding to the user selection

You've set things up so that when the view is first created — or when the user taps a control — the `AirportController`'s `selectTrans:` method is called, allowing the `AirportController` to hook up what the view needs to display with what the model has to offer. Listing 17-4 shows the necessary code in all its elegance.

Listing 17-4: selectTrans

```
- (void)selectTrans:(id)sender {
iPhoneTravel411AppDelegate *appDelegate =
        (iPhoneTravel411AppDelegate *)[[UIApplication
        sharedApplication] delegate];
bool realtime = !appDelegate.useStoredData;
if (realtime) {
  [ airportView loadRequest:[NSURLRequest
        requestWithURL:[airport returnTransRealtime:
        (((UISegmentedControl*) sender).
        selectedSegmentIndex)]]];
```

```
    }
  else  {
    [airportView loadData: [airport returnTransOffline:
          (((UISegmentedControl*) sender).
          selectedSegmentIndex)] MIMEType:@"text/html"
          textEncodingName:@"UTF-8" baseURL:nil];
    }
}
```

This is the code that gets executed when the user selects one of the segmented controls (Train, Taxi, Other) that you added to the view. If you'll
notice, the controller itself has no idea — nor should it care — what was
selected. It just passes what was selected on to the model. That kind of logic
should be (and as you will soon see *is*) in the model.

✔ You use the useStoredData instance variable (the one you created in
    Chapter 16 to hold the user preference) to see if you're using real-time
    data (that is, to see that you're not in shared-data mode). If you are
    using real-time data, you send the returnTransRealtime: message to
    the Airport object. It returns the NSURL that Web view needs to load
    the data. (The NSURL is simply an object that includes the utilities nec-
    essary for downloading files or other resources from Web and FTP serv-
    ers.) You then include that in the loadRequest: message to the Web
    view (airportView), which tells it to load the data associated with that
    NSURL.

✔ If you're using stored data, then you send the returnTransOffline:
    message to the Airport object. It returns the data which is then passed
    on as one of the arguments in the loadData: message sent to the Web
    view (airportView). (You did the same thing in Chapter 11 when you
    loaded the phone number into the ReturnMeTo Web view.)

Before I show you the code in the model that implements returnTransReal
time: and returnTransOffline:, I want to show you one other thing,
and that is the implementation of goBack:, which I specified as the selector
when I created the back button in viewDidLoad. Listing 17-5 has the details.

Listing 17-5:   goBack to where you once belonged

```
- (IBAction) goBack:(id)sender{
  if ([airportView  canGoBack] == NO )
    [[self navigationController]
          popViewControllerAnimated:YES];
  else
    [airportView goBack];
}
```

In Chapter 15, I explain how you really need *two* ways to go back from a view.
The first way is the left button on the navigation bar, which sends the user
back to the previous view controller and its view — the main (table) view.

The second way — a second Back button — is needed in order to return back to a "parallel" view — when the user touches a link in a view that sent them to an external Web page for example. In the `viewDidLoad` method, I show you how to create that button and I specify there that when the user touches the button, the `goBack:` message should be sent to `AirportViewController`.

The `UIWebView` actually implements much of the behavior I need here. When the user touches the Back button and this method is called, I first check with the Web view to see whether there is someplace to go back *to* (it keeps a backward *and* forward list). If there is an appropriate retreat, I call the `UIWebView` method (`goBack:`) that will reload the previous page. If not, it means that I am at the Heathrow content page, and I simply "pop" (remove from the stack) the Airport view controller to return to the main window — the same thing the button on the left side of the Navigation bar would do.

Finally, I need to disable links when I am in stored data mode — if the user isn't online, there's no way to get to the link. `shouldStartLoadWith Request:` is a `UIWebView` delegate method (remember I had you make the `AirportController` a `UIWebView` delegate earlier when you added the `airportView` outlet). It's called before a Web view begins loading content to see whether you want the load to proceed. I'm only interested in doing something if the user touched a link when he or she is in stored data mode. Listing 17-6 shows the code you'd need to disable links in such a situation.

Listing 17-6:   Disabling links in stored data mode

```
- (BOOL)webView:(UIWebView *)webView shouldStartLoadWith
        Request:(NSURLRequest *)request navigationType:
        (UIWebViewNavigationType)navigationType {
    if ((navigationType ==
        UIWebViewNavigationTypeLinkClicked) &&    (
        [[NSUserDefaults standardUserDefaults] boolFor
        Key:kUseStoredDataPreference]) ) {
    UIAlertView *alert = [[UIAlertView
        alloc] initWithTitle:@"" message:
        NSLocalizedString(@"Link not available
        offline",   @"stored data mode")
        delegate:self cancelButtonTitle:NSLocalizedSt
        ring( @"Thanks", @"Thanks") otherButtonTitles:
        nil];
    [alert show];
    [alert release];

    return NO;
  }
    else    return YES;
}
```

Here's the process the code uses to get the job done for you:

1. **First, check to see whether the user has touched an embedded link while in stored data mode.**

```
if ((navigationType ==
      UIWebViewNavigationTypeLinkClicked) &&   (
      [[NSUserDefaults standardUserDefaults] boolFor
      Key:kUseStoredDataPreference]) ) {
```

2. **If the user is in stored-data mode, alert him or her to the fact that the link is unavailable, and return** NO **from the method.**

This informs the Web view not to load the link

```
UIAlertView *alert = [[UIAlertView alloc]
    initWithTitle:@"" message: NSLocalizedString
    (@"Link not available offline", @"stored data
        mode")
    delegate:self cancelButtonTitle:NSLocalizedString
    (@"Thanks", @"Thanks") otherButtonTitles: nil];
[alert show];
[alert release];
return NO;
```

I create an alert here with a message telling the user that the link is not available in stored-data mode. The Cancel button's text will be @"Thanks".

3. **If you are not in stored-data mode, return** YES **to tell the Web view to load from the Internet.**

The Airport Model

You're starting to get all your pieces lined up. Now it's time to take a look at what happens when the controller calls the Airport functions.

The Airport interface, seen in Listing 17-7, shows us what methods are available.

Listing 17-7: Airport.h

```
#import <Foundation/Foundation.h>

@interface Airport : NSObject {
}
```

(continued)

Listing 17-7 *(continued)*

```
- (id) initWithName: (NSString*) airportName;
- (NSURL*)returnTransRealtime: (int) transType;
- (NSData*)returnTransOffline: (int) transType;

// "Private methods"
- (NSData*) getAirportData: (NSString*) fileName;
- (void) saveAirportData: (NSString*) fileName
        withDataURL:  (NSURL*) url ;

@end
```

The first method here should look familiar to you, since I used it back when
I created and initialized the `Airport` object in "The initialization chain"
section, earlier in the chapter. The next two methods are called from the
`selectTrans:` method in `AirportController`. The last two are internal
methods that are used only by the model itself.

If you're coming from C++, you probably want these last two methods to be
private, but there is no private construct in Objective-C. To hide them, I could
have moved their declarations to the implementation file and created an
Objective-C category. Here's what that looks like:

```
@interface Airport   ()
- (NSData*) getAirportData: (NSString*) fileName;
- (void) saveAirportData: (NSString*) fileName
        withDataURL:  (NSURL*) url ;
@end
```

In Listing 17-8, you can see the two methods called from `selectTrans:` as a
group.

Listing 17-8:   **Model methods used by the Airport Controller**

```
- (NSURL*) returnTransRealtime: (int) transType {
  NSURL *url =[NSURL alloc];

  switch (transType) {
    case 0:                                              {
      url = [NSURL URLWithString:
            @"http://nealgoldstein.com/ToFromT100.html"];
      [self saveAirportData:
                  @"ToFromT100" withDataURL: url ];
      break;
      }
    case 1: {
```

```
            url = [NSURL URLWithString:
                    @"http://nealgoldstein.com/ToFromT101.html"];
            [self saveAirportData:
                            @"ToFromT101" withDataURL: url ];
            break;
            }
        case 2: {
            url = [NSURL URLWithString:
                    @"http://nealgoldstein.com/ToFromT102.html"];
            [self saveAirportData:
                            @"ToFromT102" withDataURL: url ];
            break;
            }
        }
    return url;
}


- (NSData*) returnTransOffline: (int) transType {
    NSData* returnData ;


    switch (transType) {
        case 0: {
            returnData = [self getAirportData: @"ToFromT100"];
            break;
            }
        case 1: {
            returnData = [self getAirportData: @"ToFromT101"];
            break;
            }
          case 2: {
            returnData = [self getAirportData: @"ToFromT102"];
            break;
            }
        }
    return returnData;
}
```

When the model is called to return the data the view needs to display, it is passed the number of the segmented control that was touched (Train, Taxi, Other). It is the model's responsibility to decide the data that is required here.

To concretize all these abstract coding principles a bit, check out how you should deal with the returnTransRealtime: method. The data for each of the choices in the segmented control is on a Web site — www.nealgoldstein. com, to be precise. First the method constructs the NSURL object that the Web view uses to load the data. (The NSURL object is nothing fancy; to refresh your memory it is simply an object that includes the utilities necessary for downloading files or other resources from Web and FTP servers).

```
NSURL *url = [NSURL URLWithString: @"http://
        nealgoldstein.com/ToFromT100.html"];
```

Then the saveAirportData: method is called:

```
[self saveAirportData: @"ToFromT100" withDataURL: url ];
return url;
```

The saveAirportData method in Listing 17-9 downloads and saves the file containing the latest data for whatever transportation (Taxi for example) the user selected. It is what will be displayed in the current view, and will be used later if the user specifies stored data mode.

Listing 17-9:   Saving airport data

```
- (void) saveAirportData: (NSString*) fileName
          withDataURL:  (NSURL*) url  {

NSData *dataLoaded = [NSData
                          dataWithContentsOfURL:url];
if (dataLoaded == NULL)
                    NSLog( @"Data not found %@", url);
NSArray *paths = NSSearchPathForDirectoriesInDomains(NSD
        ocumentDirectory, NSUserDomainMask, YES);
NSString *documentsDirectory = [paths objectAtIndex:0];
NSString *filePath = [documentsDirectory stringByAppendi
        ngPathComponent:fileName];
[dataLoaded writeToFile:filePath atomically:YES];
}
```

You did the exact same thing back in Chapter 16 when you saved the current state of the application. If you need a refresher here, go back and work through that part of Chapter 16 again.

I have added an NSLog message if the data can't be found. This is a place holder for error handling that I have left as an exercise for the reader.

This is definitely not the most efficient way to implement saving files for later use, but given the relatively small amount of data involved, the impact is not noticeable. In the MobileTravel411 application, the user has a specific option to download all the data for any city, eliminating going to the Internet twice — once to download and save the data and then again to display the page.

The offline version in Listing 17-10 returns the stored data as opposed to going out to the URL. It gets the data by calling the `getAirportData:` method, which reads the data that was stored in `saveAirportData:`.

```
return  [self getAirportData: @"ToFromT100"];
```

Again, reading is the mirror image of writing. You find the path, and instead of calling `writeToFile:`, which is what you would do if you were saving the data, you call `initWithContentsOfFile:`.

Listing 17-10:   Getting the saved airport data

```
-(NSData*) getAirportData: (NSString*) fileName{

  NSArray *paths = NSSearchPathForDirectoriesInDomains(NSD
          ocumentDirectory, NSUserDomainMask, YES);
  NSString *documentsDirectory = [paths objectAtIndex:0];
  NSString *filePath = [documentsDirectory stringByAppendi
          ngPathComponent:fileName];
  NSData *storedData = [[[NSData alloc] initWithContentsOf
          File:filePath] autorelease];
  return  storedData;
}
```

`initWithContentsOfFile:` creates the `NSData` object with the content of the file. This object, content and all, is then returned to the controller, which passes it on to the Web view to load and display.

The Weather Implementation Model

The `Weather` view controllers, views, and models follow the same pattern put down by the `Airport` model. You can find the code for the `Airport`, `Weather`, and `Currency` views controllers and models on my Web site, www. nealgoldstein.com.

I want to point out some differences between Weather and the other views that you should be aware of. In the Weather view, there's no segmented control — and no corresponding `selectTrans:` message that tells the model what data is needed — so you'll need to do that in the `Weather Controller`'s `viewDidLoad` method. Listing 17-11 shows how that code looks:

Listing 17-11: viewDidLoad

```
- (void)viewDidLoad {

  [super viewDidLoad];
  UIBarButtonItem *addButton = [[[UIBarButtonItem alloc]
      initWithTitle: @"Back"
      style:UIBarButtonItemStylePlain target:self
      action:@selector(goBack:)] autorelease];
      self.navigationItem.rightBarButtonItem = addButton;

  iPhoneTravel411AppDelegate *appDelegate =
          (iPhoneTravel411AppDelegate *)[[UIApplication
          sharedApplication] delegate];
  bool realtime = !appDelegate.useStoredData;

  if (realtime) {
    [weatherView loadRequest:[NSURLRequest
          requestWithURL:[weather weatherRealtime]]];
    }
  else {
    [weatherView loadData: [weather weatherOffline]
          MIMEType:@"text/html" textEncodingName:@"UTF-8"
          baseURL:[NSURL URLWithString:@"http://
          nealgoldstein.com"]]];
    }
}
```

The only other real difference is that, instead of using stored data in the stored data mode, the Weather model method (in Weather.m) returns an HTML string, as you can see in Listing 17-12:

Listing 17-12: weatherOffline

```
- (NSData*) weatherOffline {
  NSString* htmlString = @"<div style=\"font-
          family:Helvetica, Arial, sans-serif;
          font-size:24pt;\" align=\"center\">";
  htmlString = [ htmlString stringByAppendingString:
          @"Sorry, you are offline and the weather is not
          available"];
  htmlString = [ htmlString stringByAppendingString: @"</
          span>"];

  NSData * offlineMessage = [htmlString
          dataUsingEncoding: NSUTF8StringEncoding];
  return offlineMessage;
}
```

The nib file is exactly the same as the WeatherController nib file — with appropriate class names, of course.

The Currency Implementation Model

The Currency view controllers, views, and models follow the same pattern laid down by the Airport and Weather implementation models. Again the complete code is on my Web site at www.nealgoldstein.com. There are only a few differences I need to point out.

Currency is always offline, which means it's a great way to show you how to implement static data.

The content for the Currency view is in a file I created called Currencies. html. To make it available to the application, I need to include it in the application bundle itself, although I could have downloaded it the first time the application ran. (But there's method in my madness: Including it in the bundle does give me the opportunity to show you how to handle this kind of data.)

Now, you can add it to your bundle one of two ways:

✔ Open the project window and drag the .html file you created into the project folder, as shown in Figure 17-13.

It's a good idea to create a new folder within your project folder as a snug little home for the file. (I named my new folder "Static Data.")

or

✔ Select Project⇨Add to Project and then use the dialog that appears to navigate to and select the file you want.

By using the Add to Project command, you end up adding the data as a resource.

The only thing interesting here is that you are going to use some data that you have included with your application as a *resource* (which you can think about as an included file, although it does not "live" in the file system but rather is embedded in the application itself).

In Listing 17-13, you can see that in the viewDidLoad method in Currency Controller.m, the currencyBasics method is called to return the data the view will display.

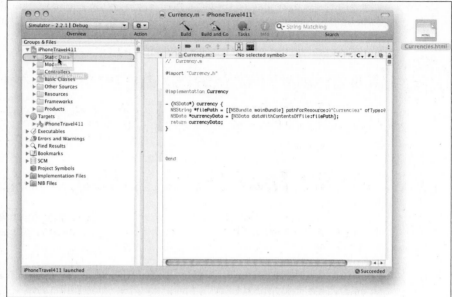

Figure 17-13:
Drag in
Currencies.
html.

Listing 17-13: viewDidLoad

```
- (void)viewDidLoad {

    [super viewDidLoad];
    [currencyView loadData:[currency currencyBasics]
            MIMEType:@"text/html" textEncodingName:@"UTF-8"
            baseURL:[NSURL URLWithString:@"http://
            nealgoldstein.com"]];
}
```

In Listing 17-14 you can see how the `currencyBasics:` method in the `Cuurency.m` file returns the resource to the `CurrencyController`.

Listing 17-14: currencyBasics method

```
- (NSData*) currencyBasics {
    NSString *filePath = [[NSBundle mainBundle]
            pathForResource:@"Currencies" ofType:@"html"];
    NSData *currencyData = [NSData dataWithContentsOfFile:fi
            lePath];
    return currencyData;
}
```

In this case, you're using `pathForResource`, which is an `NSBundle` method. (You used an `NSBundle` method when you got the application name in the `RootViewController` to set the title on the main window back in Chapter 15). Just give `pathForResource` the name and the file type.

Be sure you provide the right file type; otherwise this technique won't work.

The nib file for the `Currency` model is exactly the same as the `Weather Controller` nib file — with appropriate class names, of course.

What About That Promise You Made Us

Now that you know what it takes to develop the view controllers and models for a not-that-simple application, let's see how you can make them more generic.

This information is perhaps a bit more abstract than what you've been accustomed to. You may need to come back to it after you have more experience in creating view controllers and models. You'll also find more information on this on my Web site.

Let's start with the model and work our way backwards.

The model is responsible for providing the view controller the information it needs to send to the view to display. Now, remember that the model object I need in iPhoneTravel411 isn't about the content — for my purposes, a model object that gets weather information and a model object that gets information about the Heathrow express are pretty much the same. It's about identifying the information that needs to be displayed, knowing where that information is located, and then delivering it to the view controller.

To create a generic model, the first step is to replace any of the hard-coded logic (in the `Airport` model, for example) that determines what and where the information is that it is supposed to provide to the view controller. Instead of relying on hard-wiring, the model logic should look up the requirements for what it must provide (in a property list, data base, or table — I'll not get into the details in this discussion) based on where the user is in the application.

For example, in the `Airport` model the logic that needs to be replaced is in `returnTransRealtime:` and `returnTransOffline:`. I'll just use the former as an example — changes are in bold:

```
- (NSURL*) returnTransRealtime: (int) transType {
  NSURL *url =[NSURL alloc];

  switch (transType) {
    case 0:                                                    {
      url = [NSURL URLWithString:
              @"http://nealgoldstein.com/ToFromT100.html"];
      [self saveAirportData:
                  @"ToFromT100" withDataURL: url ];
      break;
      }
    case 1: {
      url = [NSURL URLWithString:
              @"http://nealgoldstein.com/ToFromT101.html"];
      [self saveAirportData:
                  @"ToFromT101" withDataURL: url ];
      break;
      }
    case 2: {
      url = [NSURL URLWithString:
              @"http://nealgoldstein.com/ToFromT102.html"];
      [self saveAirportData:
                  @"ToFromT102" withDataURL: url ];
      break;
      }
   }
  return url;
}
```

To make this generic, instead of using a switch statement and then having the URL (what and where of the data) embedded in the code

```
url = [NSURL URLWithString:
        @"http://nealgoldstein.com/ToFromT102.html"];
```

you would look up the URL in your handy dandy property list instead.

What would you need to have in order to be able to look stuff up? Some sort of key that the model can construct that would uniquely identify the data that needs to be displayed. You could construct that key using:

City: London, for example.

Row: The row in the table was selected — Heathrow, for example.

Level: The offset from the initial selection. All of the views you see in the iPhoneTravel411 application are level 0. In other applications — the iPod application for example — there can be more. Selecting a song from an album is similarly at level 0, and then selecting the song details is level 1.

Tab: At a given level, which view is associated with which tab. For example, in the iPhoneTravel411 application Train is 0, Taxi is 1, and Other is 2.

Status: Is the user online or in stored data mode.

This quintuple (an "ordered list" of five values) of city-row-level-tab-status would enable the model to go into a property list where all the information about the data had been specified. In the Airport example, it would be a URL (`http://nealgoldstein.com/ToFromT100.html` for example) if the user were online, or a file name/location (`ToFromT100/home directory`) if the user were in stored data mode, or even a resource name and location (`Currencies.html/main bundle` in the case of the Currency example above.).

In order for this to happen, of course, the view controller would have to pass this information to the model when the user made a selection. That means some of the information would need to be passed into the view controller when the user made the selection in the main view. So let's take a look at the view controller.

The `Airport` controller actually has most of the logic it already needs to implement the generic model. In `selectTrans:` you are already sending the tab information (the code was written that way for a reason), and the view controller already determined the status.

```
airport returnTransRealtime: (((UISegmentedControl*)
         sender).selectedSegmentIndex)
```

All you would have to do is change the method call to include the city-row-level-status.

The main challenge in implementing a generic view controller, however, is constructing the tabs at the bottom of the view — the ones that the user can select to move from, say, Heathrow Express information to Taxi information.

To implement this, you would use the same approach that you did with the model — look up the number of tabs as well as the text for each tab in a property list. In this case, to uniquely specify that for a view, all the view controller would need is the city-row-level information — which just so happens to be what the view controller needs to send to the model. Where does that come from?

Still working backwards, you come to the `RootViewController`, which is responsible for creating and initializing the `Airport` controller. The `RootViewController` has the city-row-level the `Airport` controller needs and it would simply pass that in when it created and then initialized the view controller.

Yes, there is more. Tabs not only are used to indicate the data to display, but can also implement navigation to a new level in the hierarchy, like in the iPod application. This approach supports that, but I'm not going to get into it here. You can find out more on this as well as more on a number of more advanced concepts, on my Web site at www.nealgoldstein.com.

What's Next?

Although this point marks the end of your guided tour of iPhone Software development, it should also be the start, if you haven't already, of your own development work.

Developing for the iPhone is one of the most exciting opportunities I have come across in a long time. I'm hoping it ends up being as exciting — and perhaps less stressful — an opportunity for you. Keep in touch, check out my Web site www.nealgoldstein.com for updates and what's new, and keep having fun. I hope I have the opportunity to download one of your applications from the App Store someday.

Part V
The Part of Tens

The 5th Wave   By Rich Tennant

"Hold on, Barbara. I'm pretty sure the App Store has an iPhone application for this."

In this part . . .

1 once had a boss who liked to hire smart-but-lazy people. He figured if he gave them a hard job they'd find an easy way to do it.

In this part, I show you some ways to (first) avoid doing more work than you have to, and (second) avoid redoing things because you outsmarted yourself. I take you on a tour of Apple's sample applications and point out where to look if you want to "borrow" some code to implement some piece of functionality (don't worry — it's strictly legit to do that). Then I show you where spending some up-front time doing app development the right way is definitely worth it.

Chapter 18

Top Ten Sample Apple Apps (with Code!)

· ·

"Good artists copy. Great artists steal."

– Pablo Picasso

One way to really learn how to do things on the iPhone is to look at (correct) sample code. Apple provides a lot of it. The only problem with learning from samples is that, while it can show you how to do a specific thing (like flip a view), it doesn't give you the overall architectural understanding you need to create an application.

After going through this book, you know enough to take real advantage of all this sample code. By all means, take what you can from the samples and use it where you can to jumpstart your own application development.

Here are the ten samples I like the best. You can find them at the iPhone Dev Center Web site at `http://developer.apple.com/iphone/` under the Sample Code section on the bottom left of the page. You'll have to click on View Featured, which will take you to the Sample Code for iPhone page, and then click on View All in Featured Sample Code (View All) at the top left of the page.

They all come as Xcode projects, so you can check out the code, compile the project and then load it into the simulator or even onto your development iPhone.

AppPrefs

If you want to get a good handle on preferences and how to set, access, and use them in your application, this is the place to get that grip. This app even has a table view with flip animation which explains the application on the flipside.

BubbleLevel

I can't help it. I love this application. It includes a lot of things any iPhone app developer would want to know how to do, including graphics and audio, and how to develop an application with a landscape view. It also allows you to calibrate the level with directions on the flipside of the level view. I actually keep this app on my iPhone. You never know when you might need a level to straighten a picture or build a deck.

LocateMe

If you want to extend the iPhoneTravel411 application and base the user's available options on his or her current location, you can start here. This app shows you how to use core location, but remember that the simulator shows you a world with only one location — Apple's headquarters in Cupertino, California.

NavBar

Navigation bars crop up in the book from time to time (in particular, in Chapter 17), and I show you how to add a Back button in Chapter 17. If you want to customize an existing navigation bar even more, this app has the code that shows you how to do it. You can add custom left and right buttons and even change the style of the Navigation Bar. It also illustrates how to use multiple nib files — each page has its own.

Reachability

If you're a network geek this is great — otherwise you can use this code to get your app to determine network state and check whether a particular site is available. This app also shows you, if you uncomment a line of code, how to run in asynchronous mode and notify the application of a change in device status.

SQLite Book List

This sample shows you how to use the SQLite database in a book-catalog example. (Feel free to add this book to it.) You can add and delete book entries, as well as edit them. The sample also explains how to set up the database. If your app needs to use a database, it will probably use this one.

UICatalog

This sample illustrates all the elements you'd want to use in your app's user interface. (You know — all those buttons, icons, and bangles that the user sees on-screen.) This one application shows you how to implement all of them.

URLCache

URLCache demonstrates how to download a resource, store it in the data directory, and use the local copy. Very useful for anything you want your app to do on the Web. It also includes a framework for asynchronous processing. If you need to download a lot o' data when the application starts up, this sample shows you how to tell your app to start a download and then go off and do other things until the download completes. It also includes an activity-indicator view that tells the user your application is actually at work, and not on a lunch break.

XML

There are actually two XML samples I can recommend. The first one, Seismic XML, shows you how to work with XML documents. When you launch it, it gets and parses an RSS feed. This particular feed is from the U.S. Geological Survey that provides data on recent earthquakes around the world. (I live in Northern California, so you can bet I keep this one on my iPhone as well.)

The second sample, XMLPerformance, parses XML by using the two APIs provided in the SDK. This sample allows the user to choose between the two APIs, tracks the statistics of each parse, and stores that data in an SQLite database. There's a good discussion of performance in the ReadMe file. In addition, the app's RSS feed uses the "Top 300" songs from iTunes so you can keep up to date on that.

Tables

There are a number of samples that show you how to implement the functionality inherent in the table view. I'll just list them here and you can examine them at your leisure:

- ✔ Accessory implements a check-mark button in a custom accessory view.

- ✔ DrillDownSave saves the current location in a hierarchy and then restores the current location when the user re-launches the application. (Hmm. I wonder where I've seen that before?)

- ✔ EditableDetailView shows how to insert, delete, and move rows.

- ✔ HeaderFooter shows customized header and footer views.

- ✔ TableSearch implements searching and then filtering content. This is similar to what the Mail application does when you start to type an e-mail address in the To field when you are composing an email.

- ✔ TableViewSuite shows a lot of table views.

- ✔ TheElements is a very robust application. It allows you to sort data and present it in multiple formats. It uses a tab bar, displays in plain and grouped table views, uses navigation controllers to navigate deeper into a data structure, creates custom table view cells with multiple subviews, accesses a Web site using Safari, reacts to taps in a view, flips view content from front to back, and reflects a view, Makes me tired just to think about it.

- ✔ TouchCells implements controls in a table view.

Chapter 19

Ten Ways to Be a Happy Developer

In This Chapter

▶ A bunch of developmental things I learned to do so I'll be happy later

▶ So there.

There are lots of things you know you're supposed to do, but you don't because you think they'll never catch up with you. (After all, not flossing won't cause you problems until your teeth fall out years from now, right?)

But in iPhone application development, those things catch up with you early and often, so I want to tell you about what I've learned to pay attention to from the very start in app development, as well as a few tips and tricks that lead to happy and healthy users.

It's Never Early Enough to Start Speaking a Foreign Language

With the world growing even flatter, and the iPhone available in more than 80 countries, the potential market for your app is considerably larger than just people who speak English. Localizing an application isn't hard, just tedious. Some of it you can get away with doing late in the project, but when it comes to the strings you use in your application, you'd better build them right — and build them in from the start. The painless way: Use the `NSLocalizedString` macro (refer to Chapter 15) from the very start and you'll still be a happy camper at the end.

Remember Memory

The iPhone OS does not store "changeable" memory (such as object data) on the disk to free up space, and then read it back in later when needed. It also doesn't have garbage collection — which means there is a real potential for memory leaks unless you tidy up after your app. Review and follow the memory rules in Chapter 6 — in particular, these:

- Memory management is really creating *pairs* of messages. Balance every `alloc`, `new`, and `retain` with a `release`.

- When you assign an instance variable using an accessor with a property attribute of `retain`, you now own the object. When you're done with it, release it it in a `dealloc` method.

Constantly Use Constants

In the iPhoneTravel411 application I put all my constants in one file. When I was developing the MobileTravel411 projects, I did the same. The why of it is simple: As I changed things during the development process, having *one* place to find my constants made life much easier.

Don't Fall Off the Cutting Edge

The iPhone is cutting-edge enough that there are still plenty of opportunities to expand its capabilities — and many of them are (relatively) easy to implement. You are also working with a very mature framework. So if you think something you want your app to do is going to be really hard, check the framework; somewhere in there you may find an easy way to do what you have in mind. If there isn't a ready-made fix, consider the iPhone's limited resources — and at least question whether that nifty task you had in mind is something your app should be doing at all. Then again, if you really *need* to track orbital debris with an iPhone app, go for it — someone needs to lead the way. Why shouldn't it be you?

Start by Initializing the Right Way

A lot my really messy code that I found myself re-doing ended up that way because I didn't think through initialization. (For example, adding on initialization methods after initialization is a little late in the game, and so on.) Re-read and heed Chapter 17; the initialization process is important in implementing reusable view controllers and models.

Keep the Order Straight

One of the things that can really foul up your day as a developer is the order in which objects are called. If you expect an object to be there (and it isn't) or to have been initialized (and it wasn't), you may be in the wrong method. Copy Table 19-1 and paste it into a file — and/or print it out and tack it up somewhere you can easily find it:

Table 19-1	The natural order of things
Object	*Method*
View Controller	`awakeFromNib`
Application Delegate	`applicationDidFinishLaunching:`
View Controller	`viewDidLoad`
View Controller	`viewWillAppear:`
View Controller	`viewWillDisappear:`
Delegate	`applicationWillTerminate:`

What trips up many developers is that the `awakeFromNib` method for the initial view controller (the one you see when the application starts) is called *before* the `applicationDidFinishLaunching:` method. If you have a problem with that, do what you need to do in `ViewDidLoad`.

Avoid Mistakes in Error Handling

There a lot of opportunities for errors out there; use common sense in figuring out which ones you should spend work time on. For example, don't panic over handling a missing directory in your code. On the iPhone, it's supposed to be there; if it's not, then look for a bug in your program. If it's *really* not there, then the user has big problems and you probably won't be able to do anything to avert the oncoming hassle.

There are however, some potential pitfalls you do have to pay attention to, such as these two big ones:

- Your app goes out to load something off of the Internet, and (for a variety of reasons) the item isn't there or the app can't get to it.

- An object can't initialize itself (for a similar range of perverse reasons).

When, not if, those things happen, your code and your user interface must be able to deal with the error.

Remember the User

I've been singing this song since Chapter 1, and I'm still singing it now: Keep your app simple to use. Don't build long pages that take lots of scrolling to get through, and don't create really deep hierarchies. Focus on what the user wants to accomplish, and be mindful of the device limitations, especially battery life. And don't forget international roaming charges.

In other words, try to follow the Apple's iPhone Human Interface Guidelines, found with all the other documentation in the iPhone Dev Center Web site at `http://developer.apple.com/iphone/` under the iPhone Reference Library section — Required Reading. Don't even *think* about bending those rules until you really, *really* understand them.

Keep In Mind that the Software Isn't Finished Until The Last User Is Dead

If there is one thing I can guarantee about app development, is that Nobody Gets It Right the First Time. The design for MobileTravel411 evolved over time, as I learned the capabilities and intricacies of the platform and the impact of my design changes. Object orientation makes extending your application (not to mention fixing bugs) easier, so pay attention to the principles.

Keep It Fun

When I started programming the iPhone, it was the most fun I'd had in years. Keep things in perspective: Except for a few tedious tasks (such as provisioning and getting your application into the Apple Store), lo, I prophesy: Developing iPhone apps will be fun for you too. So don't take it *too* seriously.

Especially remember the *fun* part at 4:00 a.m. when you've spent the last five hours looking for a bug. Here's a handy way to do that: My editor here at Wiley told me he knows of someone who downloaded an iPhone app with little buttons placed on-screen like the holes on an ocarina; the idea is to blow into the iPhone and *play* it that way. She's organizing an iPhone virtual-ocarina quartet. Imagine them playing "Wild Thing" — that'll keep things in perspective.

Index

BUSINESS, CAREERS & PERSONAL FINANCE

Accounting For Dummies, 4th Edition*
978-0-470-24600-9

Bookkeeping Workbook For Dummies†
978-0-470-16983-4

Commodities For Dummies
978-0-470-04928-0

Doing Business in China For Dummies
978-0-470-04929-7

E-Mail Marketing For Dummies
978-0-470-19087-6

Job Interviews For Dummies, 3rd Edition*†
978-0-470-17748-8

Personal Finance Workbook For Dummies*†
978-0-470-09933-9

Real Estate License Exams For Dummies
978-0-7645-7623-2

Six Sigma For Dummies
978-0-7645-6798-8

Small Business Kit For Dummies, 2nd Edition*†
978-0-7645-5984-6

Telephone Sales For Dummies
978-0-470-16836-3

BUSINESS PRODUCTIVITY & MICROSOFT OFFICE

Access 2007 For Dummies
978-0-470-03649-5

Excel 2007 For Dummies
978-0-470-03737-9

Office 2007 For Dummies
978-0-470-00923-9

Outlook 2007 For Dummies
978-0-470-03830-7

PowerPoint 2007 For Dummies
978-0-470-04059-1

Project 2007 For Dummies
978-0-470-03651-8

QuickBooks 2008 For Dummies
978-0-470-18470-7

Quicken 2008 For Dummies
978-0-470-17473-9

Salesforce.com For Dummies, 2nd Edition
978-0-470-04893-1

Word 2007 For Dummies
978-0-470-03658-7

EDUCATION, HISTORY, REFERENCE & TEST PREPARATION

African American History For Dummies
978-0-7645-5469-8

Algebra For Dummies
978-0-7645-5325-7

Algebra Workbook For Dummies
978-0-7645-8467-1

Art History For Dummies
978-0-470-09910-0

ASVAB For Dummies, 2nd Edition
978-0-470-10671-6

British Military History For Dummies
978-0-470-03213-8

Calculus For Dummies
978-0-7645-2498-1

Canadian History For Dummies, 2nd Edition
978-0-470-83656-9

Geometry Workbook For Dummies
978-0-471-79940-5

The SAT I For Dummies, 6th Edition
978-0-7645-7193-0

Series 7 Exam For Dummies
978-0-470-09932-2

World History For Dummies
978-0-7645-5242-7

FOOD, GARDEN, HOBBIES & HOME

Bridge For Dummies, 2nd Edition
978-0-471-92426-5

Coin Collecting For Dummies, 2nd Edition
978-0-470-22275-1

Cooking Basics For Dummies, 3rd Edition
978-0-7645-7206-7

Drawing For Dummies
978-0-7645-5476-6

Etiquette For Dummies, 2nd Edition
978-0-470-10672-3

Gardening Basics For Dummies*†
978-0-470-03749-2

Knitting Patterns For Dummies
978-0-470-04556-5

Living Gluten-Free For Dummies†
978-0-471-77383-2

Painting Do-It-Yourself For Dummies
978-0-470-17533-0

HEALTH, SELF HELP, PARENTING & PETS

Anger Management For Dummies
978-0-470-03715-7

Anxiety & Depression Workbook For Dummies
978-0-7645-9793-0

Dieting For Dummies, 2nd Edition
978-0-7645-4149-0

Dog Training For Dummies, 2nd Edition
978-0-7645-8418-3

Horseback Riding For Dummies
978-0-470-09719-9

Infertility For Dummies†
978-0-470-11518-3

Meditation For Dummies with CD-ROM, 2nd Edition
978-0-471-77774-8

Post-Traumatic Stress Disorder For Dummies
978-0-470-04922-8

Puppies For Dummies, 2nd Edition
978-0-470-03717-1

Thyroid For Dummies, 2nd Edition†
978-0-471-78755-6

Type 1 Diabetes For Dummies*†
978-0-470-17811-9

---

* Separate Canadian edition also available
† Separate U.K. edition also available

 WILEY

INTERNET & DIGITAL MEDIA

AdWords For Dummies
978-0-470-15252-2

Blogging For Dummies, 2nd Edition
978-0-470-23017-6

Digital Photography All-in-One Desk Reference For Dummies, 3rd Edition
978-0-470-03743-0

Digital Photography For Dummies, 5th Edition
978-0-7645-9802-9

Digital SLR Cameras & Photography For Dummies, 2nd Edition
978-0-470-14927-0

eBay Business All-in-One Desk Reference For Dummies
978-0-7645-8438-1

eBay For Dummies, 5th Edition*
978-0-470-04529-9

eBay Listings That Sell For Dummies
978-0-471-78912-3

Facebook For Dummies
978-0-470-26273-3

The Internet For Dummies, 11th Edition
978-0-470-12174-0

Investing Online For Dummies, 5th Edition
978-0-7645-8456-5

iPod & iTunes For Dummies, 5th Edition
978-0-470-17474-6

MySpace For Dummies
978-0-470-09529-4

Podcasting For Dummies
978-0-471-74898-4

Search Engine Optimization For Dummies, 2nd Edition
978-0-471-97998-2

Second Life For Dummies
978-0-470-18025-9

Starting an eBay Business For Dummies 3rd Edition†
978-0-470-14924-9

GRAPHICS, DESIGN & WEB DEVELOPMENT

Adobe Creative Suite 3 Design Premium All-in-One Desk Reference For Dummies
978-0-470-11724-8

Adobe Web Suite CS3 All-in-One Desk Reference For Dummies
978-0-470-12099-6

AutoCAD 2008 For Dummies
978-0-470-11650-0

Building a Web Site For Dummies, 3rd Edition
978-0-470-14928-7

Creating Web Pages All-in-One Desk Reference For Dummies, 3rd Edition
978-0-470-09629-1

Creating Web Pages For Dummies, 8th Edition
978-0-470-08030-6

Dreamweaver CS3 For Dummies
978-0-470-11490-2

Flash CS3 For Dummies
978-0-470-12100-9

Google SketchUp For Dummies
978-0-470-13744-4

InDesign CS3 For Dummies
978-0-470-11865-8

Photoshop CS3 All-in-One Desk Reference For Dummies
978-0-470-11195-6

Photoshop CS3 For Dummies
978-0-470-11193-2

Photoshop Elements 5 For Dummies
978-0-470-09810-3

SolidWorks For Dummies
978-0-7645-9555-4

Visio 2007 For Dummies
978-0-470-08983-5

Web Design For Dummies, 2nd Edition
978-0-471-78117-2

Web Sites Do-It-Yourself For Dummies
978-0-470-16903-2

Web Stores Do-It-Yourself For Dummies
978-0-470-17443-2

LANGUAGES, RELIGION & SPIRITUALITY

Arabic For Dummies
978-0-471-77270-5

Chinese For Dummies, Audio Set
978-0-470-12766-7

French For Dummies
978-0-7645-5193-2

German For Dummies
978-0-7645-5195-6

Hebrew For Dummies
978-0-7645-5489-6

Ingles Para Dummies
978-0-7645-5427-8

Italian For Dummies, Audio Set
978-0-470-09586-7

Italian Verbs For Dummies
978-0-471-77389-4

Japanese For Dummies
978-0-7645-5429-2

Latin For Dummies
978-0-7645-5431-5

Portuguese For Dummies
978-0-471-78738-9

Russian For Dummies
978-0-471-78001-4

Spanish Phrases For Dummies
978-0-7645-7204-3

Spanish For Dummies
978-0-7645-5194-9

Spanish For Dummies, Audio Set
978-0-470-09585-0

The Bible For Dummies
978-0-7645-5296-0

Catholicism For Dummies
978-0-7645-5391-2

The Historical Jesus For Dummies
978-0-470-16785-4

Islam For Dummies
978-0-7645-5503-9

Spirituality For Dummies, 2nd Edition
978-0-470-19142-2

NETWORKING AND PROGRAMMING

ASP.NET 3.5 For Dummies
978-0-470-19592-5

C# 2008 For Dummies
978-0-470-19109-5

Hacking For Dummies, 2nd Edition
978-0-470-05235-8

Home Networking For Dummies, 4th Edition
978-0-470-11806-1

Java For Dummies, 4th Edition
978-0-470-08716-9

Microsoft® SQL Server™ 2008 All-in-One Desk Reference For Dummies
978-0-470-17954-3

Networking All-in-One Desk Reference For Dummies, 2nd Edition
978-0-7645-9939-2

Networking For Dummies, 8th Edition
978-0-470-05620-2

SharePoint 2007 For Dummies
978-0-470-09941-4

Wireless Home Networking For Dummies, 2nd Edition
978-0-471-74940-0

OPERATING SYSTEMS & COMPUTER BASICS

iMac For Dummies, 5th Edition
978-0-7645-8458-9

Laptops For Dummies, 2nd Edition
978-0-470-05432-1

Linux For Dummies, 8th Edition
978-0-470-11649-4

MacBook For Dummies
978-0-470-04859-7

Mac OS X Leopard All-in-One Desk Reference For Dummies
978-0-470-05434-5

Mac OS X Leopard For Dummies
978-0-470-05433-8

Macs For Dummies, 9th Edition
978-0-470-04849-8

PCs For Dummies, 11th Edition
978-0-470-13728-4

Windows® Home Server For Dummies
978-0-470-18592-6

Windows Server 2008 For Dummies
978-0-470-18043-3

Windows Vista All-in-One Desk Reference For Dummies
978-0-471-74941-7

Windows Vista For Dummies
978-0-471-75421-3

Windows Vista Security For Dummies
978-0-470-11805-4

SPORTS, FITNESS & MUSIC

Coaching Hockey For Dummies
978-0-470-83685-9

Coaching Soccer For Dummies
978-0-471-77381-8

Fitness For Dummies, 3rd Edition
978-0-7645-7851-9

Football For Dummies, 3rd Edition
978-0-470-12536-6

GarageBand For Dummies
978-0-7645-7323-1

Golf For Dummies, 3rd Edition
978-0-471-76871-5

Guitar For Dummies, 2nd Edition
978-0-7645-9904-0

Home Recording For Musicians For Dummies, 2nd Edition
978-0-7645-8884-6

iPod & iTunes For Dummies, 5th Edition
978-0-470-17474-6

Music Theory For Dummies
978-0-7645-7838-0

Stretching For Dummies
978-0-470-06741-3

Get smart @ dummies.com®

- Find a full list of Dummies titles
- Look into loads of FREE on-site articles
- Sign up for FREE eTips e-mailed to you weekly
- See what other products carry the Dummies name
- Shop directly from the Dummies bookstore
- Enter to win new prizes every month!